Europeanization, Care and Gender

Europeanization, Care and Gender

Global Complexities

Edited by

Hanne Marlene Dahl
Roskilde University, Denmark

Marja Keränen
University of Jyväskylä, Finland

Anne Kovalainen
University of Turku, Finland

palgrave
macmillan

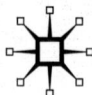

First published 2011 by
PALGRAVE MACMILLAN

Palgrave Macmillan in the UK is an imprint of Macmillan Publishers Limited,
registered in England, company number 785998, of Houndmills, Basingstoke,
Hampshire RG21 6XS.

Palgrave Macmillan in the US is a division of St Martin's Press LLC,
175 Fifth Avenue, New York, NY 10010.

Palgrave Macmillan is the global academic imprint of the above companies
and has companies and representatives throughout the world.

Palgrave® and Macmillan® are registered trademarks in the United States,
the United Kingdom, Europe and other countries.

ISBN 978–0–230–29969–6

This book is printed on paper suitable for recycling and made from fully
managed and sustained forest sources. Logging, pulping and manufacturing
processes are expected to conform to the environmental regulations of the
country of origin.

A catalogue record for this book is available from the British Library.

Library of Congress Cataloging-in-Publication Data
Europeanization, care and gender global complexities / edited by
Hanne Marlene Dahl, Marja Keränen, Anne Kovalainen.
p. cm.
Includes bibliographical references and index.
ISBN 978–0–230–29969–6 (alk. paper)
1. Social work administration—Europe. 2. Globalization—Europe.
I. Dahl, Hanne Marlene. II. Keränen, Marja. III. Kovalainen, Anne.
HV238.E977 2011
362.94—dc23   2011016887

10   9   8   7   6   5   4   3   2   1
20 19 18 17 16 15 14 13 12 11

Printed and bound in Great Britain by
CPI Antony Rowe, Chippenham and Eastbourne

Contents

Tables and Appendices

Acknowledgements

The editors would like to acknowledge the financial support provided by CINEFOGO, the Network of Excellence of the EU 6th Framework Programme.

Anne Kovalainen would like to acknowledge the financial support of the Academy of Finland. A research grant provided her with the possibility to take main responsibility for the final editing of the book during her faculty fellowship at the Michelle R. Clayman Institute for Gender Research, Stanford University. The intellectual stimulus and discussions with colleagues at the Michelle R. Clayman Institute and at Stanford University are greatly acknowledged.

This book is dedicated to all we care about, and are being cared by.

Hanne Marlene Dahl, Roskilde University, Denmark
Marja Keränen, University of Jyväskylä, Finland
Anne Kovalainen, University of Turku, Finland;
Stanford University, USA

May 2011

Notes on Contributors

Thomas P. Boje is Professor of Social Science at the University of Roskilde, Denmark. He was in charge of the CINEFOGO network of excellence 2007–10, and he has published widely on labour markets, gender and the welfare state. Among his most recent publications is *Welfare and Families in Europe* (with Peter Abrahamson and Bent Greve: Ashgate, 2005).

Susana Climent is a doctoral student in sociology at the Universidad Carlos III, Madrid, Spain. Her research interests are in gender and the welfare state, gender and migration, gender and social care.

Hanne Marlene Dahl is Professor in the Department of Society and Globalization at Roskilde University, Denmark. Her research fields include elderly care, Europeanization and globalization of care, and feminist state theory. She has several research projects funded nationally. Her most recent books include *Dilemmas of Care in the Nordic Welfare State* (co-edited with Tine Rask Eriksen: Ashgate, 2005).

Anders Ejrnaes is Associate Professor at the Department of Society and Globalization at Roskilde University, Denmark. He is working within the fields of work/family reconciliation, labour markets, ethnic minorities and European family policy and has published on European societies and European Union politics.

Kirsi Eräranta is a doctoral student at the University of Helsinki, Finland. Her research interests include gender equality policies, European governance, the social politics of fatherhood, gender and sexuality.

Majda Hrzenjak, PhD, works as a researcher at the Institute for Contemporary Social and Political Studies in Ljubljana, Slovenia. Her research interests widely cover social policies, gender studies and cultural studies. Her recent books include *Invisible Work* (Peace Institute, 2007).

Lise Widding Isaksen is Professor in the Department of Sociology, University of Bergen, Norway. Her research interests include global studies, gender and social policy as well as migration. She has published widely within these fields in edited collections and journals.

Marja Keränen is Professor of Political Science at the University of Jyväskylä, Finland. Her research interests range from democracy, political participation and participatory governance to technologies of participation. She leads an Academy of Finland project on Democracy and Governance. Her publications include an *Gender and Politics in Finland* (editor: Avebury, 1992).

Anne Kovalainen is Academy Professor at the University of Turku, Finland, and faculty visiting fellow at Stanford University and the London School of Economics. Her research interests range from gender, economy and social theories to methodological questions. She leads an Academy of Finland project on Gendered Economy. Her latest books include *Qualitative Methods in Business Research* (co-authored with Päivi Eriksson: Sage, 2008).

Janice McLaughlin is Reader in Sociology at Newcastle University, UK. Her research interests include contemporary social theory, family and disability, care, and interdependency. She has published, among other titles, *Families Raising Disabled Children: Enabling Care and Social Justice* (co-authored with Dan Goodley, Emma Clavering and Pamela Fisher: Palgrave Macmillan, 2008).

Kevät Nousiainen is Professor of Comparative Law and Legal Theory at the University of Turku, Finland. Her research interests include theory of law and gender studies in law. She has published widely on her research topics and in 2009 guest edited (with Johanna Kantola) an issue of the *International Journal of Feminist Politics*.

Egle Sumskiene is a lecturer in the Social Work department at the University of Vilnius, Lithuania. Her research interests include institutional care, care for the disabled, and human rights, stigma and discrimination. Her recent publications include 'Child and Adolescent Mental Health in Europe. Research on Best Practice' (with Dainius Puras, *Eurohealth*, 15 (4), 2010).

Joan Tronto is Professor of Political Science at the University of Minnesota. Her research fields range from political theories, gender and the ethic of care, to the history of political thought. She has authored numerous articles and books, including *Moral Boundaries: A Political Argument for an Ethic of Care* (Routledge, 1993) and co-edited (with Cathy J. Cohen and Kathleen B. Jones) *Women Transforming Politics* (New York University Press, 1997).

Fiona Williams is Professor of Social Policy at the University of Leeds. Her research interests range from care in contemporary Europe, gender, 'race' and ethnicity in social policy, to migrant workers in home-based care in Europe. Her publications include articles and books, including *Rethinking Families* (Calouste Gulbenkian Foundation, 2004), *Social Policy, a Critical Introduction* (Polity, 1989) and *Gendering Citizenship in Western Europe* (co-authored with Anneli Anttonen, Jet Bussemaker, Ute Gerhard Ruth Lister et al.: Policy Press, 2007).

Introduction

Hanne Marlene Dahl, Marja Keränen and Anne Kovalainen

This book addresses the recent, and to a large extent still much unexplored, developments concerning care in Europe. It considers care as a crucial part of European restructuring of care labour markets, the contents of care and the different forms of care that range from the EU legislation level to the diversities among the individual care workers' life situations and experiences of being cared for in present-day Europe. The book argues for a strong statement about the complexity of care research – no longer restricted within the domain of social policy research but pertinently addressed in political science and in governance, legal studies and feminist research, and thus calls for a multidisciplinary approach. The chapters in this book show the variety of care arrangements and the multitude of value judgments behind the family-, market- and state-organized care that prevails in Europe. Therefore, questions about forms of Europeanization, the diverse paths for care arrangements and the gender patterns in relation to citizenship and civil society are important for the Europe of the future.

The book addresses the complexities of care affecting many nations and through three key topics, examining the growth of migration of care workers as well as the linkages between formal, private and informal forms of care in different parts of Europe. The overall aim is to re-analyse the welfare models of Europe, which is specifically carried out in several chapters. The argument binding the articles of the book is that the renegotiations of relationships among the family, the market and the social welfare state take different forms and different shapes throughout Europe, thus requiring special attention to be given to care chains, forms of care and the embedded and embodied nature of care. In addition, the discrepancies in development within European nation-states are exposed and explored in individual chapters, in relation to the European

Union's aim of achieving cohesiveness in social policy development at the European level.

Recent research dealing with different types of care arrangements and welfare services in the fields of sociology, social policy and political science have recognized the changing or even diminishing significance of the nation-state, on the one hand, and the increasing tensions between the transforming nation-states, developments within the welfare state, and ideas of citizenship at the European level, on the other hand. The complexity of the idea of citizenship, what it consists of, and the real care-related needs of people become visible in current European development with its recent enlargement and economic crisis – both processes that articulate and carve out the differences in gendered structures of care arrangements throughout the continent. The assumption that European citizenship can be defined in terms of clearly defined rights such as care-related rights that are underpinned by a shared set of values might perhaps be misleading, or at least, misleading in its simplicity.

One key feature of the present EU is that the nation-states are adjusting to Europeanization, because the EU has been an important agency in enhancing the social rights of its citizens. Still, Europeanization is not a single, straightforward process of integration and unification of similarities, but is full of smaller processes that are closer to differentiation and even contradictory by nature. In addition, global trends have an effect at the European and the national levels: the interdependency of economic fluctuations and national possibilities to allocate budgets to care structures is clearly increasing with the current global economic uncertainty. Partly for these reasons, the continued diversity of national traditions based on gendered labour market positions, on gendered care arrangements, and developing dissimilarities is presented in all of the chapters in this book. In addition, the neo-colonial aspects of these relations that transcend national boundaries are discussed, and show a remarkable new restructuring that is taking place throughout Europe. It is therefore important to mediate the understanding of the pluralism that is characteristic of both welfare state developments and care arrangements, as well as the legal regimes underlying these two, in order to be able to highlight the variety of issues that are uppermost in citizenship discussions.

This book, through detailed descriptions from various parts of Europe, aims to increase this understanding. Our argument valorizes the varieties of care arrangements through the whole array of cared-for and vulnerable groups in different nation-states. Whatever the nature of Europeanization processes, the Europeanization of the nation-state is not leading to any grander, single version of the nation-state. Europeanization can in fact be treated as a specific form of globalization (see, for example, Rumford 2003; Delanty and Rumford 2005; Sassen 2007), thus displaying and articulating the tendencies that can unify and can be common to nation-states, tendencies that may tear them apart, as well as other tendencies such as culturally and socially embedded ideas of citizenship, good care, the role of women in care processes and positions of families, markets and the state.

Some chapters will explore in a more detailed manner the presently existing varieties of care, care arrangements and care relations in different sectors throughout various parts of Europe, in order to unveil the layered nature and national patchwork patterns of care and its general interwoven nature with different gendered positions. The chapters in this book do not aim to cover all the various forms of care throughout the whole of Europe, but to show the varieties of care and the key aspects that lead to different developments in the various regions. When analysing care arrangements, the contemporary context involves consideration of the various intersectionalities of care: the dependencies and complexities of various issues such as migration, the labour market situation of women, state dependency and independency, and welfare policies. The book does not aim to cover all functional forms of care in all parts of Europe. Nor does it cover all forms of publicly provided versus privately provided care services and the shifting balance between these two. Instead we deliver case studies illustrating the key complexities of contemporary care relations that manifest the gradual processes of convergence and divergence present in European care in relation to gender relations and welfare state formation. The sometimes overly simplistic notion of European citizenship as a passport citizenship is challenged in the chapters throughout the book through addressing the gendered nature of the complex relationships between the individual, the state and society through care and care arrangements.

Research on care tends to be functionally divided into different forms of care, such as elderly care, child care, care of the disabled and so forth. By bringing forward in this volume recent studies on various forms of care we illustrate the similarities and differences as well as the complexity of care in different institutional and cultural contexts as well as giving a flavour of the differences in understanding what good care is about in different welfare regimes. Our book provides a unique opportunity for the reader to understand the complexity of care, the diversity in care regimes and varying ideas about care in the present European context.

The articles in this book are united in their aim to show how contradictory and highly contested are tendencies toward the single notion of the Europeanization of care. Thus, rather than aiming for fully comprehensive pan-European coverage, as this is not possible, the selected cases in this book offer views on the existing differences within Europe. Care is in itself a highly contested concept since its constituent features are (and have been) debated in a lively manner over time (see, for example, Tronto 1993; Bubeck 1995; Cooper 2007; Beasley and Bacchi 2007). Inspired by Joan Tronto, among others, we view care as principally involving four schematically different aspects of care: caring about, taking care of, care-giving, and care-receiving, that is, the response to care by the receiving person (Tronto 1993). The notion of 'care' thus needs to be taken into its wider context and related to the changing citizenship and changing nation-state discourses. When the aspects of 'rights discourse' are related to the 'differences discourse', we may then specify the different conditions through which the rights can be realized.

Understood broadly, care is thus much more than the face-to-face care giving of two persons physically meeting, defined earlier by, for example, Bubeck (1995) as the key feature of care. Care involves that as well, but is not bound to face-to-face meeting and entails more societally understood tenets of care. Care takes place in informal and formal settings where embedded institutional arrangements (such as national or supranational legislation, the welfare state or the labour market) enable or define the forms of care. Thinking about care in general terms involves seeing and taking responsibility for the needs of dependent people, such as children, and handicapped and elderly persons, that they cannot possibly meet themselves. This aspect of dependency (Baier 1992) is usually identified and analysed in relation to and at the personal level of care, involving and including aspects of vulnerability, trust and mistrust (Kovalainen 2004). But care involves aspects other than the interpersonal. Care carries the socio-cultural and even legal notions of how and in what ways care is permanently and institutionally arranged, supported, organized, discussed and handled in the nation-state context. Dependency with regard to care relations extends beyond the interpersonal aspects of care, following the persons who migrate for care work, and thus extends the dependencies over state borders and nation-states. The migration of care workers changes the spatial landscape of dependencies and shows how deeply embedded care – be it formal or informal – is in economic relationships of different kinds, thus relating care closely to gender, work arrangements and informal dependencies that are often forgotten in welfare regime discussions. Here, the questions of citizenship and migration become crucially involved and entangled with the formal and informal arrangements of care, as several chapters in this volume point out.

Ideals about care have changed historically (see, for example, Wærness 1987; Finch 1989; Dahl 2005) pointing most often to the conventional element in care. Constructions of care, however, differ not only in time, but also potentially across space, be they local or national contexts, such as between different care cultures (Hochschild 1995). Care of the elderly, the handicapped and children takes place in the family/friends network and in civil society by NGOs, the state and the market. Care is regulated within and between various policy fields as social, health and family policies at both the national and intergovernmental level. Care is in this respect subject to multilevel governance, ranging from highly private and interpersonal arrangements to nation-state and supra-state level regulations.

The inherently gendered nature of care means that at the European level it is possible to argue that the new rearrangements at the European level cannot be detached from wider societal issues such as family structures, cultures of care, social policy, and labour market structures, policies and processes. Yet the gendered nature of care is in constant change: who works in the care services, who pays for it, who is employed and on what terms, and what types of shifts can be seen at the policy levels throughout Europe. The grey area of paid and unpaid care work, formal employment contracts and black labour markets in care are shifting and changing and taking the form of international care labour migration. At the same time, multinational care companies are growing as international businesses, increasing their volume in Europe and changing care services by providing care infrastructure in many countries (Kovalainen and Sundin 2008).

Often issues of gendering are related to issues of recognition and misrecognition of care work. We understand recognition often as status equality (Fraser 2003). Recognition of care-giving work therefore means the equal socio-cultural value of this kind of work on a par with other forms of work. Misrecognition of care-giving work is seen to relate to its hidden, unpaid character, but misrecognition is even identified in paid care-giving work by the state (Dahl 2004; 2009). Misrecognition in state policies are here related to new forms of governing inspired by New Public Management that marketize and standardize care-giving work – a misrecognition that revitalizes old feminist struggles about the valorization of care (Dahl 2009).

Feminist researchers have long argued for a re-evaluation of care (Bubeck 1995; Knijn and Kremer 1997). And in our view this involves not only both the right to give and the right to receive care (Knijn and Kremer 1997), but also the many aspects related to vulnerability and dependency (Baier 1992). Baier in fact questions the totalizing idea of 'care' and its stereotypical features (see, for example, Kovalainen 2004). This book addresses these various complexities of care affecting individuals in the nexus of three processes: first, through the assumed Europeanization of care and its effects; second, through the different forms of care in different parts of Europe; and third, through the varieties of care relations in Europe. It also offers unique analyses of current care relations and the more structured care arrangements and a re-analysis of the present welfare models of Europe, arguing that the renegotiations of relationships among the family, market and the social welfare state take different forms and different shapes throughout Europe, thus requiring special attention throughout the care chains, the forms of care and the embedded and embodied nature of care.

The Europeanization of care?

Can we identify a Europeanization of care, understood as an emerging, yet thin, European social citizenship, as has been suggested in recent literature (Mantu 2008; Bleijenbergh et al. 2004)? We argue that Europeanization is not necessarily one single, traceable process, nor is it a clear-cut 'mature' concept that can be used as an explanatory resource for all changes or processes: we first need to ask what is specific in Europeanization and how it differs from globalization or other processes of transformation such as cosmopolitanization, as sketched out by Beck (2002; 2006). For Beck cosmopolitanization is not the conventional type of globalization with top-down, economy-led processes, but consists of more multidimensional, contradictory processes that include new institutional forms of creating social space and new rule-creating bodies such as the International Court of Justice. This type of change emerged from the internal transformation of societies. Specific to Europeanization as a process are the legislative measures taken by the EU, the supranational regulatory body par excellence. This feature can distinguish Europeanization from globalization, even if it does not necessarily differ from it as a process.

Throughout the chapters the variety of processes that can be labelled as Europeanization will become apparent, although contradictory tendencies exist. Europeanization can be identified as taking place at various levels. At one level the Council of Europe issues directives such as the formally binding piece of legislation on parental leave (1996), and it can also issue less binding targets such as those adopted for child care provision (2002). At another level the European Court of Justice gradually pushes welfare regulation on health issues forward, thus reducing the sovereignty of the member states and creating rights for European citizens on some forms of care (Martinsen 2009). Other understandings of Europeanization highlight the convergence toward a European social model on social expenditures (Greve 1996; Heichel et al. 2005). And yet at another level it seems impossible to neglect the spread of sociocultural ideas about good care around countries within Europe, which also contributes to the Europeanization of care.

By exploring different forms of care, different care arrangements and different ideas about care in Europe from a gender perspective at various levels, we hope to contribute to feminist research on the EU and to studies on Europeanization and studies on care. Feminist research on the EU has primarily focused on gender mainstreaming (Pollack and Hafner-Burton 2000; Squires 2005) and the reconciliation of work and family life (which has mostly covered care but not other forms of family life) (Lewis et al. 2008; Lewis 2006), as well as gender relations within the supranational body (Walby 1997). Explorations of care and gender relate also to the wider questions on gendered citizenship (see, for example, Lister 1990; Walby 1997). Europeanization studies have been, on the other hand, too often focused on key fields of integration within the supranational body, such as agricultural and regional policy, thus fulfilling the conventional policy-driven approach and neglecting any issues on care. This omission may be explained by the lack of stress on social policy issues in the EU up to 1992. However, the 1992 recommendation on social protection, that is social welfare, radically changed this situation and has incrementally led to the development of EU social policy (Falkner 2008). This social policy is more developed in the field of employment than in care politics as such.

The topic of Europeanization has produced studies on how European integration affects domestic politics and policies (Radaelli and Pasquier 2008; Bulmer 2008). It has been argued by Radaelli that Europeanization consists of processes of: a) construction; b) diffusion; and c) institutionalization of formal and informal rules, procedures, policy paradigms, styles, 'ways of doing things' and shared beliefs and norms, which are first defined and consolidated in the EU policy process and then incorporated in the logic of domestic (national and subnational) discourse, political structures and public policies (Radaelli 2000, 4). This top-down approach to effects at the level of the nation-state, such as the diffusion of ideas and adaption of new policies, also includes other processes of the EU system of governance. The OMC and the procedure of social partnership are both soft regulation procedures. In the OMC the EU puts pressure on member states to reform by setting common objectives and monitoring their progress by means of peer review (Lewis 2006). It is primarily used within social policies, and there is scholarly disagreement as to its political efficacy (Borras and Greve 2004; Lewis 2006). The procedure of social partnership is a non-binding mode of regulation between labour market organizations.

Still, Europeanization can and will take place in other processes as well, as described in this book. Part of the difficulty resides in understanding how to assess the extent of Europeanization – as a process it does not stop or adopt a rigid formula but transforms into other types of activities, as well as trickling down to practices and processes. The chapters in this book each offer their own unique way of understanding the present Europeanization in relation to the practices and processes of care-related activities, be they bureaucracy and its formation or the migration of individuals within Europe.

Europeanization, however, seems to us more complicated than the division offered by Radaelli (2000) above. While one can find disparities between sectors in EU policies, some being open while others are not, the outcome is a contradiction between free movement of labour but no comprehensive regulation on social issues. In the case of care the disparity becomes extremely clear: the ideology of subsidiarity exists (the EU relegating issues of care to nation-states) whereas some policies are visibly regulated (equality being high on the agenda at certain periods of time). Furthermore, the same kind of regulation obviously lands in different places differently and is implemented in very different ways, garnering different meanings and consequences in various locations.

One of the consequences of Europeanization is that the models and the varied ways of organizing care in different parts of Europe need to be taken into consideration at the same time as the process of Europeanization modifies and changes the models themselves. Welfare state models therefore become descriptions of variation in the local contexts. At the same time Europeanization has to be described as a process that transforms and revises.

The outcome of the above is a web of local and nation-state practices and policies of care that are increasingly affected by both each other and EU regulation. This web becomes a crisscross system of different types of care, involving different traditions for organizing that care, institutional or domestic, with variation in who provides and who receives care. This crisscross system involves different parts of Europe and different types of welfare regimes that have now become senders and receivers of care labour. The problems and the challenges are still embedded in local settings that vary: the Nordic model, in this volume represented by Finland (Eräranta), the United Kingdom and Ireland (McLaughlin), as examples of the countries where cash for care has increased the number of differing solutions; Southern European informal care models represented by Spanish and Italian cases (Climent and Isaksen); and the new member states from central and eastern Europe (Slovenia in Hzrenjak, Poland in Isaksen). Through these cases we wish to show that there exists a large variation in the crisscross system of people and inter-national networks. In this system, the question of 'uneven' and contradictory Europeanization produces a puzzling patchwork of unintended consequences. The traditional idea of care as private, performed by mothers and daughters in the home, is presently being negotiated at various levels, including negotiations between the women in an Italian family and their domestic, Polish care worker about the proper way to care for an elderly female relative. Cultural ideas of good care are also being negotiated in various European policy circles framed by the social and political context of a care squeeze, between New Public Management and economic stagnation.

A post-welfare market society?

Care has surfaced on the political agenda of the EU. It has been on the minds of policy-makers in the Parliament, the Commission and the Council. Care has been framed within a horizon of a care crisis indicated by an increasing demand for care and a decreasing supply of carers (Saraceno 1997; Hochschild 2003), as well as by an increasing expenditure structure of care. The increasing demand for care is due in part to the retrenchment of welfare states linked to the dominance of neo-liberal ideas such as marketization and individualization (Larner 2000) in New Public Management (NPM) and increasing numbers of elderly people in European societies. The decreasing supply of care givers is due to increasing numbers of women in paid (part- or full-time) work and to recruitment problems in paid care (Dybbroe 2008).

Within the last 20 years we have witnessed neo-liberal policies that have redefined public care as properly belonging to the market or to the community. These new ideas about the state and care have travelled between nation-states and international forums such as the OECD and the EU (see, for example, Marcussen 2002; Sahlin-Anderson 2002) either as a result of policy learning within the EU or as ideas that have become the dominant, naturalized way of doing things (Unalan 2009). As a result of new ideas arising from NPM we have witnessed a withdrawal of some states from their care-giving obligations, an increasing consumerist discourse stressing the free choice of the user-citizen (Glendinning 2008) and the development of cash-for-care schemes (Ungerson and Yeandle 2007) as an alternative to care services.

Most visibly, the care of children has had top priority and entered the European agenda first. As previously mentioned, this resulted in a (formally binding) directive on parental leave (1996) and targets for child care provision (2002). The EU aims to have child care provision for 33 per cent of children under three and care services for 90 per cent of its children between three and school age (Lewis et al. 2008). Lately elderly care has entered the political agenda as well. We have witnessed an emerging discourse about how Europe should respond to the care crisis framed as 'Eurosclerosis'. This notion refers to a nation-state model where sagging growth in the economy, together with rising unemployment, make it impossible to renew any of the existing or prevailing structures.

EU policy-makers have looked upon the Nordic model as a normative ideal that is seen to solve some of the contemporary problems most member states are currently facing, for example Eurosclerosis (Borchorst 2008). The Nordic model is often characterized by the public responsibility for and provision of large parts of care, such as care for pre-school children and elderly care (Hernes 1987; Szebehely 2003). But the Nordic model is on the move as well: the purchaser–provider split has brought in new elements and new forms for arranging care services, and new agencies that are no longer state governed to the same extent as before. The Nordic model is facing challenges and struggling with the same demographic and economic problems as the rest of Europe.

European Union member states have to face three major challenges on the horizon: demographics, gender equality and knowledge (Borchorst 2008; Esping-Andersen 2007). The demographic challenge concerns the aging populations that are supposed to lead to financial problems for the welfare state, whereas publicly provided day care and elderly care is intended to increase women's incentives to have children (thereby increasing fertility rates), deliver higher female employment rates and provide better care for the elderly. Elderly care in the Nordic model provides cheaper care compared to other alternatives, better coverage and more equity between classes and genders (Sarasa and Mestres 2007) and is consequently seen as a preferred solution. Regarding knowledge, politicians increasingly view the EU as being in strong competition with the rest of the world, and therefore a stronger competitive and 'knowledge-based' production is seen to be necessary (Borchorst 2008).

However, which policy field care is understood to belong to is important for framing and for the solutions imagined. At the EU level the surfacing of care on the political agenda seems strongly related to issues of employability, that is of expanding the pool of available workers, seen as one of the main objectives of the Lisbon strategy (Lewis et al. 2008; Borchorst 2008). Whether care is constructed as belonging to one and/or the other policy field has vital importance for the priority assigned on the political agenda and for the way it becomes framed (Bacchi 1999). It is therefore interesting to note that issues of care are not systematically framed as a gender equality issue. Issues of gender equality are instead instrumental in relation to achieving growth and competitiveness (Lewis et al. 2008).

Four responses to the present care crisis have been imagined: a traditional, a post-modern, a cold modern and a warm modern response (Hochschild 1995). According to Hochschild these solutions are images informing social policies. A traditional model reverses industrialization and women's liberation by installing women as the main care givers (unpaid in the home); a post-modern model leaves matters as they are, reducing expectations about care; whereas the cold and warm modern models imply differing degrees of institutionalization. A 'cold' modern model institutionalizes all forms of human care, whereas the 'warm' modern model attempts a balance between institutional and private care as established (ideally) in the Nordic countries (Hochschild 1995). A fifth model is now emerging within the EU as a traditional model of care but installing paid migrant workers within the home, as outlined by British sociologist Fiona Williams in Chapter 2 in this book on migrating care workers in different European welfare regimes. Variations between EU member states depend upon the interlocking of care, migration and employment regimes. Particularly important are cultures of care that enforce or restrain the extent to which a migrant-in-the-home becomes a legitimate model for solving a care squeeze, such as is seen in Spanish case in Chapter 9 by Susana Climent in this book, in contrast to the illegitimacy of such a model in Sweden.

In contrast to the commodification of care within the home, we might look to the EU and contemplate how the model of care is envisioned at the EU level at this moment in time. As argued by Finnish legal scholar Kevät Nousiainen in Chapter 1, care at the EU level is bound by a double principle of subsidiarity. On the one hand, the EU is to be only a *subsidium* (help or aid) to the member states in matters related to care, and on the other, the state itself is considered as supplementary to the care carried out by families and civil society. Many areas of social welfare lie altogether outside EU legislative competence and see poor response in the new member states' national policies, as shown in by Madja Hrzenjak and Egle Sumskiene in Chapters 3 and 6, respectively. Due to contested EU legitimacy under the subsidiarity principle, the issue of how responsibility for child care should be allocated became a matter for self-regulation between labour market organizations. It is possible to argue that this principle protects traditional gendered responsibility for care and as such reproduces a traditional model of care as identified by Hochschild. If the 'time off' leave model is extended to care for the elderly, we will face even more disparately gendered responsibilities.

Questions about European social citizenship arise from unification tendencies, visible, for example, in the so-called activation reforms, which have throughout Europe – partly due to processes related in the European Employment Strategy (EES) – somewhat tightened up the systems of income maintenance and increased investments in human resource development (see, for example, Hvinden et al. 2001). This activation has been seen as part of the 'widening of citizens' social rights' and as one step towards 'welfare democracy' and active citizenship. These policy activation measures most often tend to forget the kinds of work that in some European countries are related to the core of women's employment, paid or unpaid, and in some European countries to the shadow economy, the informal economy and even to migratory and gendered black labour markets.

Plan of the book

The book addresses the complexities of care affecting many nations through three nexuses: through Europeanization, through different modes and regimes of care and through neo-colonial gender relations of care in Europe. These questions are analysed through the ten chapters that are thematically arranged under these topics. The initial three chapters, in the the first part 'The Europeanization of Care', cover the transformation of social citizenship in Europe, partly through social dialogue, and partly through the migration that has changed the care relations and the care crisis in Europe. The question of change processes in Europe such as the Open Method of Coordination (OMC) and the procedure of social partnership are discussed Chapter 1 by Finnish legal scholar Kevät Nousiainen. But as British sociologist Fiona Williams argues in

Chapter 2, the Europeanization of care is not similar everywhere: it depends on the interlocking of the care, migration and employment regimes, which all vary in Europe. At the same time, as argued by Slovenian sociologist Majda Hrzenjak in Chapter 3, there is a new merger, for example, between different agendas, such as ensuring high employment, solving the care crisis and creating gender equality in the EU. The transformation of unpaid work traditionally carried out in private homes by women is increasingly seen by policy-makers as having potential for job creation, and its regulation is seen as a win-win situation: it addresses the need for more and better home and family services, while at the same time provides for more and better quality jobs for hard-to-employ people. However, it appears that the idea opens up as many problems as solutions, and Hrzenjak argues that regularization as a political solution will reproduce existing inequalities concerning gender and class. Instead she argues in favour of care services provided by the state: stable 'status jobs' (that is, recognized positions) as envisioned in either the cold modern or warm modern model outlined by Hochschild.

The second part of the book, 'The Complexity of Care', deals with care in various nation-states in Europe. The four chapters offer analytical reviews of different types of welfare regimes and their various strategies towards different forms and types of care at the intersection of gender, dependency, vulnerability and the modern nation-state. A wide area of different types of care, institutional and domestic, thus comes into focus. The book, however, does not deal with care work within the state and/or contemporary re-structuring processes. Elsewhere we have shown that restructuring of care has been ongoing for a considerable time, and is mainly taking place within a nation-state context (Dahl 2005) while being formed by the transnational travelling of ideas related to neo-liberalism (Larner 2000). The backgrounds of different nation-states vary, and they therefore valorize the problem in different ways and determine the local solutions, practices and meanings attached to them. The Southern models (Italy, Spain) with a tradition of home-based care seem more willing to solve the care squeeze problem by importing women migrants. The Nordic countries on the other hand seem less willing to solve their care squeeze by employing care workers in homes, and thus the phenomenon remains an issue.

Differences between European countries have often been captured by presenting regime models of welfare state arrangements. The models vary in their conceptions of how to organize care: should care be private or public? Should it be paid or unpaid? Should it be institutional and commodified or familiarized? The values attached to different solutions have always varied; the 'woman-friendliness' of Nordic welfare states has been related to reproduction going public, that is becoming a state responsibility where care becomes paid in the institutional context of the welfare state (Hernes 1987). Care comes in so many forms that simple solutions cannot be found and, as stated, various solutions are attached to values which also differ.

Discussing different forms of care enriches the debate and illustrates how narrow our earlier focus on care has been, preferably discussing child care as pre-school care. With the demographic time bomb ahead of us, care for the elderly especially appears as a pressing issue and calls for specific feminist attention. This, of course, does not mean that pre-school care should be abandoned as a research topic. Welfare regime research has been framing the issues discussed concerning care. Two Danish sociologists, Anders Ejrnaes and Thomas Boje, in Chapter 4, on 'Family Policy and Welfare Regimes', wish to unveil the myth of stable regimes. They argue that typologies are neither stable nor sufficient. They also note that typologies are built on the specific forms of care investigated. Considering different kinds of care, other typologies would emerge. In their comparative analysis they illustrate the genderedness of care by documenting the changing patterns in women's labour force participation and its relationship to the variety of care models, and thus also to welfare regime models.

Different forms of care and different circumstances result in different solutions. A nurse in a hospital experiences different working conditions from a privately employed domestic servant. Forms of care actually vary enormously depending on what type of care is studied. In Chapter 5 British sociologist Janice McLaughlin analyses caring practices associated with raising a disabled child. Based on an ethnographic study of the mothers' strategies of caring for the disabled child, she discusses how the mothers challenge the privatization and marginalization of care, and question the ideal of the individual autonomous adult and the discomfort with dependency in considerations of citizenship.

While Mclaughlin's chapter discusses care in the family (and its connections to welfare state institutions), in Chapter 6 Egle Sumskiene discusses care by professionals in specialized public institutions, that is, care of the intellectually disabled and the mentally ill. Even here, the citizenship rights of the cared-for are restricted. Based on qualitative and quantitative data gathered from politicians, officials and NGOs in transitive Lithuania, the article discusses conceptions of modernity in the context of care. In spite of the collapse of the Soviet system, which favoured institutional care, transformation does not seem to bring along better citizenship rights for this minority of minorities. The article questions what is considered good care and what is modern care in the context of Lithuanian society, as well as how conceptions of this have changed over time with changes in Lithuanian society, from socialism to EU membership. With European enlargement, then, the increasing volume of the community also brings increasing heterogeneity.

The discussion of welfare state models (such as by Esping-Andersen 1990) and its feminist revisions (Lewis 2002; 2004a) has seen an ambivalent and contradictory content. The models can act as heuristic tools, but they can also become too-convenient conceptions of differences between countries. The regime model debate may have met its limits in the face of the enlargement of the EU: how do we classify the entering countries of Eastern Europe in the models based on data from western countries? Another problem with regime models concerns the methodological nationalism ingrained in the thought of comparing nation-states. Welfare states can no longer be treated as isolated units. Based upon the first section of the book one would have to question the utility of nation-states as stable units of analysis and the validity of methodological nationalism. Analysing official documents on the issue of reconciliation of work and family, Kirsi Eräranta, in Chapter 7, 'Changing Conceptions of Citizenship and Care in Finnish Policy Discourse', shows how Finland, earlier classified as belonging to the Nordic model, has from the 1980s to the 2000s significantly changed: as the earlier governmental rationality was that of 'a working mother' or 'citizen worker', the related rationalities of child care and welfare production have significantly changed. Interestingly, one could ask whether this is a result of Finland joining the EU and thereby increasingly being integrated into the frame and discursive sphere of EU governance.

Women form an increasing percentage of migration flows (Kofman 2003; Yeates 2009). This is due to a new international division of labour where women's wage work in developed countries creates a demand for care work. This demand is met by women migrating from other countries, perhaps leaving their families and children behind and causing a care drain in the country of origin (Hochschild 2001a; Isaksen et al. 2008). The result is the creation of global care chains defined as: '... a series of personal links between people across the globe based on paid and unpaid work of caring' (Hochschild 2001a, 131).

The existence of care chains causes much suffering and erodes the social solidarities in the sending country (Isaksen et al. 2008). Whether this is coercive or emancipating, and who benefits, is not always simple to determine. The care chain problem in Europe has both a global and a regional character since there is both migration from the outside, that is from countries outside the EU, often from former colonies, and internal migration such as from the East to West. Sending and receiving countries can vary depending on many factors. As an example, Ireland has been a sending and a receiving country at various times (Yeates 2009). Causes of migration are often related to reasons in the country of origin (Sørensen 2002) as well as to more global inequalities (Hochschild 2001a). What happens to workers in the receiving country depends on whether they are high- or low-skilled, constituting a step up or down in social strata: they either become integrated into a professional labour force or end up in a private ghetto of dependency and deprivation. We exclusively focus here upon the downward migration of low-skilled legal or illegal migrants.

The third part of the book discusses more closely such 'Neo-Colonial Care Relations in Europe'. Informally paid domestic workers, no matter whether they are migrants or endogenous women, with their activity in the domestic sphere and domestic work, reorganize notions of welfare and the relationship between care and paid work in European societies in a fundamentally private, anti-egalitarian and exclusionary way. The current discussion on intersectionality has concerned the intersection of gender and ethnicity, but many of the earlier debates were concerned with the relationship between gender and class. Both types of analysis may find continuity of tradition with the literature on the 'global care chain', in which women from some of the poorest countries of the world migrate in order to care for the children and homes of rich women in the North. In this analysis, position in the global capitalist hierarchy of countries as core or periphery, class, ethnicity and gender all combine to produce this exploitation of the specifically feminized labour of care work.

However, in discussions of intersectionality of care, the corporeality of the care-givers and those being cared about are often forgotten. The culturally embedded ideas of the corporeality of the care work and thus also the values of that work become visible in Chapter 8 by Norwegian sociologist Lise Widding Isaksen on 'Nomadic Care Workers in Europe – a Polish-Italian Example'. Care chains are conditioned in different ways and with different intensities in different welfare state models. The legalization strategies followed in some countries, as discussed by Susana Climent in Chapter 9, 'Migrant Women and Defamilization in the Spanish Welfare State', break down the traditional division in migrating policies between high- and low-skilled workers. The broader effects of this globalization of care in the form of care chains and care drain in an

emerging transnational economy of care prompts us to raise normative issues concerning rights to give and receive care for the migrating
care-givers – in short about their citizenship (Isaksen et al. 2008) and
more generally raising global issues of ethics. A new global ethics of
care is required, in Fiona Williams' view, echoing an earlier call by Fiona
Robinson (1999). The American philosopher Joan Tronto argues instead
that it is not a question of ethics but of citizenship – in Chapter 10 she
follows the ideas of Wendy Sarvasy and Patrizia Longo (2004). By relating
the issue to the theoretical space of citizenship she links it to questions
of the rights and obligations of those who belong to the community.
She illustrates in her chapter the needs for care-as-citizenship based upon
a broad view of care contributions (paid and unpaid) to the society. She
also urges us, however, to rethink who we are and those usually thought
of as the others/the newcomers – seeing us both as caring citizens and
as receivers of care. In this sense she calls for a radical new idea of the
community as global in character and deconstructs our stereotypical
notions of care giver versus care receiver.

Thematically we have outlined different ways that challenges to care
have been dealt with or should be dealt with at various levels within
the EU: migration at the level of the individual nation-states, reconciliation policies of work and family life at the EU level, and regulation of
informal domestic work. The questions related to the changing nature
of care cannot be understood as detached from the contextual understanding nor understanding of the past, present and future of care work:
how the state is participating in or distancing care from its citizenship;
the role of the voluntary and private sectors; and the changing position
of family. There is no single answer for Europe, and one cannot even be
imagined, as the chapters of this book will illustrate.

Part I
The Europeanization of Care

1
Double Subsidiarity, Double Trouble?: Allocating Care Responsibilities in the EU through Social Dialogue

Kevät Nousiainen

Introduction

This chapter reflects on the recent reform of the European Union (EU) Parental Leave Directive[1] and its history. Negotiations between the European social partners led to a revised framework agreement on parental leave,[2] implemented as an EU directive in 2010.[3]

The reform of European regulation of parental leaves is an exercise in the 'European Social Dialogue', consisting of negotiations between employers and trade unions at the EU level. The first Parental Leave Directive, which set minimum legislative requirements for the (EU) member states, was the outcome of a lengthy process, part of 'reconciliation of family and working life' in European politics, and finally the first directive based on an agreement between the 'social partners' following a procedure that was made possible by the Social Protocol of the Maastricht Treaty. An agreement between the 'social partners' can be turned into a binding piece of legislation as a directive.

A better balance between work and family life is highlighted in the EU Lisbon Strategy of 2000. Provision of care services and flexible work are other policies to be considered alongside care-related leaves, and all these policies have different equality and other effects. Care-related leaves are the focus of this chapter, however.

The history of the parental leave agreement and directive exemplifies difficulties to be met in order to arrive at EU-level regulations on care. Addressing the need for balancing work and family life is stressed in European political agendas, both in order that Europe may deal with the demographic imbalance and for purposes of gender equality. Political means for reaching the goal are made difficult by the structural problems in European decision-making. A binding regulatory action was the main means of harmonization needed for the creation of a Common Market in Europe until 1980. Since then, a turn to a 'decentralized approach in line with the principle of subsidiarity', and a method in which 'the Union, the member states, the regional and local levels, as well as the social partners and civil society, will be actively involved, using variable forms of partnership'[4] has been manifest.

The principle of subsidiarity in EU law regulates the functional allocation of legislative and administrative powers between different levels of multi-level governance. The EU is a supranational polity, with complex processes of institutionalization of such governance. The principle of subsidiarity is important as a demarcation between national and supranational policies. It is based on the idea that decisions should be made at as local a level as possible. More generally, however, the principle of subsidiarity protects individuals and local interests against the state. The principle is claimed to originate from the Papal Encyclical of 1931, which claims that 'it is an injustice, a grave evil and a disturbance of the right order, for a larger and higher association to arrogate to itself functions which can be performed efficiently by smaller and lower societies'. The doctrine resonates with the Aristotelian tradition, as well as with Thomism (Senden 2004, 79) – generally, the doctrine on which Canon law on family is largely based. It can be seen as an antidote to any type of governance based on strong public policies, but also as a bulwark against political interventions into family life.

The claim that EU policies related to reconciliating paid work and family life take place under the constraints of 'double subsidiarity' refers thus to two types of constraints on public policies regarding gendered practices of parenting. On one hand, the family is treated as an area of political non-interference in the modern political and legal doctrine. In the 19th century, the family was set apart as a natural community obeying moral laws beyond the political mandate of the nation-state. In consequence, highly segregated public and private gender roles enjoyed immunity against the legislator. The human rights instruments of the post-war period reinforced the ideology which considers government interventions into family life dangerous. Further, the specific nature of the EU as a polity with weak powers to enforce social policies and even less mandate to legislate about family law makes it difficult to introduce EU policies that aim at reallocation of care responsibilities. This chapter considers how these constraints appear in the on-going process of 'reconciliation of professional, private and family life'.

'Double subsidiarity' is brought into play in the legislative procedure on family-related leaves that shall define the minimum standard for the 27 EU member states. The material outcome is relevant even to those member states that are willing to exceed the EU minimum, because the minimum standard has an impact on structures that underpin the sharing of care responsibilities, such as provision of child care services. The choice of policy instrument – here corporatist procedure leading to binding legislation – reflects subsidiarity in the sense of reluctance to develop enforceable social rights that would exceed what is considered necessary for the economic function of the EU. Further, subsidiarity in the second sense makes it difficult to regulate family-related leaves in a manner that would effect a change towards 'adult breadwinner' families. Dual subsidiarity reads double trouble on the route to a social policy aspiration to strengthen gender-neutral parenting.

This chapter traces the history leading to the present state of the European-level regulation of parental leaves, and assesses the outcome against the expectations arising from legal and political structures. The outcome of the procedure is seen to follow from characteristics of the Social Dialogue as such, and policies that rely on suasion based on performance assessment, which both seem to predict the adoption of the Nordic parental leave model as the minimum standard of EU regulation.

The structure of the chapter is as follows: first, family-related leave arrangements are seen as a part of EU *gender equality politics* (Threlfall 2000; Duncan 2002; McGlynn 2005). Family-related leaves are considered in the light of their effects on gendered parenting and other gendered patterns of care. Parental leave is often seen as a means to be used in promoting more equal sharing of care responsibilities. From this perspective, EU gender equality policies are seen as a continuum from the gender equality law of the 1970s, which concentrated on equality rights in access to employment and working conditions and social security directly related to paid occupations, into the late 1980s, when the attention shifted to measures to help parents reconcile paid work and family responsibilities. Family-related leaves can either reproduce the existing gender imbalance in care responsibilities and paid versus unpaid work, or balance them between parents more equally. Different breadwinner models have been discussed by scholars since 1990s (Lewis 1993; Sainsbury 1994; Sainsbury 1996), and the Nordic states have came out in comparisons as ones that encourage female participation in paid work. The shift towards an 'adult worker model', based on more equal presence in paid work and care for men and women, has since become a part of the EU employment policies (Guerrina 2008).

Second, the chapter also considers the 'reconciliation dialogue' in relation to *the social objectives in European law*. European-level social policy has been a contested issue from its very beginnings, when European integration took place mainly as a project for expansion of free trade. While economic integration has provided a rationale for the promotion of social rights in Europe, such rights have protected free movement or competition. Proponents of welfare rights see market integration as a threat to the capacity of nation-states to enact social provisions. Social rights that are no longer viable at the national level could be introduced by the EU, but social policies and rights normally require legislation, which is difficult to achieve in the EU context (Poiares Maduro 2000).

Social objectives of the EU are strongly connected to the labour market, and social rights on the European level are therefore often in the ambit of *labour law*, with the employment relation as its primary focus. Labour law sets up dichotomies, such as work/family, paid work/unpaid work, formal economy/informal economy. Scholarly engagement with labour law benefits those in paid work, and excludes precarious women workers moving between productive and reproductive tasks. 'Family-friendly labour law' is thus generated from a position outside labour law proper (Conaghan 2005). The chapter reflects how the use of the social partners' agreement for enhancing family-related leaves functions in this respect.

Third, the 'reconciliation dialogue' is considered from the point of view of choice of policy instruments. In the mid-1980s, a trend of preferring soft law measures instead of legislation, and *deregulation* in general, developed in the EC. One of the outcomes of the political impasse concerning social rights was that new measures were developed for the task, among them the 'Social Dialogue' which introduced European-level corporatist negotiations leading to agreements and further to binding law.

The aim is to analyse the present 'Social Dialogue' on reconciliation of family and working life by framing the dialogue in a manner that combines insights from these frames: 'reconciliation dialogue' as an answer to gender equality, to European social aspirations, that are an annex to paid work and labour law, and as a 'Nordic' solution to European regulative deficit.

Finally, the question of the *legitimacy* of the procedure is briefly discussed. The 'Social Dialogue' makes an excellent case study on the political and legal considerations arising with the decentralized processes that have come to replace traditional legislative ones.

'Reconciliation dialogue' – from European political impasse ...

European-level attempts to introduce day-care provisions and family-related leaves were brought to the European decision-makers in the 1980s, but they failed. Proposed directives were blocked in the political process, due to unwillingness of the member states (Threlfall 2000; Duncan 2002). The first 'Action Programme to promote equal opportunities for women' of 1981[5] proposed directives on, among other issues, parental and maternity leave. The ministers of the Council approved the Action Programme, and the Commission Equal Opportunities Unit proposed in 1983 a draft directive for parental leave, granting leave of three months full-time or six months part-time for each working parent on the condition that they share the leave equally. The method of funding was left to the member States. The draft directive was presented to the Council.[6] Until the Single European Act of 1985, all social policy matters had to be resolved by unanimous Council decision. The draft directive was the first proposal for European legislation which directly affected family responsibilities, and as such, it was politically controversial. The United Kingdom is credited with blocking the first parental leave proposal (Haas 1999, 92).

The British Minister of Employment claimed that EC legislation applied only to basic labour conditions and parental leave was not part of them; the Commissioner argued in vain that sharing family responsibilities was a precondition of equal treatment in employment and therefore a basic labour condition (Rutherford 1989). The arguments against the proposal grew in force after the EC Court decided in 1984 that redistribution of work in the family was not regulated by the Equal Treatment Directive, and therefore governments had the right to assign parental leave to women only.[7] Negotiations on the directive floundered (van der Vleuten 2007, 11–116).

The Single European Act introduced qualified majority decision making concerning safety at work. Issues concerning employees' rights were explicitly excluded from qualified majority rule (Fredman 1998, 386–7, 391). Under such a regime, maternity leave fitted more easily under the legislative mandate of the Community than parental leave. Maternity leave could be introduced as a measure involving the health and safety of mothers.[8] Thus paid maternity leave became mandatory while parental and paternity leave remained at the discretion of the member states.

The informal Council on Equal Opportunities in March 1986 advised the Commissioner responsible for equality issues to cancel the proposal on parental leave. Yet, the ministers approved in the same meeting the second Action Programme for Equal Opportunities, which still contained the initiative for a directive on parental leave[9] (van der Vleuten 2007, 137–8). The 1989 Community Charter of the Fundamental Social Rights of Workers also expresses a shift from 'equal opportunity to equal pay' to 'reconciliation of employment with family life' (Hantrais 2000).

Social policy and gender issues became at that point issues presented as ones related to economic utility. In the early 1990s, demographic transition caused by ageing and low fertility, and 'flexible' labour market policies were combined in the European Commission's Equal Opportunities Unit's turn from employment to social policy (Duncan 2002, 310–11).

While parental leave was thus politically on the European agenda, a trend of preferring soft law measures instead of legislation, and deregulation in general, developed in the EC and made the use of mandatory regulation unpalatable to many member states, especially to Britain. Mrs Thatcher in her notorious Bruges speech in 1992 declared that '(W)e have not successfully rolled back the frontiers of the state in Britain only to see them re-imposed at a European level, with a European super-state exercising a new dominance from Brussels' (cited in Senden 2004, 9). The trend reflected a neo-liberal critique of state intervention in the member states, as well as Euroscepticism.

National deregulatory tendencies and criticism of the body of EC legislation formed a catalyst for the European Communities to turn from mandatory legislation to other means of governance. In a White Paper on the Internal Market in 1985 and with the Single European Act of 1986, the European Commission started to speak of 'a new legislative culture'. From the early 1990s, the new European legislative policy recommended less recourse to legislation, and other modes of governance or regulation to be adopted, of a less compelling or non-governmental nature. The change brought along increased use of soft law instruments and other alternative modes of governance or means of regulation (Senden 2004, 20–1).

The turn to 'private ordering' by use of soft law measures coincided with the rise of neo-liberal ideology, which challenged strong centralized political rule in general, but welfare state governance in particular (Dean 1999, 164–71). On the European level, the change was formulated as one allowing member states room to develop their own policies, while they could pool experience and assess achievement and performance. Indirect regulation was achieved by means of benchmarking, best practice examples and assessments (Haahr 2004). Gender mainstreaming was introduced as a response to perceived failure of tackling inequality by antidiscrimination (Beveridge 2007; Beveridge and Nott 2002).

Preference for soft law policies also coincided with a growing scepticism among feminists of law as a vehicle of social change. 'Hard law' equality rights as the self-obvious feminist policy gave way to critical considerations on what such rights actually could achieve.[10] The assumption that the limits of legal measures are reached when formal gender neutrality is achieved was often affirmed by feminist scholars; it seems significant that scepticism about legal measures has been strong especially among scholars who work in the 'Atlanticist policy' sphere.[11]

While the Maastricht Treaty strengthened the European social dimension with its Social Protocol, the protocol itself gave little in the way of effective protection to social security as a fundamental right. The UK excluded itself, and many member states were extremely reluctant to increase the European Union's competence in the social field. Neo-liberal politicians found the whole social dimension of EU undesirable.

... to an agreement to be turned into legislation

The 1992 Maastricht Treaty set up the corporatist patterns of today's European social policy, however. After that, the Commission could choose either to present a social policy issue as one concerning safety at work (in which case legislation adopted by qualified majority was binding also for the UK), or as an issue to be put before the social partners. The Social Dialogue or the social partners procedure is strongly attached to European-level labour law as 'transnational labour law', which raises issues distinct from either national or international labour law. The EU is the foremost example of such transnational labour regulation (Bercusson 2008). The Commission may send its proposal to representatives of employers and trade unions at EU level, who decide whether they want to regulate the matter. The agreement resulting from these negotiations goes to the Council, which approves it by either qualified majority votes or by unanimity, depending on the subject matter.

The new social partners' procedure opened a way out of the stalemate in the attempt to introduce EC regulation on parental leave. Britain wanted to limit parental leave to mothers, and Luxembourg also had reservations. The draft was discussed again in September 1994, but Britain made it clear that its critical attitude would not change. Commissioner Flynn then decided to reintroduce the proposal under the Social Protocol procedure (van der Vleuten 2007, 149). The Commission initiated consultations between supranational representatives of employers and trade unions in 1995, and UNICE, CEEP and ETUC reached an agreement in November that year. The Commission presented a draft directive implementing the agreement to the Council, where it became once more a matter of controversy because some delegations thought that there was too much room for interpretation. In 1996 the Council finally reached a political consensus and formally adopted the directive on parental leave, based on the social partners' agreement. Only Ireland, Luxembourg and the UK had not introduced a statutory right to parental leave at that point. Ireland and Luxembourg could not block the directive with their votes under the 11-state Social Agreement procedure. Due to its 'opt-out' concerning social policy, the UK could no longer veto the directive.

Why did the social partners succeed where a proposal to the Council did not? Both sides of industrial relations were eager to show that the procedure introduced in Maastricht was important for them so that the route opened for corporatist decision making would not be closed by the Amsterdam Treaty. There had been disappointments with the procedure since the first attempt to use the dialogue route to policy-making in the form of collective agreement on European Works Councils had failed (Falkner 2000, 713). Simultaneously, the admission of Austria, Finland and Sweden into the Community had added pressure to find solutions for the reconciliation of work and family life. In 1995, an Advisory Committee on Equality was established. Two of the six committee members were from Finland and Sweden, countries which already had legislation granting paid gender-neutral parental leave, as well as paid paternity leave (Stratigaki 2000; Haas 2003).

After some 15 years of legislative bargaining, the Directive on Parental Leave was thus achieved in 1996. As Anna van der Vleuten points out, a comparison of the directive with the existing national standards showed that the directive reflected the minimum common denominator for the 15 member states. It left all contentious and potentially costly issues, such as pay and right to benefits during leave, to the national level (van der Vleuten 2007, 150).

The new Nordic members were decisive in getting a discourse into the agenda combining the demands of the demographic time bomb with demands of gender equality, by showing that gender equality was central to achieving both high economic activity and high birth rates (Duncan 2002). The new emphasis brought to the discussion presaged the manner in which the issue of family-related leaves was framed ten years later.

The 'Social Dialogue' procedure was formalized under Articles 136–139 EC of the Amsterdam Treaty in 1997.[12] A tripartite consultation procedure between the Commission and EU-level social partners was introduced, where the Commission's proposals on social policy are processed in a tripartite consultation. This procedure also opened a route for Community-level agreements between 'social partners' to be implemented by a Council decision.

Soft law gained ground in the EU equality policy, especially after 1997. The following decade 'witnessed dramatic changes in the EU's methods of regulation with the development of regulative techniques ... the OMC (Open Method of Coordination) being the "paradigm" of the "New Governance"' (Beveridge and Velluti 2008, 191). European Employment Strategy now became the hub of development towards New Governance. The OMC refers to a mode of governance by the EU and member states through a range of non-binding measures, decided by common agreement and pursuing agreed policy goals. The strategy relies on political rather than legal means, and involves multilateral surveillance by the Commission. Peer review and 'naming and shaming' are used as means of enforcement (Beveridge and Velluti 2008). The Social Dialogue involves a dialogue between the Commission and the EU-level labour market organizations, where the Commission initiates the procedure and the Social Partners negotiate an agreement, that may then be implemented as a piece of binding legislation. In spite of the differences between the Social Dialogue and the OMC, both methods exemplify an attempt to use consensual methods for achieving European convergence.

Family-related leaves and the Lisbon targets

The Commission started first-stage consultation of the European social partners on the parental leave directive and related matters in 2006.[13] The first stage of consultation of the Social Dialogue consists of a general discussion on a 'Green paper'-type text, prepared by the Commission, to which the social partners are expected to reply. The second stage is then followed by more explicit policy proposals of a 'White paper' nature from the Commission for the social partners.

The first-stage consultation paper by the Commission on family-related leaves refers to various European policies, such as the Lisbon strategy, the European Pact for Gender Equality, and the Framework of Actions on Gender Equality the European social partners had adopted in 2005. The consultation on family-related leaves is framed as a part of a wider aspiration to social modernization of Europe.[14] The aim is to modernize the European social model by instruments including legislation, Social Dialogue, financial instruments, the OMC and equality mainstreaming.

Child care services, rather than parental leave arrangements, have been believed to be a solution that would help a more balanced responsibility to care imbalance (Guerrina 2008). Of these policies, however, only parental leave policy is in the ambit of mandatory European regulation.

The EU 'hard law' provisions on family-related leaves obligated at that point the member states to adopt a minimum of 14 weeks of paid maternity leave[15] and three months of unpaid parental leave, in principle (but not by a mandatory provision) to be shared and not transferable between the parents. According to the framework agreement on parental leave, the social partners were to review the application of the agreement after five years after it had been adopted by the Council, but the review did not take place in 2001. The European Parliament called for improvements to the existing legislation.

In the early 2000s, social exclusion was defined in the Commission policy as a problem requiring an integrated policy approach. Holding a job was considered as a key factor for social inclusion. Improvements of provision of child care and parental leave arrangements were seen as a bulwark against social exclusion, and a field where the Community should adopt measures of cooperation and coordination type. At the same time, immigration policies were seen as a solution to problems caused by the demographic deficit. Several strands of community activities in the field of employment, social policies, gender equality and non-discrimination meet in the Community Programme for Employment and Social Solidarity – PROGRESS (Wennberg 2008, 151–65).[16]

Assessing member state performance

The minimum standard for member states provided by the Parental Leave Directive left a lot of latitude to member states, as comparisons showed. In the early 2000s, after the transposition of the Parental Leave Directive had taken place, the then 15 member states were studied by Linda Haas. The countries fell into four categories defined on the basis of how government policy supported and valued care. The 'Southern Rim' member states had introduced unpaid parental leave which merely followed the EU minimum requirements. The 'Bismarckian' member states supported long 'childrearing leaves' incurring flat rate compensations, in practice to mothers in spite of the gender neutral formulation of the leave. The liberal Western Rim had introduced the EU minimum unwillingly, and used no incentives for fathers. Employers and the markets in general were encouraged to develop care provisions. The three Nordic member states, which had developed parental leave early as an instrument to promote care and gender equality, formed the fourth category. Despite the EU policies, national policies tended to reinforce the traditional division of labour between fathers and mothers (Haas 2003).

The Commission's approach to consultation shows a spill-over effect from the methods used in the OMC on employment issues, especially in terms of inviting peer assessment and offering a common problem definition to be taken up by the negotiating parties. In a manner resonant of a discourse of New Governance type, the Commission also assessed member state performance in its first-stage consultation paper in 2006, recording a great variance. According to the commission, the duration of maternity leave, the EU minimum of which is 14 weeks, varies up to 28 weeks (for example, in the Czech Republic and Slovakia), and in certain circumstances up to 52 weeks in the UK. The length of parental leave varies substantially between the member states, from 3–4 months to 3 years in the Czech Republic, Finland, France, Germany, Poland and Slovakia. The leave attracts a payment in a considerable number of member states, but not in all.

The Lisbon strategy targets stress demographic needs and the need to promote women's access to the labour market. The normative goals of further action requested by the Commission were defined by a reference to the demographic trend and low fertility rates, but by also noting that some member states have higher fertility rates combined with higher labour force participation rates than others. The Commission used data to push the point that further action to promote fathers' participation in care was needed: women continue to be the main carers of children and other dependent persons, such as the elderly, which affects the employment rate of women who have children, whereas men with children have a higher employment rate than those men who do not. The Commission referred to European statistics that show that unpaid work is performed mostly by women, and a Eurobarometer survey of 2003 which showed that the majority of current or prospective fathers knew of their entitlement to parental leave, but most of them did not take or intend to take it.

The Commission's discourse headed towards a Nordic-type parental leave as a goal for negotiations. The Nordic states were represented as good performers, able to deliver solutions that the social partners' procedure could promote at the European level. The Commission pointed out that both birth rates and labour market participation rates of women were relatively high in Denmark, France, Finland and Sweden. Arrangements aimed at persuading fathers to shoulder some part of the leave in some member states (Finland, Sweden), as well as in Norway and Iceland, were highlighted in the Commission's paper. Here, the focus was on the part of the parental leave that is non-transferable between the parents. Thus, if the father does not take the part allotted to him, the part is lost. In Norway, five weeks of the 43–45 weeks' leave is reserved for fathers, in Sweden two months and in Finland one month. In Iceland, the combined maternity and parental leave of nine months is non-transferable to three months for both parents, and three months is transferable.

The Commission's consultation paper can be considered against information on pregnancy, maternity, parental and paternity rights, provided by a report on pregnancy, maternity, parental and paternity rights by the Network of Legal Experts on gender equality law[17] presented in a report to the Commission in 2007.[18] The report shows that parental leave was unpaid in many member states, often in the ones where the leave is non-transferable. The countries coincide with those classified either under the 'Southern' or 'Western rim' categories used by Haas. Where the leave was transferable, it was usually paid or covered from a benefit, and in the huge majority of cases, taken by mothers. In the Central and Eastern European new member states, parental leave was usually long and covered by a benefit or pay, but it was also fully transferable. In 'new' member states, there is a long tradition of maternity protection. The legal experts stressed that the legal protection of pregnant workers is insufficient while the imbalance continues, because the cost to employers in the female branches functions as an incentive to discrimination.

The Legal Experts' report also sheds light on some less well known aspects of the Nordic solutions.[19] The leave systems allot a lengthy period to family-related leaves, covered by social security benefits. The Icelandic solution is the most radical in the Nordic area, as only one third of the parental leave is transferable between parents. The opposite case in terms of mandatory sharing of the leave is Denmark, where the Maternity, Paternity and Parental Leave and Benefit Act of 2006 guarantees 14 weeks of confinement-related maternity leave and 32 weeks of fully transferable parental leave. In Sweden, the Parental Leave Act deals with family-related leave, which grants parental benefits related to pregnancy and parenthood by the National Insurance Act. Before 2000, there was no division between maternity and parental leave – the Parental Leave Act was formulated in a gender-neutral manner. At the Commission's behest, the Act was amended so that an obligatory period was placed around confinement. The Act gives an entitlement to leave until the child is 18 months old. The leave is transferable, but 60 days of the sickness benefit cannot be transferred to the other parent. In Finland, the maternity leave and sickness-insurance level benefit covers approximately four months, and a similar parental leave with benefits around six months. The parental leave and benefit are fully transferable, but if the father receives a paternity benefit for at least 12 days, he is entitled to a further period of paternity benefit at the end of the parental leave.

In Norway, six weeks' maternity leave is obligatory, and the length of the entire maternity and parental leave is up to 53 weeks. The National Insurance Act contains a 'father's quota' of five weeks, which is reserved exclusively for fathers.

The parental leave system in Nordic states has been an issue to be settled through tri-partite negotiations between labour market organizations and the state. While parents' loss of income is covered from social insurance, collective agreements often contain clauses on pay during maternity, paternity or parental leave. Due to the fact that mothers take most of the leave, employers of female branches in the gender-segregated labour markets bear more costs than those of male branches. In particular, the system pushes the burden of both direct and indirect costs to public sector employers, to the state and the municipalities, because women tend to work in the public sector. In Denmark, the cost allocation between employers was achieved by a social partners' agreement that was turned into a legal act in 2006.[20] Collective agreements in Sweden often include clauses on pay during family-related leave. Cost allocation between the employers has been discussed, and parental benefits insurance has been pointed to as a solution. In Finland, a Government Bill based on labour-market-inspired preparatory work proposed that the capped parental benefit be raised for fathers, but not for mothers in order to achieve better allocation of costs between employers. The Constitutional Law Committee of the Parliament considered the proposal discriminatory against women, and the benefit was raised for both mothers and fathers. A similar measure of giving financial bonuses for men taking up family responsibilities was presented in the second stage of the Social Dialogue by one of the trade unions (ETUC's Position on the Second Stage Consultation). Trade unions seem to have no objection to proposing incentives for men even at the cost of direct discrimination against women.

Thus, all the Nordic provisions on parental leave largely respect the 'second level' subsidiarity principle in the sense that it is left mainly to the discretion of the parents to decide who does most of the actual caring. The cost imbalance between employers of female and male branches causes friction, which is dealt with by refunding employers of women. The social partners, who play a considerable role in formulating the rules, seem to pay attention to the demands of distributive justice among employers, rather than between parents. The loss of income that women face is dealt with attempts to persuade fathers to share at least a small part of the total leave, by making a part of parental leave non-transferable between parents.

The social partners' positions at the first phase of consultation

The Commission consulted the social partners on five questions, among them the parental leave legislation, and received 13 replies from social partners at European level.[21]

The organizations' replies disagreed both on taking any action and on what the appropriate level of action should be. Employees' organizations (ETUC, CESI and EPSU) preferred action at all levels including the EU. Employers' organizations (BUSINESSEUROPE, EuroCommerce, CEMR and CEEP) preferred national or local levels. Bigger businesses preferred the national level, and smaller businesses the sectoral or workplace level as the most suitable for reconciliation action. Most organizations, both employers and employees, referred to the need for better care facilities and more flexible working arrangements. The care facilities should be the responsibility of the state, however. Both employers and employees also referred to the need to encourage men to make use of parental leave, but the employers recommended information campaigns and exchanges of good practice, rather than mandatory regulations. The employees' organizations were open to evaluating the legislative provisions; ETUC proposed that the social partners evaluate the parental leave agreement and improve its provisions especially in relation to pay. The trade unions believed that both Parental Leave and Maternity Protection Directives needed to be amended, and called for an introduction of paternity leave and leave for the care of elderly persons or other dependants. The employers' organizations considered the existing EU legislation fully adequate, referring to the OMC rather than further EU legislation as a vehicle for change.

The European Women's Lobby (EWL), formed in 1990,[22] is the main formal organization representing women's interests in EU policy-making. The transnational organization represents diverse interests, and the European Commission has discouraged women's groups from operating outside the EWL (Cichowski 2007, 202). The EWL supported ETUC's contribution for encouraging fathers. Further, the Women's Lobby welcomed full salary maternity leave to be extended from 14 to 24 weeks, including extending its compulsory duration of six weeks. Parental leave provisions should incur an income equalling national average pay, and should not perpetuate the gender wage gap. A 'certain period' should be made non-transferable, and the leave extended to 24 weeks (European Women's Lobby, 14 March 2008).

In its response to the social partners in the second round of consultations, the Commission took up the issue of encouraging men to take up reconciliation measures in clear terms, and asked the social partners' views on the issue. The Commission suggested new forms of leave. Entitlement to paternity leave (a short period of leave around the time of birth or adoption) should be introduced, as well as leave for care for an elderly parent or a family member with a disability or with a terminal illness. Maternity leave could be lengthened. The payment or allowance for maternity leave should be at least equivalent to that for sickness leave.

As to parental leave, the Commission offered options to be considered. First, the parental leave could be made strictly non-transferable, by making the clause mandatory. There could be a clause requiring member states to adopt provisions which encourage fathers to take leave, fathers could be encouraged to take leave by reserving a minimum period of leave for the fathers (as in Sweden), or parents or each parent could get an additional period of parental leave, if the father takes a specified minimum period of leave (as in Italy).

The social partners' progress report at the end of February 2008 noted that there had been a consultation of national social partners, and that an ad hoc working group had been established and had convened. Negotiations between the partners continued even after the date when they should have been concluded in 2008. Finally, on 23 March 2009, the social partners' negotiation team arrived at an agreement, to be processed by the organizations before being presented to the Commission.

In the revised framework agreement on parental leave,[23] the social partners frame the issue of work-family life balance in the setting of demographic change and globalization. The parental leave framework of 1995 had been successfully and fully transposed in all EU member states, and even promoted autonomous Social Dialogue in some member states. Yet, the lack of or low level of income connected to the leave limited the use of leave entitlements. Despite the transposition of the agreement, it did not fully achieve the objectives of gender equality, reconciliation and sharing responsibilities between women and men. The social partners agreed to undertake joint action to better achieve the aims of the parental leave directive and assess maternity protection. Later, the social partners decided to leave maternity leave to the Commission. The social partners noted that the choice left to the member states to make the individual right to parental leave transferable between parents had turned parental leave into a leave for mothers, as '(e)xperience shows that making the leave non-transferable can act as a positive incentive for the take-up by fathers, the European social partners ... agree to make part of the leave non-transferable' (para 16 of General considerations).

The agreement extends the individual leave to four (instead of the earlier three) months. 'To encourage a more equal take-up of leave by both parents, at least one of the four months shall be provided on a non-transferable basis' (Clause 2(2) of the agreement). Member states should provide benefits under sickness insurance during the minimum period of parental leave.

The agreement contains a compromise resembling a Nordic-type solution. The solution will probably encourage a shift to fully transferable parental leaves, except for the 'father's month' that is made non-transferable. Social insurance rather than employers is to be responsible for the costs. Allocation of costs between employers in male and female branches of work will be on the agenda, especially where collective agreements carry clauses on pay during family-related leaves.

On purely economic grounds, it would seem to be in the employers' interests to require that family-related leaves are divided equally among different branches and tasks. This does not seem to be the case, however. At least in the Nordic states, the labour markets are gender segregated and women tend to work in the public sector. Thus, the costs of parenting are allocated to the public sector, to employers who traditionally take the burden into account in their employment policies.

Legitimacy of the social partners' procedures – a legitimate research question?

Institutionalized forms of power at the EU level increase through various channels. One of them is the Social Dialogue. It may not be considered an extremely effective manner of arriving at EU-level regulation, as only three of about 20 consultations have led to an agreement that has been implemented by a directive. The procedure is controlled by the European Commission, which delegates drafting of legislation to the social partners, and checks the outcome by verifying it against criteria discussed below.

The procedure seems to raise issues of legitimacy, however. Some aspects of legitimacy of the procedure as a replacement for parliamentary democracy at supranational level were addressed when the European Court of First Instance had to decide whether the three 'social partners' that were parties to the negotiations leading to the Parental Leave Directive of 1996 were representative (Bernard 2000).[24] The level of required representation is difficult to estimate, as trade union representation in member states is extremely varied (Bercusson 1999). The Court of First Instance argued that the Commission and Council have a duty to check that the social partners are representative as a public duty to the people, not as a private right enjoyed by potential social partners. The Social Dialogue was seen as a procedure that is comparable to the parliamentary process. The court understood democracy to require that decision-making has to be able to claim procedural legitimacy (Bernard 2000).

Political and legal scholarship that relies on the normative contents of communicative rationality, deliberative democracy and procedural legitimacy, developed in the footsteps of Jürgen Habermas, does not shy away from measuring new forms of decision-making against normative criteria. Transparency of the procedure, broader public debate as a part of decision-making, participation of citizens affected by the decision, the capacity of the procedure to learn from successes and failures, and the responsiveness of the procedure to the concerns of those affected have been offered as relevant criteria for legitimacy (de la Porte and Nanz 2004, 272–3).

European-level industrial relations lack the economic pressure that is usually the motivation for collective bargaining. The social partners' procedure is parasitic on the EU legislative process (Fredman 1998). The Social Dialogue is dependent on the incentive provided by the Commission to start negotiations, as well as on public implementation of the agreement. The Dialogue thus takes place under the shadow of public authority. It is unclear how much legislative power the Commission in fact delegates to the partners. The Commission checks that the agreement contributes to the social aims of the Community, respects the principle of subsidiarity, is in accordance with Community Law, is compatible with provisions that protect small and medium-sized enterprises, is appropriate in terms of policy, and is legitimate with regard to non-signatory social partners. Pragmatic reasons make the Commission unwilling to upset an agreement, even though it has no competence to change the text of the agreement when it is implemented (Smismans 2008, 168).

The subsidiarity principle requires that decisions should be taken as close to the citizens as possible, but the European-level social partners do not fulfil the requirement easily. Nor does the procedure fit easily with the ideology of participative democracy, because some organizations hold a monopoly on the procedure. Deliberative democracy is associated with public law instruments, not with a negotiation and agreement procedure using the private law mechanism of striking a bargain – especially if the corporatist arrangement does not rest on a polity's shared commitment to the arrangement (Bernard 2000).

The national social partners' activity rate, as well as their cooperation in the present Social Dialogue, seems to have varied greatly. The Finnish and Swedish social partners only sent a joint reply to the Commission, and the Danish partners sent both a joint reply and an additional reply from one employers' union. Austrian, Belgian, German, Italian, Irish, Latvian, Dutch, Portuguese and UK social partners replied. There were separate replies from trade unions and employers from Bulgaria, Cyprus, the Czech Republic and Slovenia as well as from France (with two replies from trade unions), Luxembourg and Lithuania. From Iceland, Hungary and Slovenia, only the employers' unions replied. From the rest of the states involved, there was no reply. Clearly, the interests of national social partners were coordinated 'at home' in the Finnish and Swedish cases, but most replies were given separately or even from only one side represented in the procedure.

Considering that parenting patterns concern a great number of people in all member states, the representation of interests and the responsive nature of the procedure are not very striking. It can be assumed that where the national social partners have been able to strike a bargain from the start of the negotiations, their position in the negotiations is strong. The employers in the case at hand were not interested in a reform that would increase mandatory regulation, least of all at the European level. The regulative interest thus rested with the trade unions, helped along by the suasion from the Commission.

The Social Dialogue procedure is far from being transparent. The positions of the negotiating parties are made public only partially, and information about how a compromise was achieved will be difficult to obtain. Public debate on the issues delegated to the social partners has also been scarce.

Many researchers into questions relating to power are reluctant to discuss legitimacy of late-modern governance. The procedure studied here can be seen as an aspect of the overall turn to a modern way of governing, which is often reframed into an inquiry on governmentality (Dean 1999; Rose 1999). One aspect of the strongly Foucauldian framework in studies on the turn to private ordering has been the reluctance to discuss legitimacy. In studies on governmentality, inspired by Michel Foucault's analysis of power, questions of legitimacy are taken to hamper a critical analysis of productive power, and need to be bracketed from the analysis (Haahr 2004, 212–14). A critical positivist analysis of power in the Foucauldian tradition aims at getting at the taken-for-granted assumptions underlying forms of governance.

After the social partners' agreement was concluded, the task of the Commission was limited to taking account of the representative status of the social partners involved, and checking the legality of the text. No changes in the text of the agreement may be undertaken by EU legislative bodies. The Commission being satisfied with both the legality of the text and the legitimacy of the partners, the agreement was turned into a Council Directive in March 2010.

To a legal scholar, the need to open the brackets around legitimacy for critical scrutiny remains quite compelling. The Social Dialogue involves a partial privatization of the legislative process. A failure to measure the legitimacy of the procedure, as well as its hidden power-knowledge formations, benefits only those who can yield the power to set the form of the procedure in the first place. That power seems far removed from the ones who need care, or those responsible for providing it.

Notes

1. Council Directive 96/34/EC on the framework agreement on parental leave concluded by UNICE, CEEP and the EAY, now ETUC. The directive was extended to the UK by Council Directive 97/75/EC.
2. Revised framework agreement on parental leave. Adopted by the Negotiating Team 23 March 2009.
3. Council Directive 2010/18/EU implementing the revised Framework Agreement on parental leave concluded by BUSINESSEUROPE, UEAPME, CEEP and ETUC and repealing Directive 96/34/EC.
4. European Council (2000) Presidency Conclusions, Lisbon, 23 and 24 March.
5. Commission 1981, COM(81)758.
6. Commission 1983, COM(83)686.
7. Case 184/83 Hoffmann.
8. Council Directive 92/85/EEC on the introduction of measures to encourage improvements in the safety and health at work of pregnant workers and workers who have recently given birth or are breastfeeding (tenth individual Directive within the meaning of Article 16 (1) of Directive 89/391/EEC.
9. Commission 1986, COM(86)758, 15.
10. *Feminists and the Power of Law* by Carol Smart (1989) is an impressive explication of the shortcomings of legislative policies. Later, the scepticism is reflected for example in the form of assumptions about the evolution of equality policies from 'formal equality rights' to 'positive measures' or 'affirmative action', and further to equality mainstreaming. Under this formula, open-ended political procedures are privileged as more effective than legislation. The assumed sequence in time (from anti-discrimination to positive measures and on to gender mainstreaming and, in European policies, to social policy) may reflect Anglo-American developments. The CEDAW Convention, as well as national developments elsewhere, have followed several types of policies simultaneously.

11. Simon Duncan describes the US-inspired 'Atlanticist' discourse on reconciliation of work and family life to be based on a model consisting of individuals in an efficient free market, where a failure to overcome social constraints is seen as an individual moral failure. The labour force must be flexible in order to withstand the competitive forces of globalization (Duncan 2002, 305).
12. Now renumbered as Articles 153–155 of the Treaty on the Functioning of the European Union.
13. First-stage Consultation of European Social Partners on Reconciliation of Professional, Private and Family Life. Brussels, 12.10.2006 SEC(2006) 1245.
14. Communication on the Social Agenda (COM(2005) 33 final.
15. Council Directive 92/85/EEC on the introduction of measures to encourage improvements in the safety and health at work of pregnant workers and workers who have recently given birth or are breastfeeding (tenth individual Directive within the meaning of Article 16 (1) of Directive 89/391/EEC).
16. Decision 1672/2006/EC, *OJ* L 315 of 15.11.2006.
17. The Commission sponsors networks of experts in the area of gender equality, among them the Legal Experts network established in 1984. As to the present tasks of the network, see http://ec.europa.eu/social/main.jsp?catId=641&langId=en
18. http://ec.europa.eu/employment_social/gender_equality/legislation/report_pregnancy.pdf, accessed 15 December 2008.
19. The information is based on reports by Ruth Nielsen (Denmark), Kevät Nousiainen (Finland), Herdís Thorgeirsdóttir (Iceland), Helga Aune (Norway) and Ann Nummhauser-Henning (Sweden).
20. Act on Reimbursement of Pregnancy Payments in the Private Sector, Barselsudligningsloven.
21. ETUC Position on the Second Stage Consultation of the Social Partners at Community level on the Reconciliation of Professional, Private and Family Life. Other replies to the Commission are referred to in the Commission's Second Stage of Consultation of European Social Partners on Reconciliation of Professional, Private and Family Life.
22. EWL is an umbrella organization that represents thousands of women's organizations in the EU member states, see www.womenlobby.org
23. Revised framework agreement on parental leave. Adopted by the Negotiating Team 23 March 2009.
24. The representativeness of the negotiation parties was considered in Case T-135/96 UEAPME v. council (1998) ECR II-2335.

2

Care, Migration and Citizenship: Migration and Home-based Care in Europe[1]

Fiona Williams

Introduction

Nannies and domestic servants had disappeared by the 1960s from all but the most bourgeois households in Europe. Domestic technology, alternative work in the industrial and service sectors, and, in the Nordic social democratic countries, an egalitarian repugnance at the very idea of employing others to provide 'service', all played a part in their demise. But by the 1990s research revealed that in Europe the demand for care and domestic work was growing again (Gregson and Lowe 1994), and in the major cities it was migrant women from the poorer regions of the world who were meeting this demand (Anderson 2000). The new employers were working mothers, and, by the turn of the century, older frail people or disabled people needing support in their own homes. This new phenomenon, which exists in many industrialized countries, encapsulates three major social changes. First is the global increase in women's involvement in the labour market. In European welfare states this is marked by a shift away from the 'male-breadwinner' to the 'adult worker' model which *assumes* all able-bodied adults, men and women, will be in paid work (Lewis 2001). In the poorer regions of the world, the destruction of local economies, unemployment and poverty have pressed women into assuming a greater breadwinning role, but without any form of state support (Pearson 2000).

The second is the emergence of care as a central social, political and economic concern, posing questions for European policy-makers such as how can responsibilities for work and care be reconciled when women are employed? How can care be paid for and how can its quality be guaranteed? (Daly 2002). The demographics of an ageing society and declining fertility have heightened the urgency of these questions. Third are the changing features and patterns of post-colonial migration and of national and supranational boundaries, involving the movement of women seeking earning opportunities, and related issues of documentation, citizenship rights and unregulated labour (Anderson and O'Connell Davidson 2003).

As such, the phenomenon is challenging in a number of respects – political, social and analytical; it is these, especially the last, which this chapter grapples with. To begin with, in a context where women globally are taking on more responsibilities to earn income without a significant rebalancing of their care responsibilities with male partners, the transnational movement of mainly women into care and domestic work represents profoundly asymmetrical (between poorer and richer regions) solution to women's attempts to reconcile these dual responsibilities. At the same time, it exposes the limits to how far care can be either commodified or socialized. In addition, this is not simply the consequence of the supply and demand for labour in a free market, but one shaped by the restructuring of European welfare states and their policies for care of older, disabled people and young children, as well as by their migration and employment policies. It therefore requires an analysis which attends to the role of state policies and the nature of citizenship. There are important questions about the legal, social and civil rights of migrants, but also about how citizenship is conceived in European work/life reconciliation policies, in intra-household personal relations, and in the discourse of gender equality. Each of these aspects is cut across by other dimensions such as nationality and ethnicity. Equally, the transnational movement of women into care work raises questions about global geopolitical inequalities and strategies for global justice.

As well as concerning itself with some of these issues, this chapter deals with two analytical questions: what is the relationship between the different scales of analysis involved in looking at recent developments in migration and care, and, in particular, how might we analyse the role of the state? It builds on a qualitative research project of the experiences of employers and migrant workers in home-based child care. This was a cross-national study comparing the UK, Sweden and Spain, with interviews carried out in London, Stockholm and Madrid.[2] The implications of this study have involved looking at the relationship between three different scales or levels: the micro level of the everyday experience of migrant workers and their employers in private households in large cities, the meso level of the national/supranational institutional context, and the macro level of the global political economy of care. This has also led, in the meso-level part of the analysis, to the development of indicators that can allow for cross-national analysis of the dynamics of this phenomenon in different countries.

This chapter begins with some empirical observations on the importance of bringing the state into an analysis of migration and care. It proceeds to suggest how we might compare this relationship cross-nationally, and then to look at the complexities in citizenship rights, and briefly in the conclusion, how to nest these different dimensions within the macro level of the transnational political economy of care.

Bringing the state into the analysis

'Global care chains' is the concept used to describe the dynamics through which migrant women from the Global South work as care and domestic workers in private homes in the Global North (Parreñas 2001; Ehrenreich and Hochschild 2003) and has tended to reflect the US experience of migration and care. In Europe there are two important differences: regionalism and institutionalism. In the case of regionalism, care chains do not only operate between the Global North and South, but, in common with a number of Southeast Asian countries (for example, from Indonesia to Singapore), they also operate within the North and within the South. The enlargement of the European Union has had a particular effect with increasing numbers of women (often without children) from Eastern and Central Europe, Russia and the Balkans entering quasi-au pair/nanny work in all parts of Europe.

This is how a manager of a nanny/au pair agency in London explained this:

> *This has changed the nanny world: they are willing to combine child care with domestic work. The term nanny used to refer to a qualified child carer, but it doesn't mean anything now. Girls come over as au pairs and stay. Now employers can get child care and cleaning for less than £9 per hour – they love it!*

This reflects an ironic situation in which the cutting of social expenditure in parts of Central and Eastern Europe, and, with it, the withdrawing of some of women's former social and economic rights has led women in those countries to seek opportunities abroad. The jobs they take as cleaners and carers broaden the social and economic rights of the women who employ them whilst offering the host countries the opportunity to keep down their care costs.

The second point is about institutionalism: it is not simply the lack of public provision that shapes the demand for child care in many European states as is the case in the US, but the very nature of state support that is available. I look at three different dimensions of this: care policies, migration policies and employment policies.

Care policies

To begin with, since the early 2000s, there has been in many parts of Europe the growing acceptance of childcare as a *public* and not simply a private responsibility, such that it can be argued that this represents the emergence of a new social right, albeit shaped in different ways in different countries (Lister et al. 2007). At the same time, the shift in a number of countries from providing care *services* (or, in the case of Southern Europe, no services at all) to giving individuals *cash* payments to buy in home-based care provision has shaped care provision for children, as well as for older people and disabled people. These might take the form of cash or tax credits or tax incentives to pay child minders, nannies, relatives or domestic workers for their services. The UK, Spain, Finland and France have all introduced some form of cash provision or tax credit to assist in buying help for child care in the home (Lister et al. 2007, Chapter 4), and Sweden has introduced tax breaks for people employing domestic help in the home. In the UK free nursery care for children aged 3–5 (pre-school) is only available in the most deprived areas, with universal entitlement to only part-time day care for this age group. However, working families within an income range that includes some professional workers can claim an income-related child care tax credit of up to 80 per cent of the costs of child care. In an attempt to regularize private use of child carers, these tax credits were extended to the employment of registered nannies in 2006.[3]

There are also forms of 'direct payments' which allow older people or disabled people to buy in support and assistance, for example, in the UK, Netherlands, Italy and Austria (Ungerson and Yeandle 2007; Bettio et al. 2006). Both of these types of provision encourage the development of a particular form of home-based, often low-paid, commodified care or domestic help, generally accessed privately through the market. Often, as in the UK, the policies are there specifically to stimulate the private sector. Where care labour has historically been undervalued and poorly paid it is often the job destination of those with least negotiating power and this is where low-cost migrant labour steps in. Indeed, in Spain, Italy and Greece, this strategy of employing migrant labour to meet care needs has become so prevalent that Bettio and colleagues

(2006, 272) describe it as a shift from a 'family' model of care to a 'migrant-in-the-family' model of care. In these ways, it is possible to discern a direct or indirect relationship between the development of such policies and the employment of migrant women as domestic/care workers. In addition, the discourse of 'choice' for those who buy in services has been very important shaping the employment of migrant workers, as explained below.

A parallel development in formal care provision has been the contracting out of health and social care to private agencies and residential homes with a worsening of pay and conditions. This has been accompanied by the campaigns in the UK aimed at nurses from India and the Philippines to perform nursing work in both the health service and private agencies, reflecting the increased employment of migrant workers in many areas of social and welfare services, both in the UK and other parts of Europe (Kofman et al. 2000).

In the research project mentioned above on home-based child care in UK, Spain and Sweden, we found that it was not only tax credits or allowances which shaped demand and supply for home-based child care, but the way in which, in the UK and Spain, these legitimized the commodification of care. Policies position mothers as individual *consumers* choosing the right care for their children according to their care preferences and this is marked in those countries where the private market dominates choices for child care. This has been reinforced through the, now commonplace, use of unregulated paid domestic help in the home. In Madrid, where working mothers receive a small subsidy to help them purchase care, mothers felt it was their individual responsibility to find resources for child care in the private market. In Britain day care is provided mainly through the market or voluntary sector; however, in spite of tax credits, nursery places are expensive, especially if you have more than one child. Searching for value for money is what mothers find themselves doing in a marketized childcare economy. One employer in London said:

> [A]n au pair was what we could afford. We had a spare room and the money was what we can afford because nannies are incredibly expensive if you pay them properly.

This legitimization works in tandem with particular child-care cultures: what Spanish and British employers of home-based care share is a cultural preference for mother-substitute care which predisposes them to au pairs, nannies and domestic helps. The research in Sweden found that employment of child-care workers in private households was less prevalent than in the UK or Spain yet domestic help was a growing industry. Employers there still used public day care for their children and framed their reasons for having help with domestic work and child care in terms of the stress of having both paid work and ongoing responsibilities for care and household work. This was also reflected in public discourse about whether or not to offer tax breaks to employers of domestic service (which in the past was regarded as morally pernicious and inegaliatarian). Whilst Sweden is one of the most 'woman-friendly' states, with longstanding paid paternity leave provisions, this discourse reflects the limitations of moves for gender equality in the home and the effects of high levels of gender segregation at work (Björnberg 2002). However, even here, the notion of gender equality was invoked by the Conservative Prime Minister in support of regularizing domestic help 'in a gender equality society like Sweden, where the vast majority of women hold jobs, families sometimes need to hire home help' (AFP, Sweden 2007).

What this points to is that the attempt to resolve work-care responsibilities through the employment of help in the home, especially where this is provided by migrant women, raises questions over the meaning of gender equality, and how institutional policies frame and deliver this: whose equality, at whose cost? Having care/domestic help in the home is only one of a range of policies that can improve work/life balance: employment-based policies (for example, flexible working, maternity leave); sharing earning and caring responsibilities between men and women (for example, through supported paternity leaves); benefits available to enable people to provide care (tax credits, carers' allowances); services (residential services, day care, meals); and environmental strategies (safe and accessible public spaces). How states frame work/life balance policies and how far they balance different institutional supports can have different equality effects (see Daly 2002; Williams 2009).

It is not only policies around care, and the care and share cultures they build on, which shape the demand and provision of low-paid migrant labour, it is also the ways these dovetail with (im)migration and employment policies. In common with care policies, the past decade has seen some important shifts in migration policies. Countries that were previously assimilationist, such as France, are becoming more exclusionary; those previously exclusionary, such as Germany, have introduced residence-based nationality rights; and those previously culturally pluralist, such as Britain and the Netherlands, are asserting the need for greater assimilation. Multiculturalist policy has been challenged in most countries.

At the same time, EU enlargement has generated much greater labour mobility. This has been combined with a greater regulation in immigration policies, especially towards refugees and asylum-seekers, with a priority on migrants who meet labour force needs. Social assistance to these groups has also been curtailed in many countries. In the UK, for example, 'managed migration' has introduced a hierarchy of migrant statuses from high to low-skilled with greater to lesser rights to settlement and benefits. This new complexity and diversity of migrant statuses has led to a greater fragmentation of citizenship rights across Europe which Ong (2006) calls a 'disarticulation' of citizenship, with some migrants having more or less access to cultural, social, economic, political and legal rights. On the other hand, within a number of countries there have been moves to tighten up on both gender and 'race' discrimination, especially since the EU issued a 'Race Directive' in 2003. Yet this is combined with a growing emphasis within the EU on surveillance of borders to control drugs, crime and terrorism.

Spain and the UK offer good examples of the dovetailing of care and migration policies. In Spain there is a subsidy for working mothers to help them buy in child care and immigration policies have quota allocations for domestic/care workers. This, combined with the regularization of over half a million illegal immigrants since 2002, has led to an implicit normalization of the employment of migrant women from Latin America, North Africa, the Philippines and Eastern Europe to fill the care deficit. Employing home-based domestic and care help is now a strategy used by a range of working women – from office workers to professionals – to enable them to stay in the labour market. In addition, the dynamics of migration law can feed into the vulnerability of workers at particular times. Thus, in Spain, it is cheaper to hire a live-in newly arrived migrant woman waiting for her settlement papers because employers can avoid paying social security, and the insecurity ties the worker more closely to her employer.

The UK does not have a quota for domestic workers, but residents of EU member states are free to enter the UK as au pairs (they are now subject to a more stringent youth mobility scheme) and there is an arrangement with nine further countries outside the EU for women aged 17–27 to become au pairs to sponsoring families for two years as long as they do not have recourse to public funds. In addition, working holidaymakers between 17 and 30 years, who are citizens from the new Commonwealth, may enter the UK without an entry clearance. Domestic workers who come in on a domestic worker visa where they accompany their employer have the right to move employers, and although they must renew their visa frequently at some financial cost, they can apply for indefinite leave to remain after five years. (This was the result of campaigns of Kalayaan, the advocacy organization for domestic workers. However, plans to restrict the visa to six months without the right to renew may undermine this). Since the 1990s there has been a growth in the (undeclared) employment of domestic cleaners (Gregson and Lowe 1994, 41), and of nannies and au pairs amongst dual full-time professional households with more than one young child (Brewer and Shaw 2004).

The role of state policies in reproducing or mitigating a pool of low-paid migrant labour has also been the focus of research on global cities (Sassen 1996; Hamnett 1996; May et al. 2007). May and colleagues' research provides a broader contextualization of the specific situation of migrant home-based care workers (May et al. 2007). They found that foreign-born migrant workers constitute 35 per cent of London's working age population but represent 46 per cent of the lowest-paid workers – domestic workers, cleaners, caretakers, porters, refuse collectors and labourers with up to 60 per cent in some sectors such as hotels and catering (Spencer 2005, cited in May et al. 2007, 155). They argue that a new Migrant Division of Labour has emerged in which migrant workers, often with dependents, work in very poor conditions and live in extreme poverty exacerbated by commitments to send remittances to family back home. Furthermore, rather than offering protection, the welfare benefits system has indirectly fuelled the situation. Processes of selectivity have, in combination with migration rules, rendered the system highly complex with eligibility to benefits based on residence and migration status. Either because of ineligibility or lack of knowledge, only one-fifth of the migrant workers interviewed by May et al. earned the national minimum wage even though 86 per cent were working in formal positions and 94 per cent were paying National Insurance contributions. Only 16 per cent were claiming any welfare benefits (either in work or out of work) including only a third with children at home who were claiming Child Benefit or Child Tax Credit.

This process, May and colleagues argue, operates in tandem with the aftermath of the deregulation of the labour market of the 1980s and 1990s which has, in places, encouraged rather than undermined precariousness and labour flexibility. In spite of measures to get rid of child poverty and the introduction of a national minimum wage, in London this still remains too low to encourage people into work. Thus, polarization in London runs alongside the continued unemployment of indigenous workers and a continuing demand from business for migrant workers to fill their demand for low-paid labour. In its turn these employment policies interact with the third part of the state dynamic which are new forms of 'managed migration' introduced by New Labour and part of a trend in a number of EU countries, described earlier, towards a hierarchy of skills amongst migrant workers (in which care and domestic work is seen as low-skilled).

In a different way, this managed migration regime and employment regime interact through what Ruhs and Anderson (2006) call 'semi-compliance', where the costs to both employers and employees of following complex immigration rules are such that workers find it preferable to remain in a twilight zone.

These examples illustrate the complex way in which the state, including the welfare state, contributes to the emergence of migrant workers in low-paid jobs in general, and its implications for the demand for migrant labour in home-based child care and domestic work, in particular. A number of processes have been identified: the encouragement of the commodification of care through cash payments and the contracting out of health and social services; the discursive legitimacy of a consumerist ethic in relation to buying in child care; the constitution of a pool of low-paid labour through explicit and implicit migration rules; forms and effects of deregulation of the labour market; and the lack of the protection of welfare benefits to cushion those designated as low-skilled migrants from exploitation or poverty.

In relation to home-based care work, a further important element in considering employment policy is what happens when the home becomes the workplace. In the UK, for example the household as a place of work remains exempt from the Race Relations Act as well as from much employee protection. The tendency, found in our research (Williams and Gavanas 2008), to see employees as part of the family can mean they have no clear contractual obligations and are open to exploitation, and this is exacerbated if they live in their employer's house. In addition, in common with other empirical work, we found, as explained further below, that that individual employers and employment agencies operated racist and racializing employment practices.

So far this has been a descriptive analysis of the relationship between migration, care and employment policies with references to the UK and Spain, and, to a lesser extent, Sweden. The next section attempts to make this more systematic by spelling out the indicators for cross-national analysis of this relationship between migration and home-based care.

Indicators of care, migration and employment regimes

The empirical research project referred to above was based upon an analysis that proposes that welfare states exist in a dynamic relationship to three interconnected domains – *family, nation* and *work* – which signify the conditions, organization and social relations of social production including caring and intimacy ('family') of the nation-state and the population ('nation') and of production and of capital accumulation ('work') (Williams 1995). Within this broad understanding, the phenomenon of female migration into care and domestic work can be understood as part of the dovetailing of child-care regimes (state policy responses to changes in family and work) with migration regimes (state policy responses to changes in work, population movement and change) and employment regimes (state policy responses to changes in production and the labour market) in different countries. The concept of 'regime' used in developing indicators for the study denotes the cluster of relevant policies as well as practices, discourses, social relations and forms of contestation. The following sets of regime indicators both summarize the dimensions in the previous discussion and also lay the basis for a more detailed cross-national analysis of migration and care looking not only at state policies but also cultural practices, discourses and possibilities for mobilization.

Child care regime indicators[4]

The indicators that were developed for cross-national comparison identified as salient the following aspects of child care regimes are:

- the extent and nature of public and market child-care provision, especially for children of under school age;
- policies facilitating parents' involvement in paid employment such as maternity, paternity and parental leave;
- the nature of direct support – for example, cash benefits, tax credits and so on;
- the care workforce (for example, conditions, gaps, skills);
- *'care cultures'*, that is, dominant national and local cultural discourses on what constitutes appropriate child care, such as surrogate mothering, mothers' working and caring part-time; intergenerational help; shared parental care, or professional day care. It should be noted that national variations in care cultures may also be cut across by subnational differences of class, ethnicity and location;
- historical legacies of care policies and practices;

- the significance of movements, organizations and mobilizations around child care ('pressure from below').

Migration regime indicators

Salient factors in the relationship between migration and care are:

- immigration policies – rules for entrance into a country (and particularly quotas and special arrangements);
- settlement and naturalization rights;
- social, political, legal and civil rights, both formal and in the 'lived experience';
- migratory care responsibilities and practices – for example, remittances;
- internal norms and practices which govern relationships between majority and minority groups: the extent to which these are framed by laws against discrimination and strategies for cultural pluralism, integration or assimilation. Application of these to care work sites (such as households);
- histories of migration and emigration to particular countries, which themselves emerge from colonialism, old trade routes, and shared political, economic or religious alliances;
- the significance of movements, organizations and mobilizations around migration and race relations ('pressure from below');
- the gendering of these processes.

Employment regime indicators

The employment factors that emerge as significant for migrant care and domestic workers, and can be tracked cross-nationally and supranationally include:

- labour market divisions, exclusions and hierarchies (in terms of skills/ gender, ethnicity, nationality, disability, age/place of work/working hours/forms of indentured labour);
- processes of deregulation/deskilling/precarious and flexible labour;
- forms of social protection (eligibility to and rates of unemployment and sickness benefits, pensions, minimum wage, rights attached to care responsibilities);
- production-related discourses – male breadwinner/dual worker/welfare-to-work/labour market activation;
- forms of mobilization, contestation and solidarity across different groups.

These indicators allow for a contextualization and comparison across countries in terms of their dependence on migration workers for care and domestic work, specifically here home-based child-care work. I summarize next some of the citizenship issues to emerge from this analysis.

Dimensions of citizenship

These indicators, then, represent the factors to take into account when comparing the social, economic, political and cultural contexts in which women migrants take up home-based service work, and working women employers hire them. In looking to the question of citizenship, these indicators reflect an attempt to operationalize a concept of citizenship which emphasizes how context – temporal and national – matters (Lister et al. 2007). Different times and places result in different vocabularies of citizenship. These vocabularies affect different social groups (according to gender, ethnicity, sexuality, disability, age and so on) in different ways, and citizenship operates at different levels – from the intimate sphere of personal relationships, the privacy of the household, to the local, national, supranational and global levels. Citizenship can also be contradictory – both emancipatory and disciplinary, both inclusive and exclusive, but the lived experience of citizenship – of rights and responsibilities, of belonging and of participation – is as important to consider as formal, substantive social, economic and political rights.

The intersection of the regimes of care, migration and employment, along with the cultural practices associated with them, frame the different dimensions of citizenship caught up in the phenomenon of home-based migrant care workers. To begin with, the problem of the public/private dichotomy which lies at the heart of the gendered critique of citizenship reveals itself in at least four ways. First, the strategy of employing domestic/care labour in the home is an attempt to minimize the constraints attached to participating fully in the public sphere of paid work. However, it is a strategy which effectively collapses the public into the private, where home becomes work and work becomes home. As such, it generates a range of difficulties, not least because, as mentioned earlier, the home is not covered by the same employment protections afforded to the workplace. We found in our interviews in Stockholm and London the problem of boundaries was expressed by employers in terms of privacy, as this employer in London explained:

There's this thing that 'they should be part of your family' but they're not. But you can't treat them as an employee. I treat them as friends, but expect

*them not to be hanging around. One came in watching TV with me in the
evening! That's my private time!*

The employer/employee relationships in Madrid were often marked by
more professional distance which acknowledged the difference in status
between the two parties. Some employees would address the employer
in the polite way: 'usted' or 'señora', while their employer would use
the familiar 'tu'. In some homes employees wore uniforms; in addition,
domestic tasks were treated much more as acquired skills rather than
dispositions. In spite of this formality there was still a view amongst
some employers that they treated their employees as part of the family.

Not surprisingly, many employees did not see things in the same way.
In Stockholm domestic helps found 'niceness' disarming and it made
them feel they could not assert themselves when they felt they were
being treated unfairly. In London, many employees felt a professional
relationship gave them a better standing. In Madrid, however, employees felt demeaned by the impersonality of their employers. Boundary
issues for them were about being 'on call' and it being too easy to over-
step agreed working conditions.

Second, the fact that the work also involves affective relations usually
associated with close relationships also intensifies the confusion as to
whether work practices are based upon informal obligation or upon contractual rights. Third, for the employees, this is further exacerbated by
the fact that their migration status – for example, where they are waiting
for visas, or where they have no recourse to public funds – makes them
dependent upon an individual employer rather than able to sell their
labour freely. Fourth, home-based work isolates the worker, makes the
work invisible, and renders forms of collective mobilization for rights
more difficult.

Of course, both employers and employees who have children share
the same problem of how to balance their care and work responsibilities.
While the employee might exercise her rights to mobility, she may, at
the same time, forfeit her and her children's rights to family reunion,
and the opportunity to see her children grow up, notwithstanding the
efforts she will make to keep up contact and to ensure their care through
a surrogate. At a wider level, trends in migration regimes also reveal new
patterns of inclusion/exclusion. Changing boundaries of the EU, whilst
effectively drawing a line between who is included as an EU citizen,
coexist with rules in which skilled workers increasingly accrue more
rights.

These patterns are cut across by differences of employment. Employees may provide housework or child care or both; they may live in or live out; they may work a few or very long hours; they may be qualified yet designated as 'unskilled', they may be a carer, cleaner or personal assistant for an older, frail person or a disabled one; they may be self-employed, or 'undeclared' or work for a private agency or local authority. As migrant workers, they may be working under a special permit or they may be undocumented. All these differences make collective organization more difficult. Furthermore, these differences are overlaid with racialized, ethnic or national stereotypes which permeate the employment of these workers, giving them greater or lesser access to different types of work and payments. In all three countries differences in rates of pay between different types of job were compounded by national/ethnic hierarchies often based upon racialized stereotypes. (There were also differences in gender according to anecdotal accounts in the UK that male au pairs were paid more). This hierarchy was also influenced by how well the worker spoke the language of the country in which she worked and the assumed compatibility of her nationality with her employer's. This is illustrated by a Slovakian au pair in London:

> ... *my friend was working for one family, she was from Slovakia and she was getting quite good money, she had about £60 a week. She worked about 30 hours or something like that, babysit twice a week and she asked me if I knew someone who could exchange with her and I knew about one girl who was looking for a job but she was from Thailand; she was a lovely girl and I brought her there for an interview and this lady required her to work 40 hours [a] week, do four babysitting [shifts] a week for £45 and I said, like are you kidding me? Is that just because that person's from Thailand and that person was from Slovakia?*

It is clear that transnational care raises many complex issues for politics and policy. These include the difficulties when care is commodified: public provision of care is necessarily expensive because it has no intrinsic productivity. When the market provides care, its costs can only rise as wages rise, and this means that care workers' wages are always being forced down by strategies such as employing those with the least bargaining power. Not only is this exploitative but it jeopardizes good quality care. But, also, the Swedish case shows that public provision of child care, whilst far preferable, does not necessarily lead to a sharing of care and domestic work within the home, or the reconciliation of work and care. Yet turning to low-paid and often migrant care or domestic workers as a solution gives rise to different manifestations of gendered citizenship.

For the migrant workers, crossing continents to earn money provides an important opportunity, but it is an opportunity to enter a world in which migration rules construct limited and different rights to social, economic, political and intimate citizenship compared with their employers. Furthermore, these limitations give rise to the likelihood of women entering the often unregulated world of domestic and care work in the home, whose conditions perpetuate the devaluation and invisibility of the private domain and its subservience to the public world. In addition, when home becomes work, and workers become 'part of the family' then tensions and power relations ensue, articulated in racialized stereotypes and hierarchies and competing moralities about what is best for the child. It is where the unequal relations of global interdependency become translated into the unequal relations of personal interdependency.

All this raises difficult dilemmas about the future of the adult worker model across Europe. In the short term, regularizing care and domestic work, improving migrants' rights of citizenship (including family reunion, rights to contracts, training and so on) are urgently needed. These need to be accompanied by policies that ensure that migrant care workers are treated with respect and as citizens and as workers, not simply units of labour quotas, or as racialized others. However, improving citizenship rights in this way, whilst essential, is not sufficient. I suggest that there is more purchase to this issue both analytically and politically if we understand this phenomenon in terms of a wider, macro transnational analysis of the political economy of care. And it is to this, and the associated question of global justice, that I turn to conclude the chapter.

Conclusion: the transnational political economy of care

The context of migration and care is one in which nation-welfare-states exist in a situation of unequal geopolitical interdependence, where it is possible for welfare states of richer countries to solve the social and cost problems of their care deficits through the resources of poorer countries. However, the transnational political economy of care comprises more than just the exploitation of migrant labour in home-based care. The transnational dynamics of child care can be understood as part of a bigger picture in which there are a number of different but simultaneous processes (Williams 2011). To begin with, the migration of women from poorer to richer regions into home-based care is part of a wider process of the *transnational movement of care labour*. The workforce of the European health and education and social services depends on skilled migrants. In 2000 in the UK 31 per cent of doctors and 13 per cent of nurses were non-UK born (Glover et al. 2001); and this was similar in France and Germany and Sweden. Migrant workers also work in both formal and home-based elder care. Brain drains and care chains enable some of the welfare regimes of the west to meet their needs for care in cost-effective ways, whilst depriving poorer nations of their skills and sources of care provision. Second are the *transnational dynamics of care commitments* as people move and leave behind younger or older people to be cared for at a distance. These create disproportionate care responsibilities across the globe. While the richer areas of the North are concerned with a 'care deficit' consequent upon women's employment, and an ageing population, in the developing world a crisis of care also exists where AIDS, chronic illness or natural disasters place enormous burdens on women who are expected to do the caring with very little infrastructural support. Associated with is the movement of wages and the remittances which migrant workers send home constitute a major cushioning against poverty for developing countries; they total twice the overseas aid that goes to poorer countries (Brown 2006, 58).

Third is the *transnational movement of care capital*. Brennan's forensic study of Eddy Groves' child-care company, ABC Learning (Brennan 2007), shows how care has become big business (see also Holden 2002 on the internationalization of companies owning long-term residential care institutions for older people). Associated with this is the *transnational influence of care discourse and policies*. One example of this is the spread of a 'social investment' approach amongst national and supranational governments, such as the EU, and international organizations such as the OECD. This urges public investment in the capabilities of human capital – mothers as workers and children as citizen-workers-of-the-future, and is to be achieved through supports for labour market activation, anti-poverty measures, and education and child care (Jenson 2008; Mahon 2008; Williams 2009). The other side of this is the *transnational development of social movements, NGOs and grassroots campaigns*. Examples here include developments in the 1990s such as Development Alternatives for a New Era and the organization of world women's conferences such as that in Beijing in 1995 (Mayo 2005). Similarly within Europe, the European Women's Lobby organizes for women's interests to be present within EU debates, one of whose lobbying themes is care.

Understanding the issue of migration into home-based care in these terms also allows us to think differently about normative implications and political strategies. Fiona Robinson has argued for an approach to global social justice which can embed, theoretically and empirically, everyday social relations of care with macro understandings of inequality (Robinson 2006a, 2006b). The implication of this is that balancing work and care is a global issue which requires global strategies. From where those of us in the developed world stand, we need a broader notion of 'work-family reconciliation'. Currently this is centred on the private sphere of the family, the contained and andocentric organization of work, and the restricted national spaces of territorial citizenship. It seems to have no place for community-based or voluntary activities, or for those practices which are part of a flourishing civil society, often impelled by interdependence or mutuality. We need bigger, more imaginative understandings of 'work' and 'care' and the geopolitical extent of both.

We do not only need time and capacity to ensure we can support and care for ourselves, and support and care for close others, but also the time and support to care for the 'world' in the sense of a wider community that is both local and global. This is where a political ethic of care can be developed in relation to global citizenship. It would see the care ethic not as a modernized form of maternalism, but as a recognition of an interdependence beyond family, of an inclusiveness wider than the current productivist work ethic, and a moral reach beyond the private household or the local community.

Notes

1. This chapter develops further work which has been published elsewhere. For analysis of the micro-level see Lister et al. (2007), Chapter 5; Williams (2007) and Williams and Gavanas (2008); for conceptual discussion see Williams (2010) and for a more developed analysis of the transnational political economy of care see Williams (2011).
2. Between July 2004 and April 2005, Anna Gavanas carried out interviews in London with 16 employees, 10 employers and eight agencies. In Stockholm, interviews were conducted with 17 employees, 10 employers and eight representatives of organizations and agencies dealing with domestic work. In Madrid, interviews, most of which were made in collaboration with Virginia Paez, were conducted with 14 employees and 10 employers as well as nine organizations. All quotations in this chapter are taken from Anna Gavanas's interviews and translations (see also Gavanas, 2006). We are grateful for funding from the European Community's Sixth Framework Programme (ref. MEIF-CT-2003-502369). This chapter also draws from an ESRC-funded study

A Theoretical Synthesis of Gender, Migration and Care, and Welfare Regimes (ref. 000-22-1514) undertaken as part of an ongoing research collaboration with scholars from Ireland, Germany and the Netherlands studying migrant work in child care and elder care in Europe, *Migration and Networks of Care*, under the Eurocores programme, 2006–9.

3. The Coalition Government elected in 2010 is set to cut back some subsidies for middle-class parents.

4. These indicators can be generalized to regimes of care that cover care for older and disabled people as well as people with mental health problems.

3

The Regulation of Paid Domestic Work: A Win-Win Situation or a Reproduction of Social Inequalities?

Majda Hrženjak

Introduction

Paid domestic work such as cleaning, child care and elderly care has a long history and is still at the crossroads of important themes for the European Union, especially with reference to irregular work, (un)employment, demographic decline, gender inequalities, the relationship between the family and the state, migration and citizenship. On the other hand, unpaid domestic work is still, to a large extent, perceived as non-work, or as a labour of love performed by women, and thus is not considered 'real' work. Furthermore, when such work is performed within the private sphere, it is not a subject of public interest; it is viewed as non-productive work that does not produce surplus value, but is primarily oriented towards consumption. The perception that domestic work is not work leads to the invisibility of the double burden shouldered by contemporary women that is that of paid productive work within the public sphere and unpaid reproductive labour within the private sphere (Hrženjak 2007). Public, political and even feminist critiques have focused primarily on the participation of women in the sphere of paid work, while the problematization of the burden of reproductive labour shouldered by women has been marginalized. The perception that domestic work is not work is also the reason for the invisibility of paid domestic work, although, according to a number of research findings (Lister et al. 2007; Lutz 2008c; Fish 2006; Sarti 2005; Ehrenreich and Hochschild 2002; Cancedda 2001; Parreñas 2001; Gregson and Lowe 1994), it is as widespread in modern society as it was in the past. It is particularly problematic that such invisible and unregulated work is mostly carried out within informal situations by groups of women who are already, to a large extent, socially excluded: older women, long-term unemployed women, young women seeking their first job, the working poor and, in particular, immigrants (Anti-Slavery International 2006; Lutz and Schwalgin 2003). There is a saying that behind every successful man there is a woman. More pertinent to our context would be to say that behind a successful woman there is another woman who does domestic work for her.

The problem of domestic work not being perceived as work has been exacerbated by the increasing demand for paid domestic work in modern EU societies and an increase in irregular employment in this area. Significantly enough, in 2000 the Parliamentary Assembly of the European Council adopted a resolution *Regulating domestic help in the informal sector* (A5-0301/2000) that urged the Committee of Ministers to 'elaborate a charter of rights for domestic workers' that should guarantee, among other things, 'the recognition of domestic work in private households as "proper work", that is to which full employment rights and social protection apply, including the minimum wage (where it exists), sickness and maternity pay and pension rights'.

A Local Dimension for the European Employment Strategy (Strauss 2000) identifies domestic work as one of the four most promising areas as regards new job positions. The European Commission White paper *Growth, Competitiveness, Employment* (1993), for instance, contained a set of proposals to increase employment and one of the priorities among them was the promotion of local development and employment initiatives including 'services for everyday life'. Thus, paid domestic work is framed as a policy for managing work and family conflict and also as a policy that works toward reducing social exclusion and unemployment.

However, the phenomenon of contemporary paid domestic work lacks studies that are based on precise quantitative evidence, though that is most likely due to the fact that many domestic workers work irregularly. According to Sarti (2005), in Germany it is estimated that in 2002 there were between 1.2 and 2.9 million domestic workers working within private households. In France, it is said that the past decade saw an 'explosion of domestic help', and the estimates were that this kind of employment amounted to 538,390 jobs in 1999. In Italy, according to Statistical Office data, there were 1,049,500 informal jobs in private households (Sarti 2005). With regard to the Central and Eastern European countries a similar situation exists; for instance, in Hungary informal data estimates about 200,000 women (Krizsan 2007) and according to the Inspectorate RS for Work in Slovenia there are about 23,000 informal domestic workers there (Hrženjak 2007). When considering current demographic and socio-economic trends, in particular the ageing of the population and increasing female employment, as well as income and quality of life imbalances on a global and local scale it can be expected that there will be further increases in the recourse to paid domestic work.

In this chapter the situations of the two groups of women are discussed: on one hand, we have employed women who are doubly burdened by productive and reproductive work and hence forced to transfer part of their reproductive labour to irregular domestic workers; on the other hand, we have contemporary paid domestic workers who are facing social exclusion and poverty, so they undertake the work of other women. In the first part of this chapter I discuss some of the characteristics of contemporary irregular paid domestic work, in particular the themes of the precariousness of the work and the intersectionality of gender, class, ethnicity and race, and employment and citizenship status which characterize contemporary domestic workers. I also touch upon how the regulation of domestic work is seen from the perspective of domestic workers. In the second part of the chapter it is argued that increasing women's participation in the labour market combined with gender inequality in the private sphere and insufficient policies for managing work and family conflict create a high demand for irregular paid domestic work in European middle-class households. In the third part I critically discuss the potential impact of the professionalization and the regulation of paid domestic services on gender and class (in)equalities, which seem to be a major part of the policy recommendation at European Union level for reducing both social exclusion and work-family conflict.

The irregular market for paid domestic work

The precariousness of paid domestic work

Anderson (2000, 30) established that two factors have the greatest impact on the quality of working and living conditions for domestic workers in Europe: their relationship with their employer (live in/live out), and their status within a country (citizenship status and work permit, legal or illegal work). The most negative aspects of paid domestic work stem from the informal employment of undocumented immigrants who live in the employer's household. 'Live-in' domestic workers in particular are frequently, although not as a rule, recruited from immigrant populations, including undocumented immigrants. These workers are under serious stress, which is caused by the constant threat of expulsion. In addition, many are burdened by debt that is either owed to an agency, to a relative in their home country, or to a member of an informal network in the host country. Consequently, a job in a household that also provides accommodation and food appears to be a good solution in a situation where a migrant finds herself in an unknown country. However, live-in jobs have many negative sides: poor wages and undefined working hours that extend to the worker being on duty around the clock, because the job usually involves caring for young children or sick or older people.

Live-in workers frequently do their work in complete social isolation. They find themselves in an unknown cultural environment and have no other social contacts or connections save for those with the members of the household. Another problem that live-in workers face is a lack of privacy; for example, some do not even have their own room, while others are asked to leave the door to their room open so that they can hear the children if they call during the night, and so on. Furthermore, live-in workers cannot have their own family and children. Or, if they do have a family in their home country, they are separated from it for long periods of time and have to leave their children to the care of relatives or hired childminders and thus such arrangements contribute to the global care chain (Parreñas 2001).

Studies on paid domestic work treat live-out arrangements as a modernization compared to live-in arrangements (Katzman 1978; Thornton Dill 1994; Ozyegin 2001). Live-out workers usually work for several employers. Those whose duties involve a combination of household work and child care may work for one employer only, but their working hours are better defined. Nevertheless, long working hours also frequently occur with this kind of arrangement. Live-out workers who work for several employers must therefore be skilful managers of time to cover the distance from one workplace to another. In addition, the time they spend travelling from one place to another is usually not paid for and is not counted as working time, although it may amount to as many as 15 hours a week, with the result being abnormally long working hours on a weekly level. Despite this, a live-out arrangement has its advantages over the live-in arrangement because there is less personal control on the part of the employer, and a domestic worker is not so critically dependent on the employer, which means that the loss of a job with one household does not lead to a complete loss of income. Nevertheless, the situation does become complicated if a live-out domestic worker herself has small children, works long hours and has a low income. The reconciliation of long working hours with child care is very difficult in such a case.

Both immigrant and local domestic workers in the European Union cope with many problems related to the quality of working conditions

(Cancedda 2001). First of all the definition of the work performed by domestic workers is too narrow[1] because it does not include a provision for care, such as child care and the nursing of the elderly and the sick. The most frequently heard complaint of domestic workers is that in addition to the child care initially agreed on, they end up performing all the household chores (Anderson 2000, 15). Moreover, given the demanding nature of the job and the responsibility undertaken by domestic workers, the problem is low wages, because low wages lead to long working hours that are necessary in order to earn enough money to cover the cost of living. The majority of paid domestic work is performed within the area of the grey economy, so wages are not systematized and can vary greatly. It is an area of class, racial and ethnic differentiation that produces more or less privileged workers. Women coming from so-called third world countries are usually paid less and treated worse than European women who can obtain more secure arrangements and have a more symmetrical relationship with their employers. In either case, these wages do not include social, health and retirement contributions, and as a result social security does not feature strongly presently within the paid domestic work segment. A domestic worker who becomes sick loses her job and is left without income and without a roof over her head. Furthermore, an employer may not feel any responsibility towards her. This area is also characterized by a large demand for flexible and atypical working hours, for example, part-time, long working hours, split shifts, and so on.

In interviews Anderson (2000, 49–56) learnt that one serious problem facing domestic workers in Athens, who come from various regions that range from Eastern Europe, Africa and Asia to Latin America, is non-payment. Domestic workers in Athens are noted as frequently experiencing psychological problems as a consequence of their immigrant status, have a constant fear of the police, are denied requests for asylum, face uncertain employment, hard work and social isolation and can suffer an employer attitude that humiliates them. Physical and sexual abuse is not rare, either. In France the majority of those having live-in arrangements are Filipino immigrants, many of whom are not documented residents. They report difficulties similar to those of their colleagues in Athens, Barcelona and Bologna, which are long working hours, working for friends and relatives of the employer without additional payment, sexual harassment, fake accusations of theft, no insurance in case of illness and so on (Anderson 2000, 76). It is interesting that the French government has actually introduced regulations on paid domestic services, for example, the Cheque Emploi-Service (CES), which was established in 1993. This is a policy tool with which the state subsidizes and supports the use of paid domestic services by households. The European Commission has recognized that France has some of the most far-reaching policies in this area in the Union and identifies the above regulation as one of the most innovative measures taken to help reconcile professional and family life (Windebank 2007). Still, it seems that this measure did not reduce irregular supply and demand for paid domestic work, especially with reference to live-in work. In fact, working conditions in the irregular market became even worse.

The United Kingdom provides a good example of the self-organization of domestic workers, particularly immigrant domestic workers. In 1979, the Commission for Filipino Migrant Workers (CFMW) was established, which provides free advice and support. In 1984, a large number of Filipino women working as domestic workers in British households came to CFMW without any resources and documents to describe their experiences and reasons for leaving the households for which they worked. The reasons included the following: they were not paid for their work, were abused psychologically (scolded and shouted at) and physically (beaten, kicked, and pulled by the hair); some were raped, and all were traumatized and frightened. CFMW realized that they could not address these issues on a case-by-case basis, so they organized a series of meetings that clearly showed that immigrant paid domestic workers were in an extremely difficult position. They invited lawyers, researchers, union leaders and public decision-makers to cooperate. This gave rise to the Waling-Waling organization, which was intended to provide support for immigrant domestic workers when they found themselves in a 'no way out' situation. The Kalayaan organization was established in 1987 in close collaboration with Waling-Waling. Its main purpose is to encourage and develop professional and political campaigns and to lobby for changes in labour legislation and immigration policies, which should provide regulation in the segment of domestic work, and immigrant work in particular. The two organizations cooperate closely with the Transport and General Workers Union, by integrating their own members within it (Alhadeff 1998, 21–2).

In literature on domestic workers a strong consensus exists that patronization, exploitation, discrimination and humiliation, which occasionally turns into real abuse and a slave-like relationship (Anti-Slavery International 2006; Fish 2006; Skřivánková 2006; Ehrenreich and Hochschild 2002) are possible due to their isolation in the private sphere, a quasi-familial relationship with employers ('one of the family') and the 'othering' of workers, which is the consequence of the racial, ethnic, class and gender segmentation of the sector. Discussions and the recognition of the fact that massive abuse can also be the outcome of the deregulation of the sector are extremely rare among scholars. On the contrary, domestic workers' organizations, like the example mentioned above and some others (the R.E.S.P.E.C.T. network, for instance) make strong efforts towards the recognition and regulation of paid domestic work as work by supposing that it would reduce the exploitation of workers and improve their working conditions as well as their social rights and protection.

The intersectionality of gender, class, ethnicity and race, and employment status

This type of female irregular work is extremely low paid and flexible. It is usually carried out by those with the fewest options, the lowest educational and skills levels and those who have limited rights of citizenship. In a multicultural context the understanding of intersectionality (how different kinds of inequalities are inter-related) is critical to any analysis of the issue of irregular domestic work, the feminization of migration and poverty, social inclusion and so on (Crenshaw 1991; Thornton Dill 1994; Schecter 1998). While much of the current discussion on intersectionality has concerned the intersection of gender and ethnicity, many of the earlier debates were concerned with the relationship of gender and class. Both types of analysis might be thought to find a continuity of tradition within the analysis of the 'global care chain', in which women from some of the poorest countries of the world migrate in order to care for the children and homes of rich women in the industrialized North (Hochschild 2002; Parreñas 2001; Anderson 2000). In this analysis, the position in the global capitalist hierarchy of countries as core or periphery, as well as class, ethnicity and gender, all combine to produce this exploitation of the specifically feminized labour of domestic and care work.

While most of the studies deal with the situation of immigrant domestic workers, only a few studies (Cancedda 2001; Meagher 2003; Hrženjak 2007) have pointed out that informal paid domestic work is not performed only by immigrant female workers, but also by local women. In the case of the latter, instead of the intersectionality of citizenship, ethnicity/race and gender factors, it is possible to establish a specific combination of gender, social class and age factors as well as unemployment status. While the main motive behind the decision of immigrants from poor countries to take domestic jobs is their not having citizenship in the host country, among the local population the main motive is their long-term unemployment status. The action project SIPA (EU EQUAL initiative) showed that in Slovenia during the past decade it has been possible to observe an increase in the supply of and demand for household cleaning services and child care, which means a type of work that had all but disappeared during the socialist era. Apart from the gendered division of domestic labour and the rapid ageing of the population, the main factor encouraging this phenomenon is social change brought about by the change to a capitalist economy in which there are particularly long working hours for professionals and long-term structural unemployment, which has resulted from the restructuring of the economy (Hrženjak 2007).

The transformation of the political and economic system during the early 1990s was marked by the restructuring of the predominantly industrial, state-owned economy into a private market and service economy. Many companies went out of business during this process, with the textile industry, which traditionally employed mostly women, especially suffering difficulties. The 'turbo-capitalist' management logic led to the massive layoffs of older women in particular, even in companies which did not collapse. Job advertisements began to feature a new requirement; 'preferred age up to 35'. Unemployment during this transition period especially affected older women with low education levels, and their unemployment continues to be a structural problem of long-term unemployment in Slovenia.[2] Contemporary informal household workers in Slovenia belong to various social groups. Many are retired women, employed working-class women, unemployed women who never sought a regular job and students. What they have in common is that paid household work is not a means of livelihood, but a source of extra income that to a certain extent may enhance their economic situation and quality of life. However, a large number of contemporary household workers are long-term unemployed women for whom this work is, beside modest social allowances, the only means of survival. Therefore, as employment appears to be the main way out of poverty and social exclusion there is a strong incentive for the transformation of unpaid work, traditionally carried out in private homes by women, into regular jobs at the European Union policy level (*Regulating domestic help*, A5-0301/2000).

Developing domestic services is viewed as a means of creating jobs for those workers who have been rendered redundant by technological innovation in industrial production. However, the idea of opening up new job opportunities in the field of domestic services and consequently the social inclusion of hard-to-employ people could be highly contradictory. On the one hand, it reaffirms existing social relations by creating hard, poorly defined and low-paid jobs that are held in low social esteem and do not offer promotion options for marginalized social groups starting from weak social and economic positions. On the other hand, it is not possible to ignore the increasing demand for paid domestic work and the fact that an army of unemployed, poor and immigrant women already work as domestic workers within the grey economy, because for them that is the only means of survival in the current system.

Paid domestic work and women's participation in the labour market

Work and family conflict – deficient policy measures

When examining the demand side, what has to be exposed is that the target measures for increasing women's employment rate, set earlier in European Employment Strategy, have been met. The employment rate for women rose from 50.6 per cent to 54.9 per cent during the period from 1997 to 2001. New targets have been set which aim to increase the female employment rate to 60 per cent by 2010 (*Report on Equality between Women and Men* 2006). The breadwinner-caretaker model has in recent decades become replaced by the adult-worker model (Lister et al. 2007, 170) all over Europe. The development of the adult-worker model is contradictory in its impact, argues Lister (2007). It offers women a place in the labour market, which is critical to full and equal citizenship in contemporary welfare states, without significantly altering men's role. Thus, because it pays insufficient attention to the care gap to which it contributes, the adult-worker model poses many problems. Consequently, despite a number of positive developments, women are facing structural discrimination in the labour market. Furthermore, the female employment rate is still considerably lower than the male employment rate and women are, to a larger extent, engaged in insecure forms of employment with less social protection. The main reason for this can be seen in women's domestic and care obligations which, irrespective of a woman's educational level, still narrows down women's possibilities. Domestic and caring activities in the private sphere also impact on women's participation in working life, career advancement, and their ability to work full-time, together with their ability for life-course integration into the labour market. Williams (2000, 7), for example, reports that the difference in the salaries of mothers and non-mothers has been increasing lately: 'Though the wage gap between men and women has fallen, the gap between the wages of mothers and others has widened in recent years.'

A number of European studies (Webster 2005) have revealed that the scope and quality of a woman's employment depends on the number of children she has, and that women, particularly mothers, prevail in part-time jobs and flexible working arrangements. An important fact, and one not often addressed in employment policies, is that women who enter into the labour market often do part-time work, which constitutes an obstacle to equality between women and men in the labour market. In 2005 in the EU 32.6 per cent of women and only 7.4 per cent of men worked part-time (*Report on Equality between Women and Men* 2006, 6), and by 2007 the situation had not changed much as the share of women employees working part-time was 31.4 per cent while the figure for men was 7.8 per cent. Of course, the variations between European countries are large in this respect. The share of female part-time workers exceeded 30 per cent in France, Ireland, Denmark and Luxemburg, 40 per cent in Sweden, Austria, Belgium, the United Kingdom and Germany and reached even 74.9 per cent in the Netherlands (*Report on Equality between Women and Men* 2008, 13), while the share of part-time workers among women was very low in countries with a so-called post-communist welfare regime; in Bulgaria, Slovakia, Poland, Romania, Hungary, the Czech Republic and Slovenia it varied from 3 to 11 per cent in 2004 (den Dulk and van Doorne-Huiskes 2007, 49). The recourse to part-time work by women is closely linked to the number and age of children, which is not the case for men. One third of women with one child and half of those women with three and more children worked on a part-time basis, while the number of children had the opposite effect on the unemployment rate among men and their numbers in part-time jobs.

Both decrease with an increase in the number of children (*Report on Equality between Women and Men* 2006, 6). The reasons are gender inequality in sharing care work as well as insufficient public care services. Part-time work does not provide a sufficient income to allow economic autonomy and full social security rights, nor does it enable women to achieve job promotion or leading positions. Women are thus encouraged to take part-time jobs in situations where this type of work is explicitly marginalized. Part-time work is, however, considered to be the solution to the work-family conflict, and is considered to be an issue that mainly concerns women. Such a view strongly limits women's choices in the labour market and influences the unequal sharing of family responsibilities between women and men. Gender inequalities in employment such as the substantial pay gap that exists between women and men, women's overrepresentation in low-paid work, part-time salaries and women's overrepresentation in the informal economy and consequently lower protection benefits make it very difficult for women to achieve financial independence through their own earnings and this reinforces the greater likelihood of females experiencing poverty and social exclusion.

The 'reconciliation of work and private life' is a concept included in gender equality policies that aim at encouraging the equal division of domestic labour in practice and raising awareness about it. As Stratigaki's (2004, 32) content analysis of relevant European documents showed, the concept of reconciling work and family life has changed over time as the meaning of the initial, fundamentally feminist, notion of an equal division of domestic labour has shifted towards a more market-based and productive idea of 'encouraging flexible forms of work for women' so that they can more easily reconcile work and family duties. The difficulty of reconciling work and private life is thus not treated as a problem in itself, but as an obstacle to women's greater participation in the labour market. Accordingly, these measures are primarily concerned with creating opportunities for women to combine child care with paid work, while little attention is devoted to the encouragement of men towards an equal division of labour within the private sphere.

In attempting to reduce the time needed for housework, women continue to resort to, or have been returning to, domestic work to relieve them from the burden of housework for at least several hours a week. The research *Working Women's Choices for Domestic Help* (Tijdens et al. 2003) revealed that a decision to hire domestic help is primarily conditioned by the number of hours a woman spends at work, her job position and the level of her income. Another important determinant is the presence of children aged four to 12. In the hierarchy of domestic chores, the most valued are activities related to child care, cooking and shopping. Accordingly, middle-class women mainly accomplish these tasks on their own, with the help of their partners. The lowest ranking in this hierarchy are labour intensive activities (primarily cleaning and ironing), which are the tasks increasingly outsourced. Contemporary paid domestic workers actually perform the work that modern society expects to be accomplished by women in their roles as wives and mothers without payment and as a labour of love. Thus, paid domestic work is held in low social esteem and has a low market value, which also perpetuates the low status of women performing it. However, the low market value for paid domestic work is not the result of the low demand for it or of the ease of the work itself, but of the low social status granted to women's reproductive labour.

Paid domestic work: a private solution to gender inequality and work and family conflict

The increasing incorporation of European women into the labour market, gender inequality in domestic work and the inadequacy of state provision for the care of children and the elderly have resulted in a greatly increased demand for domestic workers and these care roles have been fulfilled by 'other' women. The employment of informal domestic workers has facilitated changes in the economic activity rate of one group of women whose reliance on the family (for example, their mother and other unpaid female kin) can no longer be guaranteed. Informally employed, paid domestic workers, no matter whether they are migrants or local women, with their activity in the domestic sphere and domestic work has reorganized notions of welfare and the relationship between care and paid work in European societies.

In other words, the hierarchy between poor and wealthy and between migrants and natives is so strong that it affects the traditional division of roles within households and has resulted in wealthy, native men and women becoming highly involved in the labour market and poor and migrant women becoming widely employed in the domestic work sector. Today, greater gender equality for middle-class European couples in the labour market is being obtained at the cost of continuing or even widening the social gap between social classes and countries (Sarti 2005, 56), or, as Macklin put it, 'one woman is exercising class and citizenship privilege to buy her way out of sex oppression' (Macklin 1994, 34). Present trends indicate that irregular domestic workers are increasingly becoming part of the support structure that allows women to take on regular (paid) jobs in the public labour market.

It has been established by research (Webster 2005, 32; den Dulk and van Doorne-Huiskes 2007, 47) that there is a close link between high rates of female labour market participation and the provision of care (of children, the sick, the elderly) by the state. In general, where care provision is highest, so too is female labour market participation. The growth of cash-rich time-poor[3] dual-career households has inspired the demand for services offered in the irregular market of domestic and care work where women are again over-represented. Irregular work reduces tax revenue, undermines public finances and is not covered by the social protection system. This is the context in which the European Parliament's concerns with regard to the increase in demand for informal care and domestic work and their policy responses to it should be understood. According to Webster (2005, 13), besides framing regulation for paid domestic work as a way out of poverty and social exclusion, there is the underlying framework in which Employment Guidelines for the European Employment Strategy suggest that member states should seek to transform irregular and informal paid domestic work into regular and formal work.

Discussion

At first glance the regulation and professionalization of informal domestic work is seen as a win-win situation because it addresses the need for more and better home and family services in Europe, while at the same time it provides more and better quality jobs for hard-to-employ people. The protagonists of this idea are not only EU policy-makers but, as shown, also many dual-career middle-class households, who have already found a remedy for the care crisis and gender conflicts about sharing domestic work, which they have 'solved' by hiring irregular domestic workers, as well as domestic workers' organizations who believe that the regulation of their work would improve their working conditions and grant them rights related to regular work. The regulation of paid domestic work would, according to this vision, lead to the creation of new job opportunities for hard-to-employ people and increase their social inclusion, as it would represent an 'innovative' measure taken up to help manage work-family conflict. However, many authors and case studies argue against it.

In Gorz's opinion (1988, 156) the outsourcing of domestic work establishes a system in which modern servants are forced to undertake, in addition to their unpaid domestic labour, the domestic work of the privileged minority but for a low wage. He maintains that domestic help services are possible only in conditions of increasing social inequality in which one part of the population monopolizes well-paid social positions and forces the other part of the population into a position of servitude. If everyone worked less, he adds, everyone could accomplish domestic work on their own, and everyone could make their living doing their work. Gorz starts from the notion that post-industrial production freed people from the drudgery of monotonous, repetitive work and opened the door to the realm of leisure.

Yet no matter how much one would like to believe this, reality does not confirm it. A post-industrial information and knowledge society or a '24 hours society' (Cox 2006) requires as much, if not more, work and the constant processing, combining and interpretation of an ever larger amount of new information. As a result, working hours have actually been lengthening rather than shortening, creating the need for care services, child escort and transport services, food preparation and delivery services, cleaning services, and so on. In somewhat simplified terms, modern working conditions have created a class of long-term unemployed and hard-to-employ people whose low skills or other perceived negative attributes (age, illness, gender, ethnicity, citizenship status and so on) are no longer needed or desired in high-skilled automated work processes, so they are condemned to social exclusion. On the other hand, there has emerged a class of over-employed, highly skilled workers with a high income, who work more than 50 hours a week and are in constant need of domestic and care services.

Another argument against the regulation of paid domestic services is presented by Windebank (2007) in her assessment of the Chèque Emploi-Service in France. She assessed the extent to which the state supported outsourcing of women's unpaid domestic labour helps to reduce the work-family conflict and the time famine which they face. Her study demonstrates that only wealthy households are eligible for tax relief from the purchase of domestic services in the system and that in 2003 the average amount of purchased services was approximately four hours a week per household. In contrast to the very positive evaluation of the system both within France and at the European Union level, Windebank argues that the impact of these schemes is marginal; both in terms of the range of households which benefit from them and in terms of the amount of relief gained by the women who purchase paid domestic services. Furthermore, these services reinforce the gender stereotyping surrounding domestic work by transferring it from more well-off to less well-off women.

In general, Meagher (2003, 133) is in favour of the regulation of domestic services. She argues that most of the studies on contemporary paid domestic services focus either on the global macro level or on the individual micro level. In the first case the studies discuss global structural oppression and constrain thinking about remedies largely to the wholesale transformation of society. In the second case the predominantly micro-level analyses of experiences and strategies focus on domestic workers' and women's individual responses to the plight of economic and cultural problems in their working lives.

What is absent in the literature, argues Meagher, is a meso level of institutional analysis. This level of analysis would suggest remedies to domestic workers' problems that can be pursued through institutional innovations that remain relatively unexplored at the moment, although strategies aimed at changing the distribution of domestic and care work between the market, state, households and civil society as well as strategies aimed at removing the discriminatory barriers that exclude ethnic and gender groups in the labour market could be highly relevant to the problems of paid household work. Nevertheless, even Meagher recognizes that although varieties of regulation (fair contracting, protection against the personal mistreatment of workers by householders and to various extents increasing pay rates) can remedy many of the problems, the majority of workers are still vulnerable in informal paid housework because domestic occupations retain a social stigma that is difficult to consider within a transformative policy measure.

In my opinion, it is important to highlight that paid domestic work is not an unvarying phenomenon, but it constitutes a domain where various social groups meet, various services are offered and various needs are satisfied. Therefore, the consideration of paid domestic work as a uniform concept would appear controversial because it is not possible to apply the same evaluation criteria to the purchase of domestic services, which are dictated by the lifestyle of the rich social classes, as it is to those necessitated by disease and old age or the work-family conflict. Similarly, it is necessary to distinguish between the situations of undocumented migrant domestic workers, and, for example, those of retired women or long-term unemployed women, who from time to time help young families with child care and household work for the purpose of their social reintegration and the improvement of their income. Therefore, the field of irregular paid domestic services assessments and policy measures should be informed by a differentiated approach that would take into account the variety of social groups and the requirements which exist in the sector.

For instance, in Slovenia the Social Security Act contains a provision on family assistance which includes family support services, assistance at home, and social services comprising domestic help, assistance in maintaining personal hygiene and assistance in maintaining social contacts (Hrženjak 2007). Institutions for social work and some other actors (local community, social enterprises) offer domestic help services as part of social care programmes through public work mechanisms, which involve various target groups of hard-to-employ people. The standards in this case require that the employee be a nurse, housewife or social assistant. This is an important element of social policy in an effort to avoid the institutionalization of the elderly as well as a way to unburden the family. However, this policy measure is restricted to social care for elderly and disabled people and can offer only limited services due to the scarcity of workers in the care sector and insufficient state subsidies.

The discussion of the regulation of irregular domestic work, the steep growth of which is the consequence of the insufficiency of public social services, could also mean an improvement and expansion of existing social policies in the direction of more innovative, organizational, differentiated and contemporary needs-adjusted services provided by the state. Domestic services as public, social services for selected social groups (those in greater need of such services, for example families with young children, single-parent families, families caring for an additional member who needs nursing, large families, working poor families, elderly people, and so on) can have the potential for challenging market norms in two inclusive ways: by providing employment for domestic workers searching for a higher status in their work, and for households searching for quality services. For employees, these jobs need to be transformed into well-paid jobs that are accompanied by social recognition and democratic employer-worker-consumer relations. In this way the redistribution of domestic and care work between the state and family would not rely on the existence and creation of a servant underclass.

Notes

1. The International Labor Organization defines the domestic worker as follows: "*Domestic helpers and cleaners sweep, vacuum, clean, wash and polish, take care of household linen, purchase household supplies, prepare food, serve meals and perform various other domestic duties. Tasks include: (a) sweeping, vacuum cleaning, polishing and washing floors and furniture, or washing windows and other fixtures; (b) washing, ironing and mending linen and other textiles; (c) washing dishes; (d) preparing, cooking and serving meals and refreshments; (e) purchasing food and performing various other related tasks; (f) performing related tasks; (g) supervising other workers*" (ILO International Standard Classification of Occupations 1990).
2. According to Slovenian Employment Service data, at the end of October 2006 a quarter of all unemployed persons registered with it amounted to 22,696 women, who were considered to be long-term unemployed women. The data demonstrate that the most vulnerable group of women in the labour market are older women with a low education level living in urban areas.
3. It should be added, that on the other hand the findings of a research study on paid domestic work in Hampstead (Cox in Anderson 2000) has shaken the myth that domestic help is hired by cash-rich and time-poor people, and that domestic workers are cash-poor and time-rich people. Cox established that the buyers of domestic services are people with a lot of money and a lot of time, and that domestic workers are women who are already burdened by housework in their own homes. This means that also time-rich and cash-rich people employ time-poor and cash-poor people. The question which arises is to what extent is a contemporary growth in paid domestic work above all the outcome of an urgent need that has been caused by the intensification of working conditions and work-family conflicts and to what extent is it the outcome of the changing lifestyle of the wealthy social groups in Europe? Further empirical research on the demand side is required to establish the answer.

Part II
The Complexity of Care

4
Family Policy and Welfare Regimes

Thomas P. Boje and Anders Ejrnæs

Introduction

The aim of this chapter is to develop a tentative classification of family policy regimes for all 27 EU member states. This classification will be developed using four variables measuring different aspects of the strategies pursued by European households in coping with the work-family balance – child-care take-up for children aged 0–3, effective parental leave, take-up of part-time work among women and, finally, spending on family policy. Based on these four indicators we have been able to cluster the 27 EU member states in five groups representing different caring models.

Most comparative studies of welfare issues – social security, social service provision, family support and labour market policy – try to group the European welfare states into welfare regime clusters and nearly all contrast their result with the typology developed by Esping-Andersen in his book from 1990, *The Three Worlds of Welfare Capitalism*. The discussion and disagreements about how to classify the welfare states take several different directions. On the one hand, what type of welfare issues are studied causes differences in the welfare state typologies. A study of social security or social services comes out with a completely different typology compared with a study of family policy or labour market regulation. On the other hand, there are also fundamentally different approaches in conceptualization of welfare provision and the kind of mechanisms creating social prosperity and equality. Therefore we have to be cautious in developing welfare typologies and in their capability for explaining differences between welfare systems.

The prevailing welfare typologies are thus in many respects highly problematic. First, the typologies often create the impression of coherent welfare regimes, which typically is not the case. Within nearly all welfare regimes we find marked differences in the institutional and contextual construction of the national welfare systems. Secondly, the typologies are primarily based on empirical data from the Northern and Western European countries while typically the Central and Eastern European countries are absent. Thirdly, they focus on the conventional welfare providers – for example, the state and the labour market – while other important welfare providers are not included – such as family, community and organized civil society – and finally, as argued by gender researchers, most typologies exclude the family and its internal gendered dynamics. Analysing the work-family balance and how the policy regimes influence on the strategies pursued by the households illustrate some of the inconsistencies and weaknesses of the existing typologies.

The work-family balance refers to the strategies pursued by individuals and households in reconciling paid work, unpaid work and caring obligations in families. Here we shall primarily focus on strategies taken by the families in different types of welfare systems in adapting the parents' work schedules to their caring obligations for small children.

This chapter will scrutinize policy interventions at both national and EU level designed to tackle issues relating to the reconciliation of caring and paid employment. The analysis will be concentrated on the development in family-friendly policies since the late 1990s. The role of policy-making among EU countries takes different forms and operates under different constraints so that it merits separate investigation, which will not be done in detail in this chapter. Nevertheless it is particularly interesting to see how compatible and effective these policies have been at improving conditions for combining work and care responsibilities in practice. The level of commitment to family-friendly policies varies between EU countries and proposed policy reforms are sometimes not taken up nor fully implemented. In some countries family-friendly policies have had a profound impact facilitating a better work-life balance, while in other countries they may have had little relevance because they have been insufficiently implemented.

By analysing the different types of caring model in the EU, the gendering of European citizenship becomes more visible. This chapter is based on empirical data from various EU studies of family policy. It starts with an overview of the extensive literature on work-family typologies. Then follows a discussion of the different types of family and welfare policies which are pursued by EU member states in reconciling work and caring obligations. A typology of five different family policy models is constructed based on a cluster analysis and this analysis is followed by a description of the models coming out of the clustering of the EU member states.

Work-family typologies in the welfare literature

In analysing the work-family balance the concept of care is increasingly used in addition to the dichotomy of paid and unpaid work in under-standing how provision of welfare services are organized in the individual welfare states. Care can be organized as private or public services and it can be provided as paid or unpaid work. Care is thus very much part of the mixed economy involving the state, the market, the family and the voluntary sector in a specific composition (Alber 1995; Anttonen and Sipilä 1996). It is therefore not possible to understand the form and nature of contemporary welfare societies without including the provision of care. Well over a decade ago Knijn and Kremer (1997) argued for including care as an integrated part of the right to social citizenship by making a distinction between the right to receive care and the right to provide care. However, most comparative welfare literature is still dealing with the interface between work and family by focusing on the state-labour market relationship and on how to integrate women into paid labour (Lewis 1992; 2002; Esping-Andersen 1990; 1999; Boje and Almqvist 2000; Lister 2002).

The weakness of the state-market approach is, however, that it describes women's societal position, their social rights, and the impact of the welfare state policies based on women's position in the labour market and the extent to which they take up gainful employment. In most cases the state-market approach does not consider the impact of these dimensions on women's caring responsibilities and on the gendered division of paid, unpaid and care work (Lewis et al. 2008). By taking this approach and by excluding the internal gendered dynamics in the family, most analysis fails in explaining why the gendered division of paid work, unpaid work and caring obligations has been so persistent in most European countries – even in the countries with the most comprehensive family policies (Orloff 1993; Ellingsæter 1998; Pfau-Effinger 2004).

In an attempt to overcome some of these weaknesses in analysing welfare systems in a work-family perspective Lewis (1992) tried in an early critique of Esping-Andersen to synthesize the debate on national differences in Europe by outlining different types of breadwinner systems. These systems combine the gender contract in unpaid care work and the employment contract regulating gender relations in the labour market. Lewis distinguishes between three types of breadwinner systems.

The strong male breadwinner system is where the impact of motherhood is significant and reduces mothers' labour market participation markedly compared with non-mothers. The provision of child care (at least for children under three years of age) is restricted or rather expensive, parental leave is low-paid or unpaid and the tax system favours male breadwinner households. Germany and the UK are represented by this system. In the modified breadwinner system that we find in France and Belgium there are generous child allowances for families with two or more children and comprehensive and cheap child-care facilities for children which allow women a real choice between paid work or care for their children in the family. Finally there is the weak breadwinner system, which we find in the Scandinavian countries where a dual-earner household is the rule and motherhood even has a positive impact on women's labour market involvement (see, for example, Ellingsæter 1998; Leira 2002; Abrahamson et al. 2005; Boje 2007).

During recent years much effort has been expended trying to combine the different approaches to analysing the complex interaction of gender relations in the labour market, family and welfare state. One such attempt we find in Daly and Lewis (2000) where they try to construct a framework for studying welfare state variations in paid work, unpaid work and welfare by combining the breadwinner system, citizenship rights and decommodification approaches in classifying welfare systems. According to Daly and Lewis the provision of care is organized through the breadwinner system and within this system the production of caring labour can be organized as either paid or unpaid work, and it can be located outside or inside the family. Furthermore the provision of care can be a private or a public responsibility depending on how care is defined according to social citizenship (see also Daly and Rake 2003).

In order to understand the relationship between work and care – paid or unpaid – and the different means by which men and women are integrated into the labour market it has been necessary to introduce new concepts in classifying the welfare systems. The importance of care provision has, as already discussed, seldom been considered as an integrated part of the basic needs of citizens and therefore has not been included in the definition of social citizenship rights. To solve this dilemma and to conceptualize the relationship between work and care, numerous scholars (Lister 1997; Daly and Rake 2003) have recently proposed that the concept of decommodification has to be replaced and/or supplemented by the concept of re-/defamilialization, defining social citizenship rights by including paid work, unpaid work and caring obligations. However, again we are confronted with the problem of having only partly included the strategies pursued by individual households and the internal gen-dered dynamics of families. Here we need to combine studies of the institutional frame for work, care and welfare with narrative studies of the gender strategies pursued by the family members in the individual households in reconciling work and care obligations (Leira 2002; Lister 2002; Saraceno 1997).

Another attempt at defining the dynamics between work, care and welfare is that of Pascall and Lewis (2004) who map European welfare systems and their labour-market and social policies in relation to gender equality across a variety of key dimensions characterizing the gender regime. These dimensions are paid work, care work, income, time use and voice. Based on these variables they try to distinguish between dif-ferent regimes in the gendered division of labour in paid, unpaid and care work. In advocating this model they argue that gender equality pol-icies in most European countries have been limited in effect, 'because they have addressed part of the system rather than the whole. [...] But gender regimes are interconnected systems through which paid work is connected to unpaid work, state services and benefits are delivered to individuals or households, costs are allocated, and time is shared between men and women in households, as well as between households and employment'. If gender equality policies have to be more efficient in delivering equal treatment, in paid work and welfare provision, they, according to Pascall and Lewis, need to address 'the interconnecting ele-ments of gender regimes as systems, with a logic of gender quality in care work, income, time and voice, as well as in paid employment' (Pascall and Lewis 2004, 379–80).

Most recently and closely related to the increasing number of European databases on work-family relations and on welfare policy regulations – MISSOC, OECD (2003 and 2005), European Social Survey (ESS), European Community Household Panel (ECHP), and Household, Work, and Flexibility (HWF) – several European research programmes have devel-oped typologies relying on information about provision of formal and informal care, and the kind of care children receive inside the household and from someone other than their parents. Based on the time budget data from European Community Household Panel (ECHP), Bettio and Plantenga (2004) have developed a typology on care regimes including organization of care for both young children and elderly people. They have identified five different care regimes: a Scandinavian public care model; a parental choice model in Belgium and France; a Southern European family care model; a privatized part-time care model in the UK and the Netherlands; and a publicly facilitated, private care model in Germany and Austria (see also Plantenga et al. 2007). Another but similar comparison has been made by Wall (2007). Here the modelling of care regimes has been done using data on leave policies and leave arrangements for parents in 19 European countries. Three dimensions have been included in this analysis: paid parental leave take-up; type of compensation during the period on parental leave; and gender sharing of parental leave. The emphasis in describing the different caring regimes is thus on the social construction of motherhood and the relationship between working parents and the welfare system. The typology by Wall (2007) is very similar to the previous one made by Bettio and Plantenga (2004) except for two cases: the Scandinavian countries are divided into two different models – a gender-equality-oriented model in Denmark, Sweden, Iceland – and Slovenia – and a parental-choice-oriented policy model in Norway and Finland but also in France and Belgium. Furthermore, Portugal is separated from the other South European countries in an 'early return to full-time work leave policy model' (Wall 2007).

Work-family relations and the welfare policies to be analysed

The 'work-family' literature illustrates clearly some of the inconsistencies and weaknesses of existing welfare arrangements. It is in this context important to evaluate their efficiency by comparing different welfare systems, although the nature of these systems and the problems they are confronted by varies among the EU member states. During this first decade of the 21st century all European countries are redefining and restructuring the relationship between paid work, unpaid work and caring and are seeking new solutions in the provision of care – they may be private or public alternatives and inside or outside the family. There has been a growing attention among the EU member states given to the role of family-friendly policies due to women's increasing rate of labour-market participation and changing family formations. At the EU level this development has been followed up by introduction of European standards for formal child care and parental leave arrangements and by attempts at evaluating the impact of family-friendly policies on employment relations, working-time arrangements and family strategies. Altogether this has been done by the EU Commission in a concerted effort to increase the female employment rate among the EU member states – but without with much notice being given towards the impact of gender relations on the gendered division of paid work, unpaid work and caring obligations.

In this chapter we will primarily focus on three policy areas which have had impact on the nature of the work-care relationships in families and on the patterns of work take-up among men and women in the EU member states. The policy areas dealt with in this paper are:

- *Family policy and working time.* The welfare systems differ in terms of how strictly the labour market and working hours are regulated. Here we will primarily focus on how to balance time for work and for caring through part-time work.
- *Parental leave schemes as one core element of family life.* These schemes differ widely in terms of eligibility, duration and benefit. The parental leave schemes are typically extended in countries where family policy highly emphasizes family care.
- *Child-care systems are prioritized in countries where women's take-up of gainful employment is strongly emphasized.* Also here we find great differences among the EU member states concerning provision, types of child care and governance of child care.

The three policy areas are developed for different purposes and have different effects on the 'work-family balance' but they all have some impact on the strategies followed by the household in reconciling work and care (Lewis 2001; Gornick and Meyers 2003; Haas et al. 2006). First, a combination of flexible working time and family policies might facilitate organizational arrangements at workplaces and in the labour market generally. Secondly, by introducing generous parental leave schemes women – and men – have been able to obtain a reasonable family income during the first months after childbirth. The relation between parental leave and employment are complex. Long periods of parental leave seem to reduce the probability of women re-entering gainful employment while a flexible combination of working-time or leave arrangements seems to make it possible to give employees a real choice in combining work and care. Thirdly, provision of child care is essential in solving households' caring obligations. Lack of access to child-care facilities is typically what keeps people – and especially women – out of paid work in all EU countries. Ejrnæs and Boje (2010) have found a strong positive correlation between child-care coverage and women's rate of employment among EU member states but no correlation has been found between parental leave and female employment. Lewis (2004b) has reviewed a range of care strategies in different countries ranging from institutionalized services to carer allowances and care accounts in terms of 'policy bundles'. She argues that there is not a single policy solution to such complex problems as managing time and care and who pays for it. Despite a situation where many countries are attempting to cut back on welfare provision, social care has remained a growth area over the past decade. Policy-makers in most EU countries are increasingly aware of the need to reform these provisions. In particular in the context of an ageing population and lack of labour supply they try to compensate by encouraging employees to work longer and women to increase their take-up of gainful employment. Consequently, the focus in nearly all EU-initiated proposals promoting equal opportunities between men and women in work and family relations are concentrated on access to work and in removing the barriers to women moving into gainful employment – and not on equality in a broader sense (OECD 2001).

The existing policy frameworks and preferences will clearly affect the specific strategies pursued by EU member states in combining work and family obligations. However, the problem of solving the constraints produced by the relationship between paid work, unpaid work and care is defined differently in the various welfare systems; in some countries it is seen as a business issue, as for example in the UK, in others it is conceived as a private family problem, which tends to be the case in Germany, or as a universal concern that has to be dealt with by the public, as is the case in the Scandinavian countries where paid parental leave and access to child care is considered a social right.

The various policies aimed at solving work-family conflicts are not necessarily internally consistent. For example, in the Netherlands labour-market policies encourage the part-time employment participation of women, whilst taxation policies encourage them to stay at home. In Denmark labour-market as well as social policies focus strongly on full-time employment for both women and men but family policies are insufficient for establishing equal conditions for women and men in taking up parental leave and in provision of the necessary amount of child-care facilities. Nor is there necessarily consistency between EU and national-level policies. Thus, the EU tries to increase female labour market participation, whilst most new member states have cut provisions for working mothers (Brunning and Plantenga 1999; Lewis 2002). Therefore we would not necessarily expect to find coherence between the different policies at different levels.

A tentative classification of the European member states – care models

Following this short overview of the main policy instruments influencing part-time employment strategies in reconciling work and care in households we now want to analyse how the EU member states are positioned in relation to a combination of family-friendly measures and the extent to which these measures are used by families in the individual EU member states. This is done by a cluster analysis including four variables:

- Child-care take-up among children aged 0–3 as a percentage of the total number of children in this age-group;
- Effective parental leave in weeks;
- Female part-time employment rate according to the EUROSTAT definition – self-declared part-time;
- Total spending on family policy as percentage of GDP.

Based on these four variables we have made a clustering of 21 EU member states – excluded are Cyprus, Malta, Bulgaria, Romania, the Slovak Republic and Ireland due to insufficient data sources.

Clustering of the countries as we have done in this chapter helps us in focusing on specific similarities and differences between the included countries but it does not give us any definite picture of the relationship between the countries and their family policy measures. This has to be developed in the following description of the individual care models coming out of the cluster analysis. We have to be cautious in using the models coming out of the clustering because such cluster analyses are highly dependent on the selection of indicators and may change radically if other indicators are included. It is therefore very important to carefully outline the conditions for the cluster analysis by explicitly defining the different variables used in clustering the EU member states – see Appendix 4.1.

In Table 4.1 we have summarized the findings from the cluster analysis. Five different and distinctive family policy regimes can be defined in Europe based on the four variables we have chosen. In the table we give a short description of each of the family policy regimes. The characteristics of the main policy instruments – child care, parental leave, part-time employment – and the strategies used by especially mothers in reconciling work, care and households' obligations are mentioned.

Based on this overview of the five family policy regimes sorted out of the cluster analysis we shall in the following develop in more detail what are the main characteristics of the individual family policy regimes.

Cluster 1: The extensive family policy model

Four countries are included in this cluster – the two Scandinavian countries – Denmark and Sweden – and the two countries normally characterized by a pro-natalistic family policy – France and Belgium.

Table 4.1 Characteristics of European family policy regimes

Family policy regime	Country	Policy	Reconciliation strategy
Extensive family policy	Sweden, Denmark, Belgium, France	Generous payment of parental leave. High level of public child care for 0–3 years. High to medium proportion of women working part-time. High total spending on family policy	Mothers return to the labour market after one year of leave and rely on public child care
Short leave, part-time	UK, Netherlands	Short period of poorly paid parental leave. Medium provision of public child care for 0–3 years. High proportion of mothers working short part-time.	Women have often a long employment interruption when the children are small but return to the labour market on short part-time basis
Long leave, part-time	Germany, Austria, Luxembourg	Long period of relatively well paid parental leave – up to 3 years. Low provision of child care. High proportion of women working part-time.	After a long period of leave mothers return to the labour market working on part-time basis.
Family care	Estonia, Slovenia, Latvia, Spain, Greece, Italy, Portugal	Period of parental leave varies but is badly paid. Low provision of child care. Low proportion of women in part-time employment	Mothers return to the labour market after a short leave and rely on help from family or they withdraw from the labour market and do not return when their children are older.
Extended parental leave	Hungary, Poland, Czech Republic, Lithuania, Finland	About 3 years' parental leave. Low-level child care and low proportion of women in part-time employment. Finland deviates and has a greater provision of public care for 0–3 years and more women working part-time.	After a long period of parental leave women return to full-time employment.

This cluster is characterized by a high level of child-care take-up among children aged 0–3 years combined with comprehensive rights to parental leave in combination with generous payment during most of the parental leave period. The level of spending on family policy is high. These countries are, in Lewis's (1992) breadwinner-typology, classified as modified or weak breadwinner countries. There is in all four countries a strong drive for women's integration into the labour force and towards women's social and economic independence. In Sweden children have nearly no impact on women's rate of employment while employment rates for Danish mothers with one child are even higher than for non-mothers (Abrahamson et al. 2005). Mothers with children aged 0 to 5 in France and Belgium have employment rates lower than in Scandinavia. For French women it is especially the case among mothers with two or more children. These mothers get substantial family allowances, which makes it possible for them to be full-time carers. On the other hand a relatively high proportion of women in all four countries are in part-time employment. About one-third of female employees have part-time jobs, when 'part-time employment' is defined as self-declared part-time. However the majority of women in part-time jobs in this cluster of countries are working long part-time – more than 20 hours a week. The relatively generous system of parental leave does not seem to have devastating consequences for women's possibilities of re-entering gainful employment in these countries (Ejrnæs 2010).

Cluster 2: The short-leave, part-time model

The Netherlands and the United Kingdom are both characterized as a short-leave, part-time regime. In both countries the period of parental leave is short and badly paid. There is a modest level of public child care for children aged 0–3. The child-care take-up is typically combined with women working part-time. When it comes to the labour market system the two countries differ both in relation to social protection and regulation of flexibility.

The UK is characterized by a market-driven labour market with low social protection. Here we find very few restrictions for employers employing workers on low wages and variable working hours. If employees are low-paid or in part-time jobs they are not eligible for social security and the employers are not obligated to pay social contributions (OECD 2005, 214). Furthermore, British women are often forced to take up low-paid part-time jobs after maternity leave because of insufficient paid parental leave and lack of child-care facilities (Plantenga and Hansen 1999).

The Netherlands is characterized by a working-time regime which is more regulated than the British labour market concerning employment contracts and social protection. Social partners are highly involved in regulating working conditions, as in the Scandinavian countries. In recent years the Dutch labour-market system has become more deregulated in an attempt to balance flexibility and security in employment relations. This has led to more individualized arrangements and especially encouraged the majority of women to work part-time. However, without a comprehensive family policy on parental leave and with a lack of child-care facilities it has been impossible to achieve even a modest level of gender equity in terms of work and care. Consequently the Netherlands holds a low position among European countries in relation to equal opportunities.

Cluster 3: The long-leave, part-time model

This cluster includes Germany, Austria and Luxembourg, which in other typologies are characterized as conforming to the strong-breadwinner model (Lewis 1992; Esping-Andersen 1999). These countries have relatively well-paid, long parental leave. Therefore, the level of spending on family policy is also relatively high.

For most mothers the period of parental leave has traditionally been followed by a longer period outside the labour market caring for children. Part-time employment is especially widespread among mothers when they take up gainful employment after years of caring. In all three countries it is part-time employment in unstable jobs with few weekly working hours. Typically mothers in these countries have been forced to leave the market to take care of children because the provision of child-care facilities is very restricted and those that are available are primarily for part-time caring.

During recent years a growing number of women in both Germany and Austria have taken up part-time work combined with caring for children, but their part-time jobs are typically short-hours in order to fit in with the caring obligations. The growth in part-time work has taken place recently and is for these countries clearly a consequence of EU efforts to raise the female rate of employment. However, problems with getting back into regular employment after being out of work for a long period because of care obligations seem to be more serious among mothers in countries within this model than elsewhere. This is primarily because of the extended period most mothers stay on parental leave. Another serious problem for mothers who want to return to work after parental leave is the lack of part-time jobs fitting into the typically restricted operating hours of child-care institutions. Finally, the number of child-care places is restricted and for child care parents have to rely on grandparents to a large extent.

Cluster 4: The family care model

Included in this cluster are all the Southern European countries and two Baltic countries. They are countries characterized by a low proportion of women in gainful employment and consequently few women in part-time jobs. The period of parental leave varies among these countries but in all countries parental leave is badly paid, forcing most mothers to rely on a male breadwinner. In the Southern European countries the provision of child-care facilities is low and when they are available they normally have short opening hours and often they are expensive. As a consequence of low payment for parental leave and restricted provision of public child-care facilities, spending on family policy is low in the countries covered by this cluster.

Few women are in part-time work in most countries included in the family care model. This is not because they are full-time employed but because the overall female employment rate is low – in some countries, such as Italy and Greece, below 50 per cent and even lower for women in the age-group 25–45. In these countries the difficulties of rearing children have resulted in a low rate of fertility. Among the family care model countries we find a negative correlation between fertility and employment while it is the opposite among countries included in the extensive family policy model (Boje & Ejrnæs 2011).

Cluster 5: The extended parental leave model

Countries with very long periods of effective parental leave character-ize this cluster. Included in the cluster are the three Central European countries, Hungary, Poland and the Czech Republic, plus Lithuania and Finland. All countries in this cluster have a low level of take-up of child care and relatively few women in part-time work. Finland deviates to some extent, having a higher child-care coverage and more women in part-time jobs than the other countries but still with extended parental leave. In countries classified under the extended parental leave model, women typically stay at home for three years or more caring for their children. After the period of parental leave the children are cared for mostly by family arrangements or privately organized child care.

The economic situation in Central and Eastern Europe has forced both men and women in the household to contribute to the survival of the family economy. Due to the low level of wages it has been a condition for a decent standard of living that both adult household members are full-time earners and, for many, low wages have forced them to take up an extra job in the 'second economy'. The high level of employment for both men and women in Central and Eastern Europe has, however, not been transferred into a more equal division of labour within the family. Consequently, women remain principally responsible for care and domestic life both when they are on parental leave and during periods when they are in full-time employment.

In Finland the social and economic conditions are different and the possibilities for choosing between paid work and care obligations are more open than in the Central and Eastern European countries. Here we find a real choice between paid family care where one of the parents is paid for caring for the child at home or cared for in public child-care institutions. These arrangements – both family care and public child care – are relatively generously paid, which also explains the high level of spending on family policy in Finland. The parental choice in Finland between family care and public child care is also the main reason for the relatively higher level of part-time employment among mothers with small children compared to the other countries in this cluster.

Conclusion and discussion

In this chapter we have tried to classify the EU member states based on four variables describing on the one hand the household strategies followed in reconciling obligations in work life and family life and on the other hand the ambitions put forward by the welfare state in pursuing a family-friendly policy towards work-life balance. In a cluster analysis we have identified five different care models. For each of these models we have analysed the relationship between family policy and the actual behaviour of mothers given the extent of caring obligations and how the strategies pursued by these women are determined. The caring regimes we found based on the family policy variables deviate markedly from traditional welfare regimes as they have been developed in the conventional welfare state literature.

Contrary to other welfare models we do not find a uniform Scandinavian model. Finland was not clustered together with Denmark and Sweden. The longer duration of paid leave allowances and the low level of female part-time workers we find in Finland can explain the difference between Finland and the other Scandinavian countries. In Finland parents have a real choice between caring for small children themselves and being eligible for family allowances, or taking up gainful employment while the children are cared for in public child-care institutions. Neither Swedish nor Danish mothers have this choice. In Denmark the family policy is mostly orientated towards motivating mothers to take up gainful employment as quickly as possible after about one year of maternity/parental leave, while we find more flexibility between child care and work schedules for women in Sweden. Here a significant group of mothers are in long part-time employment combined with the taking-up of part-time paid leave during the first years of the child's life.

Our analysis showed that the various family policy regimes to a large extent affected mothers' care praxis and the strategies pursued by the households in reconciling paid work, unpaid work and caring obligations in families. We found that in the *extensive family policy model* mothers remain in gainful employment after six months' to one year's parental leave and rely on public institutions for child care. In the *short-leave, part-time model* the periods of leave are restricted to a few months and the lack of affordable child-care facilities often forces mothers to take up part-time jobs on short hours or leave the labour market completely for a longer period of time when becoming mothers. The period spent out of gainful employment depends on the number of children. With two or more children a significant number of mothers never come back to regular work. In the *long-leave, part-time model* mothers stay home on long parental leave – up to three years per child – when the children are young and if they return to gainful employment it is typically on a contingent part-time basis on short hours and extremely low wages partly because very few regular part-time jobs are available and partly because of a lack of full-time child-care institutions. In the *family care model* we find a widespread polarization between mothers who return to the labour market after a short leave, relying on help from grandparents and other mothers who are not participating in the labour market. In contrast to the family care model, in countries represented by the *extended leave model* mothers stay home on long parental leave when the children are young but typically they take up full-time employment when the children get older (three years old) and also here the children are cared for by grandparents to a large extent due to reduced availability of institutional child-care facilities in most Central and Eastern European countries.

In order to develop strategies for a more gender-balanced citizenship covering both paid work and caring obligations in the European Union it is important to develop typologies of care models which can cast light on mothers' constraints and opportunities in combining work and care. Policies at the EU level have to take into consideration how the interplay between different kinds of family policies and gender norms shape the relationship between paid work, unpaid work and care in different national contexts. This chapter shows that reconciliation policies can take many forms and there are huge differences among EU member states.

The central question is what implications our findings will have for the challenges of combining work and care at the EU level. The findings show that different caring regimes constrain mothers' choices in different ways. In all care models, except for the *extensive family policy model*, we find a shortage of child-care provision for children below three years of age. In order to increase women's engagement in paid work and give women more choices in combining work and care all EU member states have to invest in more public and affordable child-care facilities. In the *extended leave model* an increased possibility for taking part-time leave could give women more options in combining work and caring responsibilities and help mothers towards an earlier return into the labour market. Furthermore, in several of the caring models it is important to ensure that women – and men – who take parental leave have a protected right to return to their previous job after the end of the leave period.

Besides the need for more public and affordable child-care facilities, parents in the *family care model* also need better opportunities for paid parental leave and part-time work in order to help mothers to reconcile work and caring obligations. These measures could avoid the tendency towards a polarization between women who are in continuous employment and women who are not participating in the labour market at all. We find this polarization most clearly in Italy and Portugal, where there are very different strategies among women in solving the conflicts between work and caring obligations. In both part-time models – *short-leave, part-time* and *long-leave, part-time* – the restricted provision of child care on a full-time basis for small children forces mothers to change their employment status and instead find a part-time job on a short-hour basis and often with a low salary and unstable employment conditions. In these two part-time models better employment protection for parents on parental leave and equal rates of payment for part-time and full-time jobs are needed. In many EU member states mothers returning from parental leave are offered another type of job – often dead-end positions – in another branch of the company, which can have a devastating effect on all efforts aiming at gender equality in both paid work, unpaid work and care.

Appendix 4.1 Family policy, child care and parental leave and female part-time employment among the EU member states

	Child-care coverage aged 0–3 2003*	Effective parental leave weeks, 2002–2003*	Female part-time employment 2003**	Total spending on family policy: % of GDP 2004**
Extensive family policy model				
Belgium	60[1]	18	39	2.0
Denmark	56	47	33	3.9
France	43	48	30	2.5
Sweden	41	78	36	3.1
Part-time model				
Netherlands	35	11	74	1.2
United Kingdom	26	21	44	1.7
Continental model				
Germany (including ex-GDR from 1991)	7	49	41	2.9
Luxembourg (Grand-Duché)	14	54	31	3.9
Austria	9	63	36	3.0
Family care model				
Portugal	19	20	17	1.3
Greece	7	13	8	1.7
Italy	6	24	17	1.2
Spain	10	50	17	0.7
Slovenia	27	53	8	2.0
Estonia	22	80	12	1.7
Latvia	16	50	13	1.2
Parental leave model				
Czech Republic	8	117	9	1.6
Lithuania	18	152	12	1.1
Hungary	6	152	6	2.5
Poland	2	88	13	0.9
Finland	21	107	18	2.9

Sources: *Plantenga et al. (2007) **Eurostat (various years).
Note: 1. An estimate.

5

Modes of Care and Mothering: How Does Citizenship and Care Intersect in the Lives of Mothers and Disabled Children?

Janice McLaughlin

Introduction

British feminists have long argued that welfare policies in the UK rely on gendered assumptions about care responsibilities, which maximize the role of women as carers while minimizing the role of the state (Graham 1983; Lewis 1992; Ungerson 1987; 1990). The introduction of community care in the UK in the early 1990s is one such example of a shift away from institutional care towards care within the community, which quickly became care within the home, by women (Baldwin and Twigg 1991; Orme 2001). Welfare policies have been able to rely on women to be informal carers through a range of social norms, cultural expectations and material practices which have positioned women as the presumed primary carer (Finch and Groves 1983; Finch and Mason 1993). Changes in household structures, women's involvement in the labour market and changes in gender norms have seen some move away from women taking on the caring role to the exclusion of other aspects of life and identity (Lupton and Barclay 1997; ONS 2007; Sullivan 2000; Ungerson 2000). However, feminists argue that social conditions, gender norms and welfare policies continue to create traditional demarcations of gender roles within the home (Charles 2000; McKie et al. 2002; O'Brien 2007).

Skeggs (1997) is one of the key writers who explore how gendered social and material processes continue to place women in the role of family carer. She examines how the contexts within which individuals are involved in caring activities frame and influence what is seen as care, who is seen as a carer, how care is performed and how it is received. Significantly, in an argument similar to that earlier proposed by Finch and Mason (1993), Skeggs argues that in social conditions of inequality and lack of material resources and options, women can internalize the caring role via incorporating it into their sense of self.

Being the carer offers an identity others validate as legitimate and valuable when other identities are not available. Therefore, processes of both self-regulation and agency within gendered and class boundaries influence the patterns of care that women continue to enact and how they and others read it as part of their identity as women, mothers and workers. Therefore exploring the social, cultural and political contexts within which care occurs is important to understanding its significance (Kittay 1999). This also recognizes that these processes and relationships between caring, identity and social position will be played out differently in varied national contexts; crucially in contexts of different modes of welfare provision. Therefore it should be acknowledged that the specific connections between caring identities and roles and welfare provision made here are specific to the UK. Nevertheless there will be overlaps with other European countries created by the common pattern of a shrinking welfare state now found in many countries.

The focus of this chapter is mothers looking after disabled children. This is done for several reasons. First, Traustadóttir (1991; 1995) argues that when a child is disabled equalities of care responsibility can quickly disappear as the more intensive care is still directed towards women. Second, in the past there has been hostility towards feminist work on care within disability studies. Disability writers have long argued, going back to the community care debates, that feminists are much more interested in the 'plight' of the informal carer than they are of what happens to the disabled person (Begum 1992; Keith and Morris 1995; Morris 1993a).

This was seen very clearly when some feminists advocated a return to institutionalized care as a way to resolve the problems created by community care; institutional care which disability activists argue is a key factor in the marginalization and exclusion of disabled people from society (Rummery 2002). This chapter will bring together a discussion of women as presumed primary carer for a disabled child, with an appreciation of the implications for the disabled child in this way of 'fixing' the 'problem' of who looks after them.

The final reason for the focus on disabled children is that it is a useful vehicle within which one can discuss contemporary shifts within the organization of care. New methods of providing and distributing care within the welfare system in the UK (echoed in other European countries too) are reopening the debates about who should care for those in need of care and how should that be paid for. These shifts are very visible in the care of disabled children and have significant implications for how they are cared for, and by whom.

For the purposes of this chapter I am going to discuss just two shifts in welfare provision that directly affect the care of disabled children. The first is the greater emphasis being placed on early intervention programmes for disabled children, which advocate identification of disability or 'developmental delay' as early as possible, followed by therapies in the home, by 'informal carers', with the aim of minimizing the severity of the disability. The second is what has been referred to as the increasing 'conditionality' of welfare provision; that is the increasing requirement for recipients of welfare to prove their eligibility to receive welfare assistance for the caring responsibilities they have (Dwyer 2004).

This chapter will explore early intervention and conditionality from the perspective of mothers who are witness to their significance in their daily lives and the care of their children. Through examining the perspectives of women providing such care in these contexts, the chapter will discuss what these changes imply about how care and disability is framed within contemporary welfare practices. In doing so it will seek to draw connections between what care is said to constitute and who provides it, with broader questions about citizenship and social recognition of dependency for both mothers and disabled children.

The chapter draws from an Economic and Social Research Council-funded study[1] of families with disabled children, before moving on to that discussion I will provide a brief description of the study.

The study

The study examines the perspectives and experiences of parents with very young children, using methods drawn from ethnography in order to explore the cultural, social and material practices and relationships that make up and inform the parents' lives with their children. The research, which took place over three years, was based in two English regions; at the centre of the fieldwork were 33 families who were involved in the study for more than 18 months. A series of three in-depth narrative interviews (tape recorded with consent) were undertaken. In addition, observations of a number of formal and informal care encounters also took place. Alongside the work with the families, mixed focus groups with professionals working in health, education, social care and the voluntary sector also took place.

The basis for a family's inclusion was that they defined their child as having specific care and support needs and that the child was within the age range used in the study. The study was framed in terms of parents, rather than mothers, because we did not wish to presume, and indeed replicate, the gendered division of labour. Therefore, recruitment sought both mothers and fathers; unsurprisingly the majority of people who contacted us to participate were mothers. Throughout the study mothers were in almost all cases the main carer of the child (the shifting gender dynamics around parenting and care are explored elsewhere [McLaughlin 2006; McLaughlin et al. 2008]).

Mothers as therapists

Early intervention, although operationalized in different ways, has become a common theme in the treatment of disabled children in much of the western world. It begins in the merits of earlier diagnosis of childhood conditions and moves on to introduce treatment protocols as soon as possible after a diagnosis. Treatments place great significance on informal carers participating in therapies and treatments. Across the boundaries of healthcare, social services and education, early intervention has become a defining framework for how young disabled children are looked after. Portage workers, physiotherapists and others visit homes to provide therapies, train informal carers in the techniques, and monitor progress. Often therapies are designed around everyday life; bath-time, feeding and chatting with the child become opportunities to work with the child to improve their mobility, physical dexterity and language acquisition. The assumption is that mothers will incorporate these therapeutic activities into their caring role.

However, do mothers want to turn themselves into therapists and their home into a medical venue? From our study there were often times when mothers were concerned about taking on therapy roles, whether as part of helping their child's development, or simply to keep them alive, as part of their portfolio of care. For example, Frank was first released from hospital after being born premature, still dependent on oxygen and tube feeding, technological supports Debbie, his mother, willingly took on in order that he could come home. Later, once Frank had improved and was no longer on regular oxygen, he suffered a serious infection that placed him back in the hospital and back on oxygen. Once the immediate crisis passed the hospital consultant moved to get the child back in the home as soon as possible. A plan was developed that would see his mother again in charge of monitoring his oxygen; this time Debbie, along with her husband, said no:

> ... we'd dealt with oxygen, but not at those levels, and there's only so much you can cope with. We knew what was normal, for us 'normal' was the low levels of oxygen, whereas Frank was on high levels of oxygen. It gets

to the point where you have got too many things to think about, I couldn't do it, we didn't want to do it ... we'd had a period of nearly a year where he'd had none of that, he wasn't on oxygen. And then when it came to the point where we might have to do some of those things again, you don't want it. You're tired, it's then not normal ... it's then a medical problem and somebody else will have to deal with it. (Debbie, IV1)

Debbie was concerned that their involvement in the medical manage-ment necessary to keep Frank alive left little space or time to be his parents: *'if we'd come home and he was monitored continuously, you get to the point where we would be watching the monitor and not Frank'* (IV1). Such interventions were someone else's responsibility and did not belong in the home, where they turned an intimate family space into a medical arena. The intensity of medical intervention, in particular the presence of technologies that kept Frank alive, became, from Debbie's point of view, a barrier to parental care and response (Place 2000). Debbie's deci-sion is counter-intuitive to the assumption that mothers will always want their child home as soon as possible and will willingly take on the role of nurse or therapist in order to do so. In many cases this is what mothers would choose to do, but the actions of Debbie also highlight the implications of home-based therapies. Such therapies necessitate a change in identity for both mothers and the intimate space of the family, which is not without cost. Home visits occur in a space that has a set of multiple intimate and complex meanings around family lives and iden-tities (Levine 2005), yet it is within this space 'that professionals impart their expectations of children's development' (Leiter 2004, 840).

In addition, mothers did not always agree with the therapies being pressed on them and their child. In particular they queried those treat-ments unwilling to break free of medical models of development:

The portage worker is an example of somebody who did nothing construc-tive to help. One time she brought me a chart to fill in and tick off tasks each day: achieved, not achieved, partially achieved, which is just too con-trolling and you can't do that. I felt she was policing how much I was doing each day, because she seemed to be disappointed with the level of progress that Joe was making. And, after that my feeling from her was always this hidden agenda of, well you're not doing enough that's why you're not mak-ing progress, that's always what I got from her. (Kay, IV2)

Kay eventually asked the portage worker to stop coming; her decision came from a view that setting and achieving goals for Joe, made against markers of medically defined physical and mental development, was being privileged over broader criteria of what creates a child's quality of life. In addition the portage worker did not seem to allow Joe any choice or agency over whether he wished to participate in such treatments.

The societal and medical assumption is that the 'good mother' incorporates medical care into her caring portfolio; the implication of this is that at times mothers felt that they had little choice but to participate. Lisa, whose three-year-old daughter Zoe has cerebral palsy, spoke of striving to follow the treatments and exercises prescribed by the physiotherapists in order for her to improve. She put a huge amount of pressure on herself in order to prove to others that her child was developing. At the same time she questioned her ability to aid her child:

> *She has her physiotherapy, which I do with her. I don't do half as much as I'm supposed to because she just won't tolerate it at all ... It's like I've been taking her up to Pelican school because I really want her in there and in order to do that I've got to prove to the education authority that she will benefit from their methods ... I know if she went to school there, and I wasn't there she'd just do fine. But because I'm there she just wants to be sitting on my knee and just wants cuddles and wants us to give her a drink and she just screams ... I quite often feel I'm not the right person to look after her, [pause] because I feel like she's not coming up to her potential with me because she's still so much a baby. (Lisa, First Interview)*

Lisa follows the prescriptive requirements of physiotherapy for the promise of Zoe being allowed into the school that is her first choice; she is following this ritual to perform the role of the good and compliant mother (a role she feels others doubt she can achieve because she is young and single).

What lies behind the push for early intervention? It is perfectly feasible to argue that a key aim is to improve the quality of life for young children with disabilities as they develop and to enable them to become participants in society. However, in the concerns some mothers have with it and with the processes embedded within it there are potential issues. While some interventions are geared towards keeping the child alive, others are concerned with improving the child, helping them get closer to normality. It is within the drive for normality that concerns about this mode of medicalized care can be raised. From a disability studies perspective it is possible to argue that the prioritization of seeking normality is influenced by the importance of being normal to being recognized by others – state actors and social actors – as a legitimate citizen. The push to get better increases the requirement for children and their parents to work to overcome their disability, or they will be judged as different, other and less than those defined as normal. Psychological and medical therapies directed to get the child's development closer to normality help secure the importance of being normal to being able to participate in society. It emphasizes that the child should adapt to the social require- ments of a society ill-equipped to deal with disability, rather than looking at adapting society to the differences created by impairment. Mothers are being encouraged to ensure their children can get closer to normality and therefore become as adults legitimate citizens who are not a 'burden' on society. It is understandable that mothers participate in the regulative adaptation of their child, whether this is behavioural adaptation to be more 'acceptable', or physical therapies aimed at helping the child speak or walk. Mothers recognize the social consequences of not being able to do these things and therefore they participate in activities which will shape their children into acceptable citizens.

While in contemporary society disability is being incorporated into the social body in ways that promise citizenship rights, at the same time other social processes, such as early intervention, appear to heighten the importance of being 'normal' to also being seen as a citizen (Asch 1999; McLaughlin 2003; Rapp and Ginsburg 2001). The danger is that thera- peutic practices associated with seeking improved development make it more difficult to recognize other forms of development and quality of life. When mothers reject some of the practices of early intervention what they are potentially doing is challenging this model of citizenship on behalf of their children and beginning to posit a different way of understanding what the purpose of care is and what its aims should be.

Conditional care

As has been seen in other research with mothers with disabled children (Traustadóttir 1991; 1995) mothers play multiple caring roles. The assump- tion, drawn from gendered norms and discourses, is that mothers play such multiple caring roles because they are mothers. However, mothers do not necessarily see the ever-expanding list of activities added to care as being something they automatically should do and indeed be able to do. In her first interview, Jane (IV1) commented: *'you're more of a carer than a parent: carer, psychologist, teacher, you name it you've got every role to play.'* Looking closely at the language and narratives generated by mothers we can track aspects of the care they are excepted to provide for their disabled children, which they define as outside of what they perceive as the 'normal' care mothers should provide.

For example, mothers noted that their caring role would continue into their child's adult life; however, this was not always presented as a natural extension of the mothering role:

> *I know he's only seven but I'm quite aware that he might not leave home when he's 16 or 18 and, go off to university and things like that. He could be a lot more based at home. If not all his adult life, for a much longer time than you would expect. I think of myself as a carer. I think it's just, it's another one of these, like, balls that you're trying to juggle, as well as being a parent, you're not a parent of a child who can even dress himself and things like that, Jack still needs a lot of help getting socks and shoes and can't do buttons, things like that. (Jane, IV3)*

Part of the attempts to keep such caring distinct from being a mother is read through the previous expectations they have for what mothering involves, crucially that it has a normal trajectory towards the child developing into an independent adult (Gray 2001; Rehm and Bradley 2005; Taylor 2000). This trajectory is not as clear-cut for those with disabled children, and the added responsibilities they associate with this are not something all mothers defined as their caring role as mothers. If the additional caring activities are not a continuation of being a mother, then from their perspective it is not obvious or essential that it should be their responsibility to carry on these additional responsibilities.

It is important to be specific in identifying what are the 'additional responsibilities' mothers define as not their responsibility. The areas mothers most often highlighted as problematic are those they felt were a direct product of the inadequacy and complexity of the welfare services meant to support families with disabled children:

> *I used to spend Monday afternoon every week fighting for services for Joe, or arranging appointments, or administrative stuff. And then instead of just being his mum, I'm his case manager, I'm his physio, I'm his speech therapist, I'm his advocate. (Kay, IV1)*

Kay (IV1) went on to say:

> *... the amount of time I must spend in an administrative role, not being his mum, not being a carer, but writing letters of complaint too, I wrote to the local MP about 10 o'clock last night about getting adaptations to*

the house, because we're not entitled to any help with that, so we're still carrying him up and down the stairs. It's all of that kind of stuff; it's very wearing and very stressful. (Kay, IV1)

Alongside the increased care a disabled child may require, mothers also find themselves having to take on the role of fighter or negotiator with welfare services in order to get support and resources.

The burden of care, from the mothers' perspective, is the time taken up chasing after services, such as Disability Living Allowance (DLA), direct payments, respite care and educational resources, which they have an expectation is an entitlement they should automatically receive. It is this expectation which shapes their view that having to battle for support is outside of their care responsibilities. However, what they find is that in order to receive such services they are required to fill in long and complex assessments, so that others can judge whether they do have a right to receive them. Form-filling is hardly new to social services. However, within current welfare practices in the UK there is a significant level of micro-collection of data meant to represent life, which intervenes in the allocation of citizenship rights. The DLA entitlement is mediated via medically shaped bureaucratic processes. The current methods of evaluating whether families qualify for DLA require accurate and medically validated measurement of how severe the disability is and how much care it requires. It necessitates the production of minute levels of detail about the 'burden' of caring for a disabled child in order to qualify for support. Across 52 pages parents go into extensive detail about their child, solely focused on the medical condition and what limitations the child faces. It is no surprise that mothers (and many professionals) find the DLA form a complex task, but also one that they find literally exhausting because of the intimate scrutiny it demands of their child's difficulties:

His DLA's up for renewal again, so I usually start about six months beforehand, and start writing a diary, and I'll get in touch with Disability North and get one of their advisors, she'll go through filling the forms out for us, because if you put one word that's wrong it'll have consequences. (Angela, IV3)

Mothers struggle with the time taken up getting care support for their child; this is not a product of the disability. Instead it is increasingly prominent in mothers' lives due to the requirements of conditionality within welfare – that is, the need to participate in the collection of detailed information in order to get support, which previously would have been an entitlement to receive: '[*Sarah*]: ... *red tape bureaucracy, form-filling, sometimes does take precedence over life, or just living.' (Sarah and Nick, IV3)*

Conditionality also echoes some of the problems associated with early intervention, in particular the emphases given to medical criteria of limitation. Children are recognized via the same categories that early intervention seeks to resolve, which identify their failure to live up to certain social ideals of acceptable living and capability. In the process medical categories dominate in authorizing 'entitled bodies' (Kelly 2005, 197), framing the child in particular ways, which both signal them as flawed citizens, and also restrict their rights to be supported and cared for. The DLA provides no space to do anything other than catalogue inadequacy, fixing the child in the category of the disabled other to normal society. Welfare mechanisms for attributing rights, in the UK and other European countries, demand a level of categorization that strips the individual of broader aspects of who they are and what contexts inform their social position. As conditionality (Dwyer 2004) increases as an element of welfare provision, the implication is that having to pursue services and rights of citizenship will continue to grow as an element of the caring portfolio of mothers of disabled children.

The transformative potential of care

So far the discussion has been focused on how care practices can emerge from or contribute to limitations in access to citizenship rights and recognition. However, forms of care mothers are involved with and how they articulate that as part of their subjectivity hold out the possibility of challenging prescriptive versions of citizenship.

If we look at the kind of care identity women articulate we can also see care's expansive possibilities and political potentialities. Mothers talked of a changed life, where accomplishment, as well as exhaustion, was now part of not just what they did, but also who they were. As part of changed subjectivities mothers talked of seeking out new ways of developing the skills they had acquired. So, for example, Jemma talked of going to college to train as a classroom assistant to work with children with learning disabilities after spending time volunteering in her daughter's classroom. As mothers' skills and experiences developed they were often likely to develop other extended roles.

Caring for a disabled child generates a level of change that goes broader than how carers think about their own identity. In addition, it is closely connected to changing views regarding social responsibility and disability. Mothers find new meaning and senses of self in their caring role, in particular fighting injustice against their children and others becomes an important part of what they define as the caring role and is embedded in their identity:

> Well, I have changed, I have become more assertive and not letting things lie, and really pushing ... and I think getting out there and finding out the information for yourself, and finding out your rights and your wrongs, and talking to other parents who've been through similar things before you, that's definitely helped. (Angela, IV1)

In defining their caring role, mothers include their battles with statutory services regarding conditionality. As Corinne (IV1) asserted: '*but like a normal person, her rights need to be respected as well, as the rights of a normal person are respected.*' Mothers spoke proudly of their strategies for getting what they can for their child. Such changes are not confined to women from educated, middle class backgrounds; in a way the most acute transformations and desires to challenge what others 'offer' came from mothers (such as Angela) from relatively underprivileged backgrounds. Such mothers challenge both the gendered and classed discourses that assume they are unable to articulate the care needs of their child.

Therefore the caring identity of mothers of disabled children is not always perceived as a private role; it can sit in the public realm of the care plan meeting and the statementing process required for resources to be allocated to the child when in school. Transformative care activities engage with re-evaluation of identity, the future, family templates and biographies, and political and ethical values. In becoming carers, mothers, along with their children, move through transitions which ultimately broaden care to encompass political dimensions which, through collective friendships and bonds, mean that they actively seek to incorporate political values and activities into the caring role they embed in their lives and their identities. There is an echo here of Baier's (1995) exploration of care, morality and trust; in particular that an appreciation of care values in the public sphere is required to produce a politics and rights discourse which moves beyond the poverty of liberalism and contract theory. Care activities sit within a political discourse able to challenge rights discrepancies and to identify the child and family as full members of society.

Mothers are thus politically active on behalf of their children, seeking recognition for their rights as future citizens. Their version of citizenship draws their private caring practices into the public sphere, alongside a continued belief in entitlement to receive care from that public sphere. As such they are mediators on behalf of their children; however this also involves the children as active participants themselves. A key theme for mothers who rejected some forms of support for their children and advocated others was seeking modes of care that enabled the child's agency to be incorporated in what was done, by whom and how.

Conclusion: citizenship, recognition and dependency

In the previous sections the chapter has sought to explore particular aspects of the care mothers of disabled children are expected to provide and receive under contemporary welfare provision and regulation. Mothers are encouraged to participate in medical therapies that seek to make children as normal as possible as a condition of them – mother and child – being seen as useful citizens. Meanwhile assessments of welfare eligibility emphasize the significance of medical criteria as a way of classifying disability in order for parents to receive any state support in caring for their child. When mothers resist the conditions placed on them and their child's recognition by state welfare, they seek in their care practices to include a challenge to contemporary forms of narrowing the scope and boundaries of formal care. This connection forges the link between the feminist interest in the gendering of care responsibilities and the disability movement concern with the modes of care made available to disabled people. Capturing the difficulties mothers face when others refuse to care for them as well as their children also captures the social exclusion of people who experience disability. Mothers can be important political actors who challenge, through their care activities, the privatization and marginalization of care for disabled children. In the values of care articulated by them, and some fathers, alternatives to the conditionality of what is offered to them can be seen. What these different frames point to are alternative frameworks for recognizing disability and care within welfare citizenship.

The dominant mode of recognition in contemporary western society continues to be that of the individual autonomous adult; this is the figure which both early intervention and conditionality judge a child's potential against. The difficulty for disabled people has been the connection made in liberal models of citizenship (Rawls 1985) between individual autonomy and having the rights of citizenship (Silvers and Francis 2005; Silvers et al. 1998). When disabled children are expected to fail to live up to the vision of the fully autonomous individual as they develop they continue to be seen as 'outside the range of human acceptability' (Landsman 2003). The only choice then provided is to overcome such failings, through early intervention for example, as the route through which to obtain citizenship recognition. Mothers who incorporate early intervention therapies into their caring role do so both out of a wish to improve the quality of life of their child, and also out of an attempt to give them access to the category of the modern citizen.

The only way then for disabled children to acquire citizenship rights as they develop towards adulthood is to prove their ability to overcome disability and not require care and support. What lies unsaid in this is a discomfort with dependency:

> We admire the powerful wheelchair racer, the accomplished deaf drummer, the renowned paraplegic artist, the popular blind singer. They have disabilities, to be sure, but they have overcome them in ways that society values – by having an unusual talent, by being competitive and successful, and above all by being apparently independent. (Levine 2005, 378)

Dependency is neglected in considerations of citizenship, when citizenship is framed as the right of the autonomous individual (Baier 1995). This lack of recognition places both disabled children (and adults) and those assumed to be their 'natural' carers (women as relatives or formal carers) outside of both the public sphere and the rights of citizenship. Assumed to lack the abilities of the autonomous individual due to either being a receiver or a provider of care, disabled people and the women socially positioned as their carers are then also denied the rights of the individual (Morris 1993b).

The women in this research study provide an alternative to this model of citizenship and exclusion, one based on the modes of care they reject and propose. If it is acknowledged, as they do within a politicized discourse, that relations of dependency and 'mutual vulnerability' (Baier 1995, 109) are central to the human condition, then dependency and citizenship are brought together, producing new ways of thinking about entitlement and the priorities and location of care. An injustice is maintained when care is seen as a value of the private domain geared towards overcoming impairment. When this occurs connections of dependency, which allow the allegedly autonomous individual to function in the public sphere, are kept hidden (Nelson 2002). Caring is a social practice (Sevenhuijsen 1998), which emerges from the 'reciprocal dependencies' (Fine and Glendinning 2005, 616) inherent in the human condition and denied by false models of individuality and autonomy. By drawing care into the public realm, as mothers do, they highlight what should be understood as 'mutual vulnerability' rather than private dependency, requiring as a response a willingness to incorporate interdependency into our ties of citizenship and responsibility (Lister 1997; McKie et al. 2002).

Note

1. 'Parents, Professionals and Disabled Babies: Identifying Enabling Care (RES-000-23-0129)' (www.shef.ac.uk/inclusive-education/disabledbabies/). The full project team comprises: Dr Janice McLaughlin and Dr Emma Clavering (University of Newcastle); Professor Dan Goodley, Dr Pamela Fisher and Dr Claire Tregaskis (University of Sheffield).

6

From Traditional to Modern Care? The Case of the Intellectually Disabled and Mentally Ill in Modern Lithuania

Egle Sumskiene

Introduction

Public care services remain one of a few areas where modernity and its consequences are still questioned these days. The arguments of those supporting informal traditional family care and those giving priority to the formal modern services provided by professionals are both equally strong. However, it is important to stress that the question of modern versus traditional caregiving is not entirely a scientific discussion. Caregiving directly influences a majority of society; it is a task of many trained professionals and forms a part of social policy. Caregiving is connected with decision-making on many levels: family, institutional, regional and national policy.

The beneficiaries of caregiving services include a number of different groups; children, the chronically ill, the elderly and people with various disabilities. These social groups require many different types of services and have varying needs in terms of attention and daily care. Consequently, this chapter focuses on caregiving services for mentally ill and intellectually disabled adults. According to Marshall, social citizenship rights are directed towards inclusion of all citizens in society (Marshall 1975). The intellectually disabled and mentally ill constitute a group of individuals experiencing exclusion and restrictions of their rights. Despite the differences within the group, the mentally ill and intellectually disabled are, in relation to caregiving services, discussed as a single social group.

Due to a range of different demographic, social and economic factors, caregiving has become a societal matter of concern. The distribution of caregiving services between various potential beneficiaries depends on a number of variables: the current development and direction of social policy, the economic situation, dominant societal values and traditions, the existing social structure, and other similar factors. Thus, the services are influenced both by new structures of modern society and the traditional understanding of caregiving. The analytical field of investigation of this chapter is the development from traditional to modern care for the mentally ill and intellectually disabled. The rationales and motivation for implementing certain changes will be discussed, as will the question of considering both the requirements of modern-day society and traditional understandings of caregiving.

Certain social groups are highly dependent on caregiving services and support in their daily life. Depending on the type and extent of the disability, individuals will require different types of services, such as help and care in the home on a daily basis, regular activities at a daycare facility, or specialized care in a residential institution. These services may be provided by family members, friends, neighbours, volunteers or professional caregivers; however, caregiving should not be regarded simply as the relationship between a caregiver and the person cared for. It is a complex matter that defies easy classification; it does not belong to a particular sphere of medicine, social work or family life. In modern society, the question of caregiving involves various fields of scientific expertise, social groups and spheres of life. The answers to the question of caregiving become of crucial importance to all.

Various authors have investigated the field of caregiving, employing different approaches; however, there are two predominant schools of thought on caregiving. One perspective favours familial care and stresses the emotional, intimate aspects; the other approach rests upon the paradigm of modernity, meaning caregiving is viewed as a public service that should be provided by professionals in specialized institutions. In their opinion, provision of modern caregiving can be measured by using such criteria as economic efficiency.

The number of disabled in Lithuania is steadily increasing. In 1998 the number of mentally ill was 15,300 and by 2004 it had risen to 21,700. The number of intellectually disabled in 1998 was 6,300, and in 2004 it was 7,300. Approximately 6,000 of these people live in residential caregiving institutions, and 500 mentally ill and intellectually disabled people are on waiting lists (Social Statistics of the Ministry of Labor and Social Affairs). According to a World Health Organization report, the need for care during the next decades will increase by 400 per cent, especially in developing countries (WHO 2003). The mere scope of the problem calls for immediate and direct attention. There is a strong and pressing need for research and analysis within this field, both internationally and within Lithuania.

Caregiving in context

Traditional caregiving is understood as informal services provided free of charge to family members or close relatives without special knowledge but on the basis of emotions, empathy and sympathy. Two main reasons for establishing this special contact were close relations to the person in need of care and his or her disability or illness.

Modern caregiving is one of the most important spheres in modern social policy. It is defined as everyday support for the elderly, disabled and infants. Caregiving services can be paid for or free of charge; they can be provided by professionals or informal caregivers; the care can happen in the home or in an institution, combining various forms of care and private and public resources. The change from traditional to modern caregiving can be seen as happening in three stages.

The first period (before World War I) is characterized by domination of traditional services. Large extended families took care of their ill, elderly and the youngest members. Non-governmental organizations (NGOs) tried to support people living in poverty who could not be taken care of by their families. The first manifestations of modern caregiving were care and discipline homes for the disabled, the elderly, minors, or families in poverty. During this period extended families had the prime responsibility for care in Lithuania. Rural communities traditionally cared for those left without family care. The first care institutions, called *spitoles*, were founded in the 16th and 17th centuries next to monasteries or churches. The local community or landlords usually contributed financially. In modern terminology, these *spitoles* could be considered small community-based residential care institutions whose aim was to meet the basic needs of individuals left without family care.

The second period is distinguished by the formation of modern professional caregiving. Governments implemented programs intended to benefit World War I veterans. The end of World War II brought fundamental reforms and the establishment of the welfare state. Formal care was financed by the state, and, thus, caregiving gradually began shifting from being traditional and family-oriented to being a professional service. In Lithuania this period could be subdivided into two parts. Following the Act of Independence of Lithuania in 1918, Lithuania was creating its own system of social care and supporting tens of NGOs, public and religious organizations that actively operated in providing care. After World War II, Lithuania lost its independence and became part of the Soviet Union for the next 50 years. Every citizen of the country had to work and contribute to the welfare of the Soviet Union. Working mothers were unable to take care of their small children or disabled or elderly family members. Therefore, family care was changed to institutional care, such as kindergartens, boarding schools, and residential care institutions for the elderly or disabled. The disabled and mentally ill were often forced into being institutionalized.

The third and final stage in the shift from traditional to modern care began at the end of the 20th century, following the restitution of Lithuania's independence. This phase was driven by search for an optimal combination of traditional and modern caregiving. The catalyst for this final and current stage were the country's economic downturn, its increasing need for care, and the criticism levelled against the residential caregiving institutions. Social policy turned toward family care by introducing cash for caregiving. The current situation in caregiving is distinguished by promotion of family care and the decline of dualism of paid and unpaid labour (Knijn 2004). This shift in social policy was the government's response to the cry for a new social care system to replace the Soviet system of care, which was highly institutionalized and violated patients' rights.

There are four domains that characterize the change from traditional to modern caregiving:

1) change of family responsibilities and expectations towards the public sector;
2) institutionalization of specialized care for mentally ill and intellectually disabled individuals;
3) development of market relations in the area of caregiving;
4) the importance of caregiving ethics in a risk society.

Family and public responsibility for care

The division of responsibility for care between family and state was gradually developing in western countries in the 20th century, whereas Lithuania's progress was set back by two major historical events. The first was the occupation and annexation of Lithuania by the Soviet Union after World War II. During that period, traditional care was suddenly and radically replaced by state-funded institutions and services. As a result most residential care institutions were built in the 1950 and 1960s, and the number of patients has been growing steadily since then.

The second historical event that affected the structure of caregiving was the restitution of Lithuania's independence in 1990. At this time, the state gradually began transferring the responsibility for public caregiving services to private and non-governmental sectors. The pressure that previously existed to place a disabled family member into a care institution disappeared. Families now had more options from which to choose, including sought-after services such as day care, respite care, and care in the comfort of the home.

While this reform offered a wide variety of services and more choices for disabled individuals and their families, it was also met with some resistance. The state's diminishing role presented a new set of challenges to families of the mentally ill.

Irrespective of the particulars of the state's role, the development of modern society had an impact on the traditional family. In the welfare state, caregiving services commonly fall under the auspices of the state. Naturally, this is a heavy financial burden for welfare states and is a remnant philosophy of the great prosperity some countries enjoyed in the middle of the 20th century. This economic upturn allowed welfare states to create new social services and benefits, modelled after the traditional extended family, which provided the majority of caregiving services for its members. Today welfare states find themselves in the midst of economic stagnation – downturn even – which makes it a challenge to maintain some of their social programs and struggle to find the balance between the increased need for caregiving and decreased ability of families to provide care for their loved ones who are mentally ill or intellectually disabled.

The divisions between family and public sector responsibilities for care are not clearly, and caregiving services hang in the balance with neither families nor the public sector capable of sustaining the burden of increased responsibilities. The family will be able to provide care only on the condition that it will receive maximum support from outside. Family care in the majority of cases is understood as women's responsibility. Social citizenship in this case means creation of proper conditions to combine work and care for intellectually disabled or mentally ill family members. As Giddens (1992) argues, there is no way back to the traditional family. This statement can be extended in summing up that if the state expects traditional caregiving services from the family, then it must provide the family with maximum support and modern services.

Residential caregiving

Caregiving for intellectually disabled and mentally ill individuals in large residential caregiving institutions is a central component of reforming the system of social care in Lithuania and other post-Soviet countries. According to the World Bank there are 7,400 residential care institutions in post-Soviet countries. Lithuania is also regarded as a country with a highly institutionalized care system. The proliferation of institutions created the perfect setting for practical implementation of defectology, the school of thought that views the mentally ill and intellectually disabled as defective, as incapable of being trained, educated and socially integrated. Consequently, these individuals need to be isolated, and their condition can be only improved with medication. According to Tobis (2000) residential institutions had a dual function: social protection and social regulation. Thus, institutions provided both social services and isolated 'abnormal' individuals.

The development of modern caregiving and changes of care during the period of reflexive modernity raised questions about the order of society and supporting institutions. Modernity made it easier to diagnose, treat, educate and provide professional support for intellectually disabled and mentally ill people. Unfortunately, at the same time it sabotaged the daring plan of modernity to care for the intellectually disabled and mentally ill by having them concentrated in one area. According to Ruškus (2002), caregiving in specialized residential care institutions was the beginning of the modern segregation of intellectually disabled and mentally ill individuals. Achievements of science and professional services influenced physical segregation and exclusion of the disabled in residential care institutions. The period of reflexive modernity created favourable conditions to replace residential care with community care. Unfortunately it is a difficult process. Modernization is often achieved through standardization, an institutionalization of differences, regulations and protection against risks, elements that are difficult to integrate into residential caregiving.

For these reasons, reforms concerning residential caregiving have been met with resistance. In Lithuania, as in other countries of Eastern and Central Europe, several obstacles to successful deinstitutionalization have been identified (Germanavičius et al. 2005). Primarily, there prevails a positive public opinion supporting these forms of care and treatment. Secondly, institutional care and treatment is promoted financially and professionally whereas national infrastructure for community-based services doesn't exist. Finally, there is no legislation protecting the rights of the mentally disabled nor is there an independent authority in place for monitoring and supervising them.

Social citizenship is very much restricted in big residential caregiving institutions. Residents of these institutions are excluded from the society; their rights to privacy, freedom of choice, work, family, partnership and parenting are ignored once they are placed in residential care. Their need for treatment, clothing and sleeping accommodations are met satisfactorily, although lacking in various ways; however, the need for social relations, love, recognition and self-realization remains unsatisfied.

The market for caregiving services

The key feature of development of modern care is the marketization and, as a natural component thereof, the economization of caregiving services provided by the family as well as the public sector. The market is a response to the development of modern society and the weakening of families and their ability to care for their mentally disabled relatives. It is a search for the most sensible and effective solution, and it aims to respect and encourage the individuality of the members of that society. The public sector's role in creating a market for caregiving services is very important. Although the state loses its direct responsibility for providing services, it still remains in charge of the difficult task of quality control, ensuring accessibility and financing, setting standards and so on. Therefore, the creation of a market of caregiving services can be regarded as a modification of the public sector's responsibility and not as a reduction of it.

The introduction of market mechanisms in Lithuanian care services is in its infancy. Current social services legislation anticipates privatization, but their stance remains rather weak. In part, this is due to the general distrust of the ability of market forces to meet the individual needs of care services. Also, social services reforms tend to focus on the structural and financial aspects of care services, which leaves little room for creating a system of individualized care.

A market for modern caregiving services is a natural outcome of the development of society; however, it is not necessarily the best answer to the need for care, which has not changed for centuries. What has changed are the demographic characteristics of the need for care. With greater life expectancy, the number of elderly and disabled is much higher. When introducing a market for caregiving services it is important to remember that caregiving also has ethical considerations. Therefore, it has to be analysed not only from the perspective of modern rationality but also from the normative side, as the economic aspect of care is connected with efficiency and effectiveness but not with equality and equity. As Nussbaum (2003) argues, the implementation of a care market and the introduction of other changes which may weaken the positions of care receivers is only possible after the fundamental ethical obligation is accepted.

Caregiving ethics

Without an ethical background, the social and financial support for caregiving would not have a strong foundation or a clear direction. As Peeno (1996) argues, every social, medical, political, professional and economic solution in relation to caregiving has an ethical component. The requirements of caregiving ethics have changed in developing societies. In traditional society ethics were founded in an intuition-based understanding of how to provide for intellectually disabled and mentally ill individuals. Nowadays caregiving ethics provide arguments for decisions about financing the integration of the disabled which requires correct application of the achievements of science and involvement of the disabled in the decision-making. The right to give and receive care has become an important part of social citizenship. According to Knijn and Kremer (1997), inclusive social citizenship consists of the right to time for caregiving, such as paid parental leave or the right to receive care, for example via social services for children, the elderly or the disabled.

Summing up, caregiving ethics aim to enable disabled individuals to become equal members of society and at the same time oblige every member of society to take part in this integration process. In Lithuania, the development of modern care for intellectually disabled and mentally ill individuals has its own set of unique challenges which have not yet been properly analysed. In an attempt to begin bridging this gap, qualitative and quantitative data – including an opinion poll of politicians, officials and NGOs – has been collected. The opinion poll attempted to measure the attitude toward the development from traditional to modern care, and an analysis of its findings follows.

Contemporary attitudes toward the care of the intellectually disabled and mentally ill

The goal of the research was to collect information about the attitudes of professional caregivers toward the development of the Lithuanian caregiving system. The poll sought to discover how they perceived: 1) the direction of development of the system; and 2) the changes that have occurred in the past decades. Additionally, those polled were asked to explain what kinds of obstacles they have encountered and what the positive and negative developments have been. The analysis of the opinion poll was conducted from October 2005 to February 2006. Research questionnaires were sent to 60 heads of Social Support Centers of Lithuanian municipalities, 10 heads of Social Support Centers of Lithuanian counties, and 60 heads of regional centers of the Lithuanian

Welfare Society for the Intellectually Disabled, 'Viltis'. Seventy-four questionnaires (57 per cent) were returned.

To achieve the research goals a research study of experts was also carried out. According to Meuser and Nagel (1991), expert opinions are the most valuable data for gaining insight into social problems in general, and issues concerning socially vulnerable groups and inequality in particular. Five experts participated in the research. These experts exercise important functions and their decisions often directly influence the welfare of the mentally ill and intellectually disabled. Following is a discussion of the findings of the expert interviews.

The role of the family

According to quantitative and qualitative research data, respondents acknowledge the problems of traditional caregiving within the family and the importance of public services provision for mentally ill and intellectually disabled individuals. Qualitative research carried out by various experts points to a number of health problems that caregivers may typically suffer from: *'Parents or carers have psychosomatic problems, e.g. increases in their blood pressure, development of [a] gastric ulcer or depression. The reason for this is long years of caregiving without support from outside. This could be called a chain reaction'* (citation from the qualitative research material).

However, the family remains the most important provider of care and the social expectations towards family care remain very high. Furthermore, any development in the sphere of care services should be directed towards higher involvement of family. Two thirds of respondents (67 per cent) think that the state should strengthen family care and only one fifth (21 per cent) expects the contrary. Development of community care is based on increased family responsibility: *'most of the residents of residential care institutions have their relatives alive. Families should be involved in organizing the process of deinstitutionalization'* (citation from the qualitative material). However, family care should be strongly supported from the outside: one expert argues that *'help has to be organized to allow carers to realize their potential to work, to earn, to pay taxes'*.

Benefits of social citizenship are very important for caregiving families because care for the disabled is very demanding and the disabled may need lifelong care. Furthermore, compared to the number of mainstream institutions serving 'healthy' families and individuals, the number of integrated day care facilities, schools and temporary relief services offered to families functioning as caregivers is scarce. In divorced families, women are often left alone to take care of the disabled child and they usually face stigma, fear and labelling in the society, which increases the burden of care. In modern society traditional and natural institutions such as the family grow weaker and their functions become replaced by services from the outside, provided by the public sector. On all occasions the role of the public sector is not to replace but to strengthen traditional family care. Hence, in the eyes of the respondents modern services are not a real alternative to traditional caregiving services. They support traditional care provided by the family and assisted by the state: *'Residential caregiving is a problematic and hard-to-reform part of the social welfare system.'*

When speaking about residential caregiving institutions, respondents primarily stressed the societal importance of these institutions rather than the needs of the disabled. They cited structural rather than individual reasons as crucial for the predomination of residential caregiving: lack of community caregiving services (82.9 per cent) and financial assistance mechanisms beneficial to residential care (74 per cent). A lower number of respondents emphasized an individual perspective: less than one third of respondents (29.2 per cent) stressed that residential caregiving fitted individual needs the best and only 12.9 per cent named it as a 'preferable choice by disabled persons'.

Fear, stigma and intolerance of the disabled indicate that long decades of their isolation influenced society's opinions and attitudes. Therefore society justifies their isolation and the violation of their rights and dignity. As experts point out, *'residential caregiving institutions are the heritage of the last centuries. The tradition of residential caregiving for the disabled emerged regarding isolation of the disabled as useful both to the disabled themselves and to society'*. The construction of institutions for disabled adults requiring care was informed by the best of intentions. The underlying logic was the idea that individuals with special needs are serviced more efficiently when concentrated in one location. Consequently, the duty of taking care of the disabled members of society disappeared: in many cases they were excluded so successfully that the external world fully forgot about their existence (Kröger 2001).

Experts are critical about the role of improvements in the physical conditions of the institutions. According to them this process is even more harmful to the system of care: *'during the last decade a big budget was allocated for these institutions and many improvements have been made. Now politicians and officials are afraid as they cannot find arguments for investments made to finance this ineffective system* (interview materials).

The assessment of respondents to quantitative and qualitative research is very ambivalent, as is their attitude to the role of these institutions in society. Residential caregiving institutions are a natural product of the development of modern society: the family is unable to provide traditional care, society is afraid of the disabled. Hence the concentration of the disabled solves many problems. Firstly, it decreases the family responsibility for care and instead provides disabled persons with universal, standardized services. Secondly, society becomes protected from the risk of dealing with the disabled. Finally economic rationality is anchored in a new sphere of modern society. Eventually, however, the perspective and needs of the affected disabled individuals also needed to be considered; this perspective was not part of the planning and development of modern residential caregiving services. Hence the current situation facing residential institutions is quite problematic and the future remains highly unpredictable.

Involvement of commercial care providers and development of the caregiving market

Respondents' opinion on involvement of commercial care providers is positive: almost half of them (43 per cent) support their participation in provision of care. It is important to mention that one third of respondents (30 per cent) did not have an opinion as to whether they agree or not with the involvement of the market sector in provision of caregiving services. However, as one of the experts in the qualitative research expressed it: *'if you live in a country with a state monopoly for 50–70 years and you see the consequences of it – you have no doubts that a market is necessary.'*

Although it was expected that it would be the family that would resist modern changes and the creation of a caregiving market, analysis of qualitative data has shown that the commercial sector's position in caregiving is weak because of the monopolistic attitude within the public sector, which does not want to step aside and make way for the market competition. According to the expert research: *'Officials and politicians realized that international and national legislation obliges them to provide care for the disabled in their living area and that a caregiving market is a long lasting issue. That is why a cruel fight is going on today. The state will slog it out to monopolize the provision of caregiving services.'* This situation can be explained by the Soviet heritage when families were pressed not to take care of mentally ill and intellectually disabled relatives. The main responsibility rested with the paternalistic state and thus the state fell into a habit of being responsible for all aspects of the lives of the disabled. After the fall of the regime, services provided by NGOs are more innovative and qualitative compared to those provided by the public sector. However, the public sector tends to dominate the market and block out innovative approaches. Among them is the marketization of caregiving. According to modernization theorists like Giddens, the public sector might be expected to welcome marketization of caregiving, while families would resist it. However, the survey results indicated that the development of a market was blocked not by traditional caregivers, but by the public sector which aimed at keeping the whole responsibility for caregiving for itself.

Problems of caregiving ethics

In traditional societies negative attitudes and corresponding behaviour toward disabled people was influenced by individuals' unexplainable, unpredictable behaviour as a result of mental illness and intellectual disability. Although in this respect society has become more sophisticated over the centuries, qualitative and quantitative research has shown that many attitudes still reflect the eighteenth and nineteenth century ideas which led to feelings of fear mixed with sympathy towards mentally ill and intellectually disabled individuals. In a religious context, it was believed that the mentally ill were possessed by demons and that mental illness was something sinful, and therefore ill persons should be isolated. However, Christianity also required mercy, support and compassion. Besides such traditional ethics is another equally important aspect that might be called a core attribute of modern society – economic requirements. In many cases this is even more dominant than the traditional ethics of care.

Data from quantitative research show that the largest proportion of human rights violations of the disabled occur on the social level, in relations between the disabled and the rest of society, whereas violations at the organizational and individual levels occur less frequently. Thus, the dignity of mentally ill and intellectually disabled persons is less likely to be violated by those taking daily care of them than by society at large, where there is often a perception of mental illness or intellectual disability based on prejudices and fears. Awareness of the incapacity to function caused by objective clinical or medical factors is supplemented by groundless ideas about disability; together these can invoke disrespect towards the dignity and rights of the disabled.

In spite of the fact that caregiving ethics are regarded as fundamental to making every decision about care provision, they are not necessarily progressive and do not unfailingly support the integration of the disabled. Furthermore, their requirements frequently yield to the requirements of economic rationality. As experts argue: '*Lithuanian society divides people into valuable and people of no value. A person is rated according to his economic value. We speak about reforms a lot but when we have to work on them we merely decide that economics is much more important than a human being.'*

The beneficiaries of care services have no say in relation to decisions about caregiving services; therefore their influence is minimal. Even when it is clearly possible to predict the needs of the disabled they are ignored. In summarizing the assessments of the respondents to the qualitative and quantitative research on the existing caregiving system and its need to reform, it becomes obvious that residential caregiving should be replaced by care in the family. However, at the same time respondents believe that traditional family care suits the needs of mentally ill and intellectually disabled people less than the professional caregiving services.

The voice of the disabled is rarely heard and sometimes legislative measures (based on notions of incapacity) are used to divest the disabled of their rights to take part in decision-making about their own lives. Decision-making is based not on their needs but on economic requirements. Society consents to a reduction in resources allocated for the disabled since they do not pay any dividends. Hence services for the disabled are planned not on the basis of their needs – diversity, complexity and individuality – but on the basis of the economic capacity of the state. Therefore, in order to save state pecuniary resources, reform of caregiving services is constantly put off. This is abetted by the ethics of caregiving, which are influenced by relics of traditional society which manifest themselves in fear, uncertainty and prejudice, as well as by more modern economic motives.

Conclusions

Responsibility for care for the mentally ill and intellectually disabled is not clearly divided between the family and the public sector. Although the structure of the family has changed, it is still considered the main provider of care. At the same time, the role of the public sector has increased. However, its main function is to strengthen traditional family care and not to replace it with modern services provided by professionals. Residential caregiving institutions are a product of the development of modern society. Their functions and purposes are oriented more towards the need of modern society for safety, rational action, structuring and institutionalization than for the needs of their direct target group – the mentally ill and intellectually disabled. They also fit perfectly with the working methods and goals of the Soviet ideology to make society cleaner and safer.

In the period of reflexive modernity favourable conditions were created to replace residential caregiving with community care. In Lithuania and other post-Soviet countries this process started after collapse of the Soviet regime. However this is a difficult process as the main characteristics of residential caregiving respond to residual traditional fears and prejudices and the requirements of modern society for safety and rationality. Hence residential caregiving still has many supporters in society in general and among decision-makers. Involvement of commercial care providers is welcomed with the expectation that a market in caregiving services will improve the quality of life for the disabled and improve the whole system of caregiving, by decreasing family responsibility and introducing more flexibility, rationality and efficiency.

Although it was expected that it would be the family that would resist modern changes and the creation of a caregiving services market, analysis of qualitative data showed that, in fact, the commercial sector's position in caregiving was weak because of the monopolistic attitude of the public sector, which did not want to step aside and make way for market competition.

The requirements for caregiving ethics have changed. In traditional society caregiving was based on an intuition-based understanding about support for the mentally ill and intellectually disabled. Christianity and community feeling had an important role in these traditional ethics of care. During the Soviet period, the subject of caregiving ethics was avoided, along with other sensitive subjects in this field. Nowadays caregiving ethics back up the search for reasons for the allocation of the financial resources necessary for the integration of the disabled and require the appropriate use of the achievements of science and the involvement of the disabled in the decision-making process.

The beneficiaries should be at the centre of the ethical argument, but the results of the research in this chapter correspond to the results of similar research conducted in other European countries. The system of caregiving for the mentally ill and intellectually disabled and its development reflect the changing needs and possibilities of the rest of society but not the interests of the disabled, in the following ways:

a) beneficiaries cannot influence provision of caregiving services. Sometimes legislative measures (incapacity) are used to divest the disabled of their rights to take part in decisions which directly impact their own lives.

b) Even when it possible to predict the needs of the disabled they are not considered.

c) Decision-making is based not on their needs but on economic requirements.

Thus the system of care in Lithuania has not significantly developed during the years of independence and many aspects of the Soviet ideology remain unchanged. Although the disabled represent a socially weak minority, their role is crucial for the development of the society; the need to take care of the disabled, and the principles of normalization and integration catalyse development of certain disciplines and professions: medicine, psychology, social work, social pedagogy, pharmacy and so on.

Intellectually disabled and mentally ill persons form a social group whose social citizenship rights are very much restricted even compared with the other socially weak groups. Unfavourable opinions within Lithuanian society towards the mentally ill and intellectually disabled are influenced by two main factors. The first of them is the legacy of the traditional society (traditional attitudes, stereotypes, prejudices, fears) and the second is the result of the modern society (economical rationality dominating disabled people's rights and their human dignity). Both factors seem to be very strong and deeply rooted, which leads us to assume that this situation will not change soon and that people with mental health problems will not be able to enjoy the benefits of social citizenship in the foreseeable future.

7
Changing Conceptions of Citizenship and Care in Finnish Policy Discourse on Reconciliation of Work and Family Life

Kirsi Eräranta

Introduction

Since the 1990s 'reconciliation of work and family life' has been discussed as a central concern of social policy both in Finland and the European Union. In the EU, the concern for ageing populations and the resulting unsustainable dependency ratios has led to the advancement of policies that both encourage a more active participation of citizens, women in particular, in the labour market, and allow them to have children and raise a family (Duncan 2002). Being high on the policy agenda, the issue of work/family reconciliation represents an interesting case of European government (Walters and Haahr 2005) and the debate on social citizenship and care (Lister 1997) in the EU. It also provides a possibility to analyse and illustrate the ways in which European policies are articulated and negotiated in the local contexts of the member states – in this case in one of the Nordic countries, which are often considered as forerunners in the development of reconciliation policies.

Questions of citizenship are significant for our political imaginaries, for 'the way we define citizenship is intimately linked to the kind of society and political community we want' (Mouffe 1992, 25 in Lister 1997). In this chapter, I look into work/family reconciliation as a policy discourse through which citizenship is articulated, contested and redefined in the context of welfare state redesign. Drawing from Foucauldian analytics of government as well as from feminist theories on citizenship and care, I analyse the regimes of rationality through which the issue of work/family reconciliation is problematized – rendered problematic and intelligible – and defined as an object of government in Finnish policy documents on the topic. I focus particularly on the ways in which citizenship is

123

articulated and redefined in the texts, over a period of time from 1980 to 2008.

Overall the analysis suggests that two contradictory developments in relation to the Nordic, egalitarian tradition of citizenship have characterized Finnish reconciliation policy discourse over the years. On the one hand, the child-care policies reflect a move away from 'egalitarian' citizenship ideals. As Rianne Mahon (2002) has observed, Finnish 'neo-familialist' care policies include public but less generous support for long child-care leaves, which makes the choice of temporary house-wife-mother role acceptable, even attractive. As a result, these leaves tend to contribute to gender and class inequalities. In this respect, Finland seems to have followed a diverging path from the other Nordic countries, especially Sweden, and thus moved closer to the more conservative European welfare states.

On the other hand, the promotion of family-friendly workplace policies, as well as the introduction of a 'father's month' (an incentive for male parents) in Finnish family leave policy, seems to echo, at least partly, a 'Nordic model' of gender equality and citizenship. Such a model is based on the idea that formal equal opportunities legislation is insufficient to guarantee the substantive equality of citizens, and that more active measures are needed (Bergqvist and Jungar 2000, 178; Gordon 2006). Paradoxically, both in the case of workplace policies and the father's quota, the social policies and policy coordination instruments of the EU have provided national actors means for pursuing this course of action.

Citizenship and care

In this chapter I approach citizenship as a 'creation of techniques of social discipline' (Burchell 1995, 543) and an important component in the (self)government of populations, groups and individuals. It is not limited to the state but involves multiple, and conflicting, authorities and agencies (Foucault 1991; Dean 1999; Helén and Jauho 2003). As such, citizenship is closely linked to the notion of biopolitics, which is based on organizing the necessary conditions of life and securing the vital resources and processes of a population. Historically, men have been tied to citizenship through their soldiering (Hobson and Lister 2002, 27). Later, the ability to work, and reproductive capabilities and care work for women, have offered grounds for claiming citizenship.

As the Nordic conception of citizenship combines elements from two historical traditions of citizenship, the liberal and civic republican traditions (see Holli 1992), I pay attention to the key categories of both of these traditions (Lister 1997). First, I analyse citizenship as a status defined by individual citizenship rights, especially social rights, which is typical of the liberal social rights tradition. Second, I look into citizenship as a practice, accentuating citizens' civic duties and obligations to the wider society, which is characteristic of the participatory republican tradition.

A central aspect of gender-differentiated citizenship is care (Lister 1997; Hobson and Lister 2002). I illuminate the multiple dimensions of care rights, responsibilities and practices with the concept of social care. Mary Daly and Jane Lewis (2000) have defined social care as 'the activities and relations involved in meeting the physical and emotional requirements of dependent adults and children, and the normative, economic and social frameworks within which these are assigned and carried out'. At the macro level, the concept draws attention to the relationship between services and cash benefits. It also highlights the division of care labour, responsibility and costs between the family, the market, the state and the voluntary/community sectors. At the micro level, the concept of social care brings to light the distribution of care (giving and receiving) between women and men and among families, as well as the conditions under which care is carried out, and the state's role in affecting such conditions.

Methods and materials

The empirical data consist of Finnish policy documents (including seminar reports and project publications) on the 'reconciliation of work and family', published between 1980 and 2008. The dataset was obtained by searching several national bibliographies and databases (such as FENNICA and FINLEX) for the keywords of 'work' and 'family'. Additional material was identified through references in these texts. In this chapter, references to the empirical material are indicated in *italics*.

My research strategy draws primarily on Foucauldian genealogy (Foucault 1984; 1991; Dean 1998). While my analysis does not cover broad periods of time, the approach is historical. First, I identify and analyse the particular 'regimes of rationality' that underpin the problematizations of work/family reconciliation in the policy texts. By regimes of rationality I refer to the distinctive ways in which truths about the problem are formulated, which involves the 'construction of domains of objects, strategies and procedures, concepts and vocabularies, and specific forms of knowledgeable or authoritative actors or subjects' (Dean 1998, 192). I focus particularly on the ways in which these rationalities define rights, obligations and practices of citizenship, and the possible shifts in them. Second, I try to locate these regimes of rationality outlining citizenship within certain 'regimes of practices', that is assemblages of various discursive, technical, social and institutional elements (Foucault 1991; Dean 1998, 188). I thus analyse not only the elements of policy discourse on work/family reconciliation but also the historical principles that make the discourse useful or problematic at a given time and place (see Lehtonen 2003).

Changing problematizations of the reconciliation of work and family

To illustrate the historical transformation of the rationalities and conceptions of citizenship in the policy discourse on the reconciliation of work and family life, I first contrast two policy memoranda, from 1983 and 2001 (*STM 1983:28; STM 2001:28* [for this and other empirical data quoted in this chapter, see Appendix 7.1 below]). The documents exemplify some central changes in the problematization of work/family reconciliation – the ways in which it is made problematic and intelligible as an object of government. In the memoranda, I identify two regimes of rationality (Dean 1998, 192–93), in which the understanding of domains of objects, policies and measures, and particular forms of authoritative actors is different.

The first document, a memorandum of the *Working Group on Work and Family Life* from 1983, appears to be the very first publication in Finland that focuses precisely on the reconciliation of work and family life. The working group was set up by the Ministry of Social Affairs and Health, and it consisted exclusively of female ministry officials. The assignment given to the working group was to prepare a commission for a prospective committee on parenthood and paid employment.

As the name of the working group indicates, in 1983, the dichotomy of paid work and family was already well established. These two areas are not represented as the only important spheres of life, however. The starting

Table 7.1   Changing problematizations of the reconciliation of work and family

	Memorandum 1983	Memorandum 2001
Central objective	Enable (female) parents' labour-market participation	Enable (male) parents' participation in child care
Instruments	Various measures, especially day care	Parental leaves
Reference group	Nordic countries	EU countries
Members of the working group	Officials of the Ministry of Social Affairs and Health	Representatives of different governmental departments and labour market organizations

point for the proposed committee is 'an identical responsibility of women and men for childcare and housework as well as their equal right for paid work, education, civic activity and leisure' (*p. II*). This reflects a framework of citizenship that has been strong in the Nordic countries, which emphasizes participation in different spheres of life: polity, market and family (Hobson and Lister 2002, 35). Similarly to the Nordic sex-role movement of the 1960s, the memorandum points at the importance of active participation of both men and women in society and in the public sphere, that is political citizenship as a practice (Lister 1997, 23–29; Holli 1992). And social rights to paid work and care, guaranteed by the 'women-friendly' welfare state, are understood as a precondition for participatory citizenship (Holli 1992, 82–83). The key reference group discussed in the text are the other Nordic countries. One of the tasks of the working group, for example, is to collect 'both domestic and foreign, above all Nordic, accounts for the use of the possible committee' (*p. II*).

In the 1983 memorandum, the main objective is to enable (female) parents of young children to participate in the labour market, as can be read in the following extract. The text discusses various public services and subsidies for families that enable this kind of reconciliation: maternity allowances, day care for children, a home care subsidy, and a home help service, for example (*pp. 6–13*). The importance of the supply and improvement of municipal day care services is highlighted (*pp. 11–12*). Moreover, different working time arrangements and part-time work are mentioned (*pp. 18–19*). The conclusion is:

> *The working group proposes the appointment of a committee whose assignment is defined as follows:*
>
> *1) to clarify the needs for change in working life that are required for meeting the familial responsibilities of working parents of young children*
> *2) to clarify the developmental needs in the daycare system and childcare forms, starting with the premise that childcare and familial responsibilities should prohibit or hinder as little as possible parents' participation in employment; and*
> *3) to clarify the ways in which public services for families with children may be directed and improved so that they support working parents of young children. (p. 20)*

In practice, the proposals of the working group had little direct success, as the planned committee was never set up. Overall, the discussion on the topic remained relatively marginal in the policy documents of the 1980s, although some reforms were made in the latter part of the decade.

The memorandum of the *Working Group on Reconciliation of Work and Family Life* from 2001 tells a different story. The group was set up by the same ministry, the Ministry of Social Affairs and Health, but it included both male and female members, who represented different administrative sectors and labour market organizations. The task of this tripartite working group was to explore the possibilities of reforming the existing family leave system in the following ways:

> *The working group was assigned to investigate the possibilities of creating a system that would guarantee fathers a right to one month's parental leave of their own, and that would guarantee a right to take maternity or parental leave on a part-time basis. In its report the working group should also deal with the annual holiday costs caused by parental leaves by paying attention e.g. to how effective the redistribution of the annual holiday costs of family leaves is and how to simplify the application process and whether the costs of temporary care leaves to employers could be relieved through funding from sickness insurance. (Documentation page)*

The memorandum focuses exclusively on paid work and family, and does not mention any other spheres of life, such as voluntary work or political activism. In concentrating on social rights to parental leave only, it comes to represent citizenship as a rather passive status, and the government and 'social partners' as the active respecters and supporters of the private sphere of individuals (Lister 1997, 14–15). While Sweden and Norway are still important for benchmarking, in the discussion of the 'father's month' in particular (*p. 36*), the EU now constitutes the key reference group in the memo (*pp. 31–33; appendix 2*).

The aim of the reforms proposed in the text is 'to improve the chances of parents of young children to take part in caring for their children and to make the use of care leaves more flexible' (*Documentation page*). To these ends, the working group proposes changes in parental leaves and related administrative practices. Over the subsequent years, most of these reforms were brought into effect. In general, the problem of reconciling work and family had moved higher up on the policy agenda from the 1990s onward.

Overall, these two policy texts illustrate significant differences in the problematization of work/family reconciliation and in the rationalities and conceptions of citizenship it involves. Political citizenship and civic participation are present in the 1983 memorandum (see also, for example, *Työaika naisnäkökulmasta 1982, 36*) but practically absent in the 2001 memo, where the focus is on social citizenship and social rights. The two texts also give a different picture of the functions, roles and responsibilities that diverse social actors have in facilitating such rights and work/family reconciliation. To overstate a bit, the perspective shifts from the welfare state, which provides day care and other public services for working mothers, to employers who grant parental leave to male employees. In 2001, different governmental units and the so-called social partners – the labour market organizations representing capital and labour – are represented as important players in the field. This illustrates an increasing trend toward decentralized co-operation and partnership that cross bureaucratic boundaries in policy-making and implementation.

Child care: social rights and the step from care services toward cash benefits

As the policy discourse on the reconciliation of work and family life defines citizenship primarily and increasingly in terms of social rights, I next turn to discuss these rights in more detail. I demonstrate how modifications in the concepts and vocabularies used to discuss and make sense of citizenship rights in the texts are indicative of more general changes in practices of government, namely a gradual shift from a service-oriented welfare state toward a more transfer-oriented one.

In the relatively few policy texts that focus on work/family reconciliation in the 1980s, social rights are explicitly mentioned mainly in discussions on family leaves. The rights frame is often used in the context of gender equality, especially when addressing men's right to parental leave (*KM 1980:23, 98; STM 1983:28, 6, 15, 17*). However, even though the *Act on Children's Day Care* had come into effect already in 1973, the right to daycare is mentioned only in the following statement: 'After parental leave and possibly after new extended home care leave, families should have a right to get their child in municipal daycare, if desired' (*STM 1983:28, 11*).

As the choice of words implies, the actual right of all citizens in need of municipal daycare was not fully realized in the early 1980s. Furthermore, public daycare was still commonly discussed in terms that underscored not so much individuals and their rights but rather the obligation of authorities to organize daycare for children under school age. For example, the 'daycare system is to be developed', the quality of 'daycare services improved', and the 'supply of daycare places increased' according to a nationwide plan (*KM 1980:23, 100; STM 1983:28*). This reflects the collectivist tradition in Finland, in which public welfare services are understood as tools for reducing social and regional in-equalities. In this line of thinking, trust in authorities is high, and citizens do not have to attend to their interests actively (Pylkkänen 2007; Holli 1992). Overall, the texts discuss the welfare state as the provider and regulator of child-care services, observing that it has not entirely reached its goals yet.

In the 1990s, the 'rights talk' increases in the discussion on subjective right to daycare. In 1990, children under three years of age were given an unconditional right to municipal daycare,[1] and in 1996 the right was extended to all children under school age. I suggest that the increased emphasis on the 'subjective' nature of the right in the 1990s relates to efforts to guarantee certain universal rights of citizens to social services in the context of increasing municipal autonomy (see Pelkonen 1993). In general, an individualistic rights-frame typical for liberal regimes had gained ground in Finland as a result of international and EU legislation (Pylkkänen 2004; 2007).

However, the extension of the right to daycare did not proceed according to the planned schedule (*STM 1992:13, 13; TM 1994, preface*). In the early 1990s, Finland experienced an economic crisis, which resulted in high unemployment and severe cuts to welfare services. At the time, the public sector was also criticized for its alleged bureaucracy and inflexibility. The restructuring policies were inspired by ideas and techniques typical of new public management, its principles and different activities. The reform of state subsidies in 1993 increased municipal autonomy and variation in the provision of basic services, including contracting-out and using private child-care services (Simonen and Kovalainen 1998).

From the mid-1990s, references to daycare become increasingly brief and scarce in the growing number of policy texts on work/family reconciliation. The now achieved right to daycare, as well as questions concerning its availability and quality, are largely ignored in the texts of that time, and the focus shifts to questions of work and of family leaves (for example, *TM 1994; STAKES 1999; STM 2001:28*).[2] In the 2000s, the few references made to daycare demonstrate significant changes in concepts and their meanings around the theme. The former 'daycare system' has become a 'childcare system for small children'. The substance of the 'subjective right to daycare' is presented in a novel way, accentuating the options of private care. As the following extract indicates, some suggestions had also been made to dissolve the unconditional right to daycare:

The childcare system for small children enables a family to choose between home care and daycare, as regards children under the age of three. Concerning

children over three years of age, the subjective right to daycare remains for
families, either in the form of a right to municipal services or an allowance
for private care. (Perhe ja työ 2004, 37)

Since 1997, it had been possible for families to receive a private child-care allowance for providing their children with private care. In the policy texts this reform is legitimized by liberal ideas of consumerism, that is, increasing parents' freedom of choice in child-care options (*STM 1994:11; Perhe ja työ 2004, 35, 37*). The partial reassignment of responsibilities to parents (and to social care professionals) is justified by their individual autonomy and right of self-determination (see also Simonen and Kovalainen 1998). The welfare state is now represented primarily as the legislator, coordinator and financier of child care, in the form of family leaves and allowance for private care.

It is noteworthy that in the 1990s, during the creation of the child-care system for small children, no reference is made to the reconciliation of work and family life in the preparatory texts. Neither the committee report (*STM 1994:11*), nor the numerous government bills (such as *HE 121/1995*) justify this reform by the need to help parents find an optimal work-life balance, for example. Instead, the texts refer to the possibilities of choosing the 'most convenient childcare arrangement' (*STM 1994:11, 10*). It is not until 2004 that the child-care system for small children, as well as the home care allowance and the private child-care allowance – the cheaper alternatives of child care – are rhetorically connected to the reconciliation of work and family in the texts. For example, increases in home and private child-care allowances are rationalized by suggesting that this would 'improve the possibilities of families to reconcile work and family' (*HE 162/2004*; see also *STM 2007:1, 38–39*).

It is my interpretation that in the 1990s, the improved options of private and home-based child care were discursively strongly connected to the retrenchment of the welfare state. Hence, it was not intelligible to justify them by reference to the yet relatively marginal discourse of work/family reconciliation, which until then had stressed citizens' social right to public services. In the public discussions of the early 2000s, however, politically active 'pro-family' forces had gained ground, highlighting the value of parental (maternal) care (Mahon 2002). The topic of work/family reconciliation had also become popular.

By 2008, the list of family leaves with cash benefits – all justified by the need to facilitate reconciliation – has become long. During the infant's first year, the parents are entitled to maternity, paternity and parental leave, including partial parental leave (2003) and the father's quota (2003). After that first year with the baby, they have access to child-care leave until the child turns three years old. Then there are other options such as partial child-care leave (that is, reduction of working time) (1988), temporary child-care leave (1988) and absence for compelling family reasons (1998), the latter being a European newcomer in the Finnish family leave system. In addition, people who take care of other family members are entitled to job alternation leave (1995). Many of these leaves have been further developed during the 1990s and 2000s, and this has created new possibilities for the re-familialization of care.

In the 2000s, therefore, the policy discourse on work/family reconciliation seems to have partly changed and has been used to practise a child-care policy that is different from that of the 1980s. This policy is based on a new kind of mixed economy of social care, which offers – besides publicly provided child-care services – cash benefits for stay-at-home parents and other private carers (Simonen and Kovalainen 1998).

Family-friendly policies: toward responsible corporate citizenship?

In the 1990s, new ideas and reasoning about the responsibility of the employer to facilitate its employees' work-life balance gained ground in Finnish policy texts. This reasoning appears to draw on the ideas of 'corporate social responsibility' and 'corporate citizenship', according to which corporations are to take responsibility for protecting, facilitating and enabling the social rights of citizens – and thus assume some of the functions previously expected mainly of the government (Matten and Crane 2005). Although the uneven realization of parents' rights as employees had been already discussed in a Nordic co-operation plan for gender equality in the late 1980s (*NU 1989:6F, 28–30*), a more active promotion of relevant workplace policies started along with the processes of European integration.

For example, the reform of the Finnish *Act on Equality between Women and Men* (1987) began in 1991. The Act was criticized by gender equality experts for not producing tangible results and for leaving private industry untouched (Bruun 2000, 106; *STM 1992:13*). Moreover, it was time to synchronize the Finnish equality legislation with the equality directives of the European Community (*KM 1992:35, 2*). The report of the committee responsible for the reform affirms that 'attention must be paid more than today to the facts that may impede this reconciliation in working life' (*KM 1992:35, 50, 97*; see also *STM 1992:13, 14*).

Eventually in 1995 – the year Finland became member of the EU – the term 'reconciliation of working life and family life' was taken up in Finnish law. In the revised Equality Act, it is stated that it is the 'employer's duty to promote gender equality', and it stipulates that the employer must 'facilitate the reconciliation of working life and family life for women and men' (*Laki...206/1995*). In general, the employer's obligations to promote equality were tightened in the revised act, although no sanctions were specified (Ahtela 2004; Bruun 2000, 106). The Equality Act is still the only act in Finland in which reconciliation is mentioned.

All the documents that focus on work/family reconciliation published during the period of 1994–1998 under public administration call attention to questions of work, and indicate links to the EU as well as to equality issues (for example, *TM 1994; STM 1995; TM 1998*). However, expressions of concern, ambivalence and even mistrust toward employers' duties to promote work/family reconciliation can also be identified in the texts. In the following extract, a clear distinction is made between Nordic public policies for work/family reconciliation, and the 'family-friendly' corporate policies of other, less developed welfare states:

> *In Finland, the reconciliation of work and family life has been perceived mainly as a challenge for social policy. An extensive daycare system and family leaves make it easier for parents of young children to take part in the labour market. In countries where the tax-paid welfare state is weaker than the Nordic model, the workplaces have their own policies for the reconciliation of working and family life. Especially under labour shortage, companies attract employees with a 'family friendly' image. (KM 1999:1, 47)*

Despite such doubting remarks, the monopoly of the public sector in supporting work/family reconciliation was increasingly called into question in Finland, and companies were encouraged to promote equality and wellbeing for their employees by introducing family-friendly measures. Two 'technologies of involvement' (Walters and Haahr 2005, 123–4) were of particular importance here (see Eräranta 2009). First, labour market organizations were encouraged to take the role of partners in the active 'social dialogue' on the topic, and more generally, in implementing EU regulations on working life in tripartite cooperation (Bruun 2000, 107–8). In the late 1990s and the 2000s, they participated in the preparations for relevant social policy reforms, as well as in large publicity campaigns for a more equal use of family leaves. Second, from the mid-1990s onwards, several European Social Fund projects aiming to facilitate work/family reconciliation were implemented in organizations. In one of the early project publications, the purpose of development activities is outlined as follows:

> *An awareness of meanings of work/family reconciliation, a family friendly approach as well as new innovative means to reconcile these spheres of life are needed. New practices must also be economically cost-effective, and contribute both to the wellbeing of employees and to the increase of [business] productivity. (TM 1998, 1)*

In the policy texts on reconciliation from the 1990s and 2000s, family-friendly workplace policies are often described in terms typical of corporate social responsibility or corporate citizenship (see Matten and Crane 2005). As the above extract illustrates, the proponents of these policies refer not only to the legal responsibility of firms to obey laws, but also to their economic responsibility to be profitable and their ethical responsibility to support the wellbeing of employees, employees' families, and communities. The development of work/family initiatives in organizations is delineated as strategic activity that ultimately helps to improve economic performance. It is rendered intelligible as an investment in the social environment of companies. For example, a 'family friendly collective agreement policy' is called for, because 'support for families with children would have an effect also on birthrate and, in the long run, on the availability of [the] labour force' (*Aikalisä perheelle 2002, 20*). Similarly, adequate workplace policies are argued to provide a 'competitive edge' for the firm, because the 'public image and recruitment opportunities are improved, as the organization gains a good reputation as an employer taking care of its employees' (*STAKES 2004, 13*).

In some project publications, organizational work/family policies are also explicitly referred to as a form of corporate social responsibility (for example, *MONIKKO-hanke 2008, 63*). Whereas different working time, child-care leave and telework arrangements are commonly accepted in the publications as suitable reconciliation measures, sick-child care services offered by employers apparently do not meet the criteria for socially responsible work/family arrangements, as the following extract illustrates:

> *The HR manager of another IT company had considered care service [for sick children] and discovered that it is not a child friendly arrangement in the end. S/he expected that it will probably be left out of services offered to employees. [...] This demonstrates [...] a HR policy that aims to bear social responsibility. (SITRA 2003, 77–78.)*

Overall in Finland, this kind of 'socially responsible' role of the employer seems to have emerged gradually through cross-border influences and policy learning, in the context of welfare state redesign, economic liberalization and increased flexibility requirements for employees. On the one hand, in going beyond formal equal opportunities legislation and advocating proactive measures toward equality of outcome, the promotion of family-friendly workplace policies appears to follow the Nordic tradition of citizenship. On the other hand, since the workplace policies – in practice often varied, motivated by self-interest, and primarily directed at women – question the exclusive responsibility of the public sector to guarantee citizens' work/family balance, they seem to undermine some basic tenets of the Nordic citizenship model. One may ask, how do the principles of universality and equality between the classes, regions and sexes, once so central to Nordic welfare regimes, match with the voluntary workplace policies of diverse, profit-seeking companies?

Conclusions

In this chapter, I have analysed the ways in which citizenship is redefined in 'Europeanizing' Finland, by examining policy texts on the reconciliation of work and family life from the 1980s to the 2000s. Currently in Finland, this discourse seems to be as much about care as about paid work obligations, which might be in contrast to some other European countries. In the policy texts, the 'citizen worker' is first and foremost a bearer of social rights to an increasing number of care leaves and services. While in the 1980s political citizenship is still visible in the texts (particularly those concerning gender equality), from the 1990s onwards it disappears, and the role of the citizen becomes rather to function as an active participant in the market (citizen consumer) and/or in the family (citizen carer).

In the policy discourse on work/family reconciliation this new re-articulation of citizenship is combined with a discursive shift toward a mixed economy of social care. The social right to public day-care services, guaranteed by the 'women-friendly welfare state', is largely ignored in the later texts on reconciliation, while the rights to family leave, enabled by 'family-friendly companies', receive more attention. Citizenship becomes increasingly defined in terms of a relationship to the market (labour market or the market of care services) and to the family. This re-privatization and re-familialization of care implies, above all, that families are to assume more responsibility for the care of their children. And employers and organizations are requested to support their employees' care responsibilities by offering family leaves and flexitime arrangements. Overall, the analysis indicates that whereas the changes in Finnish child-care policies have by and large been legitimized with reference to national developments, the active promotion of family-friendly workplace policies has been explicitly connected to, and thus makes use of, the social policies and policy instruments of the European Union.

Appendix 7.1: Empirical materials used in this chapter

Aikalisä perheelle (2002), Työmarkkinajärjestöjen kampanja perhevapaiden tasa-arvoisen käytön edistämiseksi –raportti, (ed.) Mira Stenholm, available at: www. akava.fi/upload/pdf/-MiraStenholmpdf.pdf.

HE (121/1995) Hallituksen esitys Eduskunnalle laiksi lasten kotihoidon tuesta annetun lain muuttamisesta.

HE (162/2004), Hallituksen esitys laeiksi lasten kotihoidon ja yksityisen hoidon tuesta annetun lain sekä elatusturvalain muuttamisesta.

KM (1980:23), Kansainvälisen lapsen vuoden 1979 Suomen komitea. VN: Helsinki.

KM (1992:35), Tasa-arvolain uudistamistoimikunnan mietintö. STM: Helsinki.

KM (1999:1), Isätoimikunnan mietintö. Sosiaali- ja terveysministeriö: Helsinki.

Laki naisten ja miesten välisestä tasa-arvosta annetun lain muuttamisesta (206/1995).

MONIKKO-hanke (2008), Perhe työssä, työ perheessä. Työn ja perheen yhteensovittamisen rajat ja mahdollisuudet työorganisaatiotoimijoiden, perheen ja sukupuolen näkökulmasta. Merja Turpeinen & Minna Toivanen. MONIKKO-hanke: Helsinki.

NU (1989:6F), Pohjoismaisen tasa-arvoyhteistyön toimintasuunnitelma vuoksiksi 1989–1993. Pohjoismaiden ministerineuvosto: Kööpenhamina.

Perhe ja työ (2004), Eduskunnan Naiskansanedustajien verkoston julkaisu 4, Kustannusliike Susi: Helsinki.

SITRA (2003), Pomot ja perheet. Työelämä ja perheiden hyvinvointi. Riikka Kivimäki & Katri Otonkorpi-Lehtoranta, Edita: Helsinki.

STAKES (1999), Elämää Euroopassa. Työn ja perheen yhdistämisen moninaiset tavat ja haasteet, (eds.) Minna Salmi & Johanna Lammi-Taskula. Työelämän ja perhe-elämän yhteensovittaminen –projekti, Seminaariraportti, Stakes: Helsinki.

STAKES (2004), Elämän kirjoa työpaikoille. Käsikirja työn ja perheen yhteen sovittajille. Jarna Savolainen, Johanna Lammi-Taskula & Minna Salmi. Stakes: Helsinki.

STM (1983:28), Työ- ja perhe-elämätyöryhmän muistio. Sosiaali- ja terveysministeriö: Helsinki.

STM (1992:13), Valtioneuvoston tasa-arvolakia koskeva selonteko. Sosiaali- ja terveysministeriö: Helsinki.

STM (1994:11), Pienten lasten hoitojärjestelmän kehittämistyöryhmän loppuraportti. Sosiaali- ja terveysministeriön työryhmämuistioita: Helsinki.

STM (1995) Työn ja perhe-elämän yhteensovittaminen Euroopan unionissa. Direktiiveistä käytännön toimenpiteisiin. Author: Eeva Raevaara. Tasa-arvon työraportteja 2/1995, Sosiaali- ja terveysministeriö: Helsinki.

STM (2001:28), Työ- ja perhe-elämän yhteensovittamista selvittäneen työryhmän (PEVA II) muistio. Sosiaali- ja terveysministeriö: Helsinki.

STM (2007:1), Tasa-arvo valtatiellä. Hallituksen tasa-arvo-ohjelman 2004–2007 loppuraportti, Sosiaali- ja terveysministeriö: Helsinki.
TM (1994) Täyttä elämää. Seminaari työn ja perheen yhteensovittamisesta 23.5.1994, (ed.) Riitta Martikainen. Työhallinnon julkaisu 78, Työministeriö: Helsinki.
TM (1998), Yritysten perheystävällisyys. Menetelmiä ja ehdotuksia perheystävällisyyden arvioimiseksi ja lisäämiseksi. Katriina Koskela. Työhallinto 191, TM: Helsinki.
Työaika naisnäkökulmasta (1982), Työaikakomitean varjokomitea: Helsinki.

Notes

1. The decision on this right was made in 1985, together with the integration of an alternative option, the child home-care allowance, in the family leave system (Hiilamo 2005).
2. Similarly, the policy texts on reconciliation no longer mention the public home help service as a solution for urgencies in which a sick child needs a caretaker or a home tidying-up (for example, *STM 1983:28*, 8). Instead, parents are encouraged to buy commercial household services (tax deductible since 1997) to manage their everyday life (for example, *STAKES 1999*, 2) or take a temporary child-care leave.

Part III
Neo-Colonial Care Relations in Europe

8
Gendering the Stranger: Nomadic Care Workers in Europe – a Polish-Italian Example

Lise Widding Isaksen

Introduction

Advertisements with headlines like 'Una donna Straniera' (a female stranger) can often be read in local newspapers in Sicily. Local people know that this means someone is looking for an Eastern European woman willing to work as a housemaid in private homes and take care of elderly persons. This is an expression of Italy's changed role in international migration, from being a sending country to becoming a receiving country. In 2007, nearly four million migrants lived in Italy. This is a considerable increase since 1997, when there were only one million migrants in Italy (ISMU 2007). In 2005, 64,000 work and residence permits were issued to Polish citizens in Italy (Nere 2006). Many of them are women working as professional healthcare workers in public and private hospitals. Jobs as domestic workers in the informal economy have also attracted thousands of Polish women to urban and rural areas in Italy.

Here I will analyse the global housemaid phenomenon by using qualitative data from Sicily, and I will discuss in particular how the social and emotional role of a Polish housemaid is negotiated and created in a Sicilian middle-class family context. The theoretical perspective is inspired by Georg Simmel's essay 'The Stranger'. In his text a stranger is a person and/or a nomadic trader who arrives in local contexts to offer services and goods as a response to a demand. Strangers are integrated into the economy: 'As long as the economy is essentially self-sufficient, or products are exchanged within a spatially narrow group, it needs no middleman: a trader is only required for products that originate outside the group' (Simmel 1908). Care deficits are a lack of self-sufficiency and develop a sense of scarcity in local communities. Demands for care open the doors for migrant carers (Hochschild 2002). Care has become a service produced in the global economy of care. This story analyses a Polish care worker in Italy and how she learned to feel and behave like a 'Polish housemaid'.[1] I will argue that local Sicilian traditions of community help are the cultural 'raw material' and the historical source on which contemporary Sicilian families base their solutions to local care problems by hiring women, no longer from a neighbouring *village*, but from a neighbouring *country*, in this case Poland.

The key informants in my fieldwork (the Pilati family) were one of the local families that hired a care worker from Poland to care for an elderly relative. Aunt Pippa was 88 years old and bedridden, suffering from cancer and incontinence. Her sister had died some months earlier with a similar diagnosis. The sister had been the mother of the middle-aged siblings Rita and Nick in the Pilati family. Rita and her sister-in-law (called here Helene) had taken care of Pippa's sister in shifts. No brothers, sons or grandchildren had shared the work with them. In local gender ideologies, care work is seen as a 'women's problem' (Andall 2000). These middle-aged family women had long shouldered the extra burden of this care work, but, coming on top of their paid work in the labour market and unpaid domestic work in their own homes, it had been a frustrating experience. Due to the physical and emotional stress involved, both of them had gained weight, developed sleep problems and experienced exhausting marital conflicts. Hiring a live-in care worker was in this case a middle-class way of maintaining bodily and mental health and also a strategy for balancing the social and internal systems of gendered divisions of labour.

Lene told me that Ewa was in her early fifties, and the family had been introduced to her at a shelter for homeless women organized by the Catholic Church in a neighbouring village. East European women looking for care work often lived there. Local families in need of temporary care workers saw the shelter as an informal labour agency. According to the local gossip, 'the female strangers', as they were called, demanded less pay than local care workers and were known to pay more respect to elderly people than local Italians. The Catholic priest had assured the Pilati family that all the care workers' papers (residence and work permits) were in order.[2] They trusted him and, after a short meeting between the Polish Ewa and Aunt Pippa, they decided to hire her. No written contract was signed and job instructions were given in informal talks and practical instructions. As a white, married, middle-aged and heterosexual woman, mother and grandmother, the family expected Ewa to have sufficient competence to care for Pippa. However, they did not want her to work in a 'Polish' manner, so they instructed her to do the housework and the care work according to their own standards.

In this context, public care was a stigmatized and unattractive solution. Private family care was the hegemonic norm and it was expected of Ewa that she should follow up and perform the care work as it had always been done in the family. Pippa and her sister used to clean the house every day. The sisters had had a fixed weekly menu based on local produce for more than twenty years. Ewa had to clean the house every morning and go to the local market to buy fresh fish, meat and vegetables. The Pilati family wanted her to use her practical and mental competence from her own care work back home as the basis for care work performed according to Sicilian norms.

Local gender ideologies

In Sicily, the sharing of housework between men and women is still a non-issue. Many men in local communities would rather take on a second job if the family has economic problems instead of letting their wives work. The Italian gender models are based on variations of masculine dominance and feminine subordination (Andall 2000). In the Pilati family, the daughter Rita had a full-time position in a public welfare office. Her brother worked in the county administration as a bookkeeper. He had a second job as a musician (piano and guitar) in the tourist industry. Most of this work was done late at night, and because of his heart problems he needed help from others to carry the instruments.

The Pilati family saw themselves as a decent family because they managed to find a private solution to their care problems. They avoided using public services, which would have stigmatized the family and given them a bad reputation as cold-hearted and ignorant people. Employing other women to do care work in private homes is an attractive alternative for families suffering from what they subjectively experience as a care deficit.

In the Pilati family, one of the male relatives was married to a Polish assistant nurse. This woman, Sonya, was a skilled care worker with experience of oncological treatment and care for terminally ill cancer patients in public hospitals in Poland. In Sicily, she worked in the informal community care system and took temporary jobs in people's homes. She did not take live-in jobs because they were, according to her, entry-level jobs for unskilled immigrant women. Sonya had achieved a good reputation as a competent and reliable care worker, and the Pilati family based their image of Polish women as warm, loving and caring persons on her.

After having worked a couple of months for Aunt Pippa, Ewa asked for an appointment with Lene Pilati to discuss her job instructions. She felt the work was harder and more energy-consuming than she had expected. Being a middle-aged mother of three grown-up children and grandmother to two small children, Ewa's energy had limits. At the meeting with Lene, she said she was exhausted, expressed her frustrations and demanded a change. Aunt Pippa's incontinence caused serious sleeping problems for her. Ewa had to walk her to the bathroom several times every night. Pippa was a heavy and overweight woman, and Ewa experienced that lifting and helping her in and out of bed was too heavy for her. The aunt was sleepy and hard to manoeuvre, and Ewa felt as if her bodily energy was being pushed to its limits. Instead, Ewa proposed that she could do more housework during the daytime and asked the family for permission to use incontinence diapers at night. Diapers would mean more stable sleep for both of them.

Lene Pilati discussed the idea with the rest of the family and with Pippa's doctor. The doctor was worried that diapers would worsen Aunt Pippa's sore skin problems in the back area and could not recommend their use. The family felt Aunt Pippa's dignity was at risk and decided that the use of diapers was not an acceptable solution according to their ideas of good care. Besides, the Pilati women shared an image of Aunt Pippa's 'civilized dignity' being better taken care of when the toilet could be used instead of diapers. However, Ewa insisted that good care could be organized differently. By presenting an alternative vision of the organization of the work she made the difference between care as *work* and care as *love* more clear.[3] The Pilati women's ideas about the use of diapers stemmed from experiences from the period when they cared for Pippa's sister. She had also been incontinent, but until her last day refused to use diapers. For the family women, the care was an obligation and they saw themselves as close and loving family members. Ewa referred to Pippa not only as a lovely person, but also as a source of work. She could not see that the quality of their particular relationship would be harmed if diapers were used. For her, the relationship to the aunt was embedded in a context of paid labour and not in a context of love and family care.

Power and dignity

Interestingly enough, in the discussions about the aunt's dignity, the issues of wetness and the smell of urine and other bodily fluids related to incontinence were absent. The odours of the old woman's body, the sounds from the body while sitting on the toilet seat and her need for help to use toilet paper were excluded from the agenda. The risk of infantilization and how the old woman herself experienced the exposed nakedness of the sexual areas of the body in front of a 'female stranger' were not explicitly verbalized. However, it seemed as if the Pilati family had a mental picture of the aunt 'as she used to be', as an imaginary rationality (Lacoff and Johnson 1980) that structured their actions and minds. Their picture of Pippa was of a proper and non-leaking person, well-dressed and mentally present as she walked on her own two feet to the toilet in the middle of the night. They thought she still had the capacity to perform the role of a civilized person with bodily control if Ewa helped her. By stressing Pippa's role as a respectable woman, they embodied her social class and moral authority (Skeggs 1997). Pippa was given the capacity to have a moral authority, and a class distinction between the two women was drawn.

In the talks about a possible re-drafting of the job instructions, their attitudes to 'body work' were revealed (Wolkowitz 2006). The body work in question involved intimate and messy contact with bodily products, touch and close proximity. From other studies, we know that exactly this kind of body work is stratified as the lowest of the low in hierarchies of care, particularly when it is performed for incontinent elderly women in private homes (Isaksen 2002). The outsourcing of intimate body work to Ewa stratified the power relations and linked intimate labour to a relatively powerless position. When Lene Pilati had taken the final no-diaper decision, she would not give Ewa the message herself. Thinking that the issue was of an intimate and taboo-like nature that would be difficult to verbalize in a decent way, she called up Sonya, the other Polish care worker in the family. She was asked to explain to Ewa in Polish that she was employed *especially because* of all the body work at night. 'This is what *Polish women* do as domestic helpers here in Sicily,' was the message Sonya was sent to give. The undertext is that Ewa was expected to act according to their expectations of a performance of the role as '*Polish*' in the '*Pilati way*'.

Ewa did not succeed 100 per cent in changing her working conditions, but the Pilati women understood her exhaustion and complaints. Instead of allowing the use of diapers, a technical solution was found. They rented a wheelchair with a toilet seat and installed it in Aunt Pippa's bedroom. Paradoxically, the toilet wheelchair materialized the leaking body the family wanted to keep socially invisible. However, Ewa did not fully approve of the solution because it neither helped her to get more stable sleep nor reduced all the lifting of the heavy body. She still had to help Pippa in and out of bed and onto the wheelchair several times every night.

Hochschild (1983) writes that feelings of disappointment and stress have a power dimension and a gender dimension. Disappointment is 'low' and related to a discrepancy between demanded and achieved control. Imagined female dignity is linked to hegemonic gender constructions and social stratification. Ewa contested the existing power relations in her workplace and the standards of work performance requested, but the middle-class Pilati women had the power to define standards and norms. Ewa's ideas about workplace democracy initiated a dialogue. Her opinions about *how* the work could be performed differently were listened to, but in the end she had to accept the conditions the family decided on for her.

The language the Pilati family used in the interview about the negotiations illustrates the local categorisation of domestic maids into ethnic categories. Images were linked to the 'Polishness' that was seen as a commodity they purchased as a service. The service included body work, housework, cooking and cleaning on a 24-hour basis. Since they thought Polish people paid more respect to the elderly than locals did, they saw Ewa's services as a qualitatively better alternative than local care. The family paid for a middle-class decency that is associated with a clean home, proper food and a dressed and clean aunt-body taken care of in the family. In other words, the family based the respect they pay to local norms that govern the performance of the 'correct female presentation of civilization' on a service purchased on the global market.

Intimate labour and welfare rights

Ewa attached ideas of social and welfare rights to her role as a worker. When her daughter gave birth to her second grandchild, she asked for unpaid welfare leave to go home to visit and welcome the new baby. However, the Pilati family had the idea that 'good care' included a stable presence. Aunt Pippa would probably be stressed if another care worker came to replace her Polish carer. She was told that if she went home to Poland to pay the traditional visit after childbirth, she would lose the job. Lene Pilati said it was easy for them to find another care worker who was willing to provide stability in caring for Pippa. They already knew a Romanian care worker in the neighbourhood. She was looking for a new job and demanded less pay. In this evaluation, the market price for the care was based on the norm of 'the cheaper, the better'. The Pilati family saw the women as strangers and traders in the global economy of care and took the idea of 'free choice' for customers and price competition among traders for granted. Ewa and her relationship to Pippa were not included in their reflections and priorities. Afraid to lose the job, Ewa stayed. A few weeks later, Aunt Pippa died and Ewa left Italy and went home to Poland.

This narrative sheds light on the existence of a plurality of ideas and differentiations in cultures of care. Ewa saw her care as *paid work* and, as a worker, expected to have a democratic right to influence how the work was organized and to be granted welfare leave when necessary. She was an active agent who struggled to change her working conditions and to follow her own ideas of individual life organization. She had different ideas and attached different meanings to what 'Polish' work could be like. She resisted being defined as 'a particular type' as Simmel would have formulated it. By confronting the categorical image of 'Polish women' as humble, unskilled and poor housemaids, she made the intersections between gender, ethnicity and class visible.

In a sociological perspective, Ewa can be 'the stranger' who is *not* perceived in terms of what she *does*, but by virtue of what is *done to her* (Simmel 1908). She did not have enough power to define her own reality in her everyday life (Berger and Luckman 1966) and had to adjust herself to the conditions given to her. The Sicilian middle-class family and local gender normativity constructed and structured her participation in local social life. The social construction of 'dirty work' as 'Polish body work', and the low social status linked to it, stratified the power relations in which Ewa's social and cultural role was created. She had to perform the role of temporary care worker, providing the stability on which the Pilati family based their social and economic integration. The contradictions between the norms of stability and nomadic temporality illustrate that she is neither 'in' nor 'out' and attach, therefore, a marginal profile to her social role.

Plural economies

By seeing care workers as traders and sellers of services, the service production can be related to global markets. In this context, the financial possibility of hiring a paid care worker was related to the Italian welfare state's cash allowance of €400 a month for families with dependent elderly members living in their own homes. The Catholic Church received state support for its shelter for homeless women, where nuns worked as voluntary unpaid care workers lodging immigrant women and helping them find a job. Nuns have long traditions of following up and taking care of immigrant women (Yeates 2009). The Italian welfare services subsidized private solutions and facilitated the development of market demand for cheap household labour. Local care crises were solved with assistance from an informal (and perhaps also illegal?) labour agency organized as a voluntary and altruistic service by the Catholic Church. The international currency situation made payments in euros 'gold' compared with the value of the Polish zloty. Immigration policy structured the inflow of immigrants. On the local level, people experienced new expansion in the tourist economy. This caused harder working conditions for local musicians caused by the arrival of performers from former Eastern European countries who worked for lower pay. Local musicians had to work longer hours and take on more jobs for less pay. Increased economic insecurity gave rise to a need for several sources of income.

Immanence and transcendence

Simone de Beauvoir, in her book *The Second Sex* (1949 [1970]), defined the feminine gender role as immanent and dominated by lack of risk-taking and by stagnation. Transcendence was attached to masculinity and linked to ideas of innovation and ability to cross social, cultural and political borders. The story about Ewa and her struggle to get more control over her working and living conditions reveals that global care workers have transcendent capacities since they cross social, geographical and cultural borders. But the role given to them as care workers seems to be based on immanent norms of femininity.

The stranger has a transcendent social role. But a stranger is also a part of a collective's culture of immanence in the sense that there will (always) be human relations where the basic condition is a mobile spatial life and the *symbol of mobility* (or nomadism) is the cultural significance of the human relations the stranger is connected to. The maintenance of local cultures (as in Sicily) is achieved with support from strangers and immigrants who bring possibilities for both immanence and transcendence.

A transcendent aspect here are the 'new eyes' Ewa brings to the Pilati family when she insists that intimacy is the service she sells as *paid work*. Previously, her work was done within the family as 'a labour of love' (Finch and Groves 1983) and was invisible in the local gender ideologies as *work* associated with welfare rights. Local community care had mainly been based on help from neighbourhood wives on an informal day-to-day basis and linked to reciprocity and norms for mutual help between local women. However, women from the neighbourhood did not work as live-in carers for elderly people. Their paid-by-the hour services could not solve the new care deficit problems due to the gap between supply and demand for 24-hour live-in care for the very frail elderly. The normative changes migrant care workers may bring to local cultures can give rise to a new diversity in intimate social relations. The growth of multicultural and paid care work may make possible the development of a new morality based on what Rosenmayr and Køckeis (1963) called 'intimacy at a distance' in Sicilian culture.

Globalization, class and gender

In Sicily, care workers had traditionally been recruited from neighbouring villages and the local community. Today, *neighbourhood* wives are replaced by *'neighbour-country'* wives. In Central Europe, the traditional neighbourhood wives came from lower social classes and many travelled from one village to another to find temporary care work and housework (Verdier 1981). A nomadic lifestyle was normal, and employers preferred 'female strangers' because of the intimate nature of the work. The norm was to keep intimate labourers at a distance socially and geographically. Global markets bring a new care economy and an institutionalization of temporality. The emotional costs for the workers can be a limitation on the possibility of listening and following one's own feelings and ideas about how quality care can be performed. In occupational health research, the experience of being ignored as an individual and treated as insignificant is understood to be a risk factor, since it is associated with lowered vitality and reduced health (Staland-Nyman et al. 2008).

From the employer's perspective, the change from unpaid obligations to paid care workers may improve their quality of life. Both the middle-aged Pilati women had been totally exhausted after a long period of providing terminal care for Pippa's sister. Night shifts had drained them of energy and left them tired and stressed during the day. Helene Pilati, married to a musician with heart problems, still worked many night-shifts carrying the piano up and down from stages in restaurants and in and out of the car late at night.

In Central Europe in the 18th and 19th centuries, cooks, cleaners and care workers normally travelled from village to village to work by the hour or by the day (Verdier 1981). They belonged to a culture of temporariness. The contemporary paradox is that migrant carers sell 'stability' even if they come today and leave tomorrow. They do not always have the freedom to come and go, since they are fixed in a spatial group such as, for instance, a private family in one particular social and cultural community. Their position in the group is determined by the fact that they have *not* belonged to it from the beginning. This gives them an innovative role since they *import* qualities into the group that do not and *cannot* stem from the group itself.

One innovative quality is the unity of social distance and the particular intimacy that comes with dependency built on corporality. Distance in this context means that the care worker, who is (spatially) close, is (emotionally) distant. Ewa created emotional and social stability for a family whose labour market integration is marked by a lack of stability. But as a worker she had to perform complex kinds of care for an incontinent individual. The leaking body is culturally associated with unpleasant smells and fluids and the touch of intimate body parts. Her initiative to organize the care in a different way illustrates an attitude related to intimate care as paid work for a person she did not know very well.

Global care workers can be strangers in different ways. They are normally not owners of land and usually pay no taxes. They are considered to be temporarily present and contribute to the maintenance of an immanent image. Ewa was not 'one of us' in the family, but her work kept up the appearances of a respectable middle-class family. Respectability is a key characteristic of what it means to belong, to be worthy and to be an individual. To maintain an image of respectability is an important marker of social class (Skeggs 1997). Ewa produced 'Polishness' as a particular service. This service was constructed according to the cultural hierarchical traditions in which local housemaids had been placed as servants. But the family expected from her a *particular* kind of service because of the stereotyped understanding of Polish people as paying more respect than Italians for the elderly. This was the emotional surplus value of her work. The social role she was given was to act *as if* she was local (one of them) but as a stranger she was expected to add an ethical respect that the family experienced as lost among local women. In this perspective the outsourcing of the intimate care from a local to a global market can be understood as an idea of importing more respectful and respected care to a culture where intimate elder care is losing social and economic status.

By analysing how migrant carers produce care in local contexts and perform a role according to the norms and traditions in the culture they live in, I have discussed how new interactions between global and local norms may challenge and change cultures of care. Contemporary patterns of informal care work in Sicily include the crossing of national borders and payment related to different foreign currencies. Global care workers have become an integrated part of the local economy, and the patterns of social stratification and conservative gender ideology are in flux. Images and ideas from the old culture seem to be 'the raw material' to which families expect their new care workers to adjust. But the 'surplus' value they expect from migrant carers seems to be related to an attitude that 'respect' is lost as a value in the local culture of care, but that it can be bought as a commodity from an international market.

Culturally the ageing process and loss of control over basic bodily functions might imply humiliation and a loss of social respect. The Pilati family gave Ewa a job instruction designed to prevent a loss of dignity and social respect and to cover up lost bodily control. The low social status of the particular kind of intimate care work was an important part of the forging of class distinctions between 'them' and 'her'. By 'outsourcing' the less pleasant and emotionally complex intimate work to a foreign woman they kept up an image of respectability for both the bedridden aunt Pippa and for themselves. In addition to the class and gender dimension there is an ethnic dimension. The 'respect' was attached to 'Polishness', and through the creation of the role of 'Polish housemaid' they perceived the employment of Ewa as a purchase of better-quality care for a good price and without creating socially visible changes in their middle-class reputation.

The maintenance of local cultures of care in Sicily is achieved with support from strangers and immigrants who bring possibilities for both immanence and transcendence. The immanent aspects are related to the buying of 'cover-up' services and create an image of traditional social stability and control. The transcendent aspect is the commodification of intimate values and the idea that 'respect' can be purchased from a stranger who comes today and leaves tomorrow.

Notes

1. The empirical data comes from the project 'Gender and Globalization: Care Across Borders' funded by the Norwegian Research Council 2002–2006. A part of the project studied Polish care workers in Italy. The interview with the Pilati family where the Polish housemaid Ewa worked was carried out in Sicily in December 2004. The story about Ewa was told to me by her employer, Miss Pilati.
2. This was in 2003, before Poland entered the European Community. Since 2004, Polish people have been able to move freely and find work in all EU countries.
3. For a more extensive discussion on care as labour and/or as love, see Finch and Groves (1983).

9
Migrant Women and Defamilialization in the Spanish Welfare State

Susana Climent

Introduction

Familialism or familism characterizes Southern European welfare states such as Spain. Familialism places the right and obligation of care and the performance of domestic tasks within the family and familialism's gender order assigns these responsibilities to women. Recently there has been an increase in households' outsourcing of care and domestic tasks to economic migrant women, reflecting an incipient defamilialization process in the Spanish welfare state. The legal frame of this defamilialization process via the market is the legislation on paid care/domestic work and the legislation that aims at ordering migrant women's access to the Spanish labour market. The defamilialization process of the Spanish welfare state relies on a gendered and origin-based outsourcing of care and domestic tasks.

The chapter is structured in four sections. I first provide an overview of the main characteristics of the Spanish welfare state, focusing on the concept of familialism and defamilialization. In the second section, I provide data which illustrates the incipient defamilialization process in the Spanish welfare state. This data include evidence of the increasing economic independence of Spanish women and the outsourcing of care and domestic tasks and its relationship to migration flows. In the third section, the focus is on the legal frame of this defamilialization process. I first analyse the legislation on paid care and domestic work, and, secondly, the ordering of and legislation on non-European migration, such as the 2005 regularization process of irregular migrant workers, and the links between both legislations. The concluding section outlines how access to citizenship rights is being facilitated within this incipient defamilialization process, and addresses the role of the state also in the defamilialization process.

The Spanish welfare state: familialism and defamilialization in the literature

Studies on welfare issues were fruitfully launched by the debate on the three welfare regimes characterized by Esping-Andersen (1990). As a result of the feminist critique that Esping-Andersen ignored the gender dimension in his analysis of social policy models, the importance of deepening the analysis of the role of the family in the family-state-market triad of welfare provision came to be emphasized. New analytical dimensions were incorporated in the study of welfare regimes (O'Connor 1993; 1996; Orloff 1993) and new theoretical models were developed (Lewis 1997; 1998; Sainsbury 1999; Hobson 2002). The feminist critique of the welfare regimes approach developed the concept of defamilialization in response to the concept of decommodification (which indicates independence from labour market participation for sustainable living). Defamilialization is first defined as 'the terms and conditions under which people engage in families, and the extent to which they can uphold an acceptable standard of living independently of (patriarchal) "family" participation' (McLaughlin and Glendinning 1994, 65) with the aim of focusing on 'the extent to which packages of legal and social provisions have altered the balance of power between men and women, between dependants and non-dependants, and hence the terms and conditions under which people engage in familial or caring arrangements' (McLaughlin and Glendinning 1994, 66).

The welfare regime approach has adopted the concept of defamilialization and defines it as 'the degree to which households' welfare and caring responsibilities are relaxed either via welfare state provision or via market provision' (Esping-Andersen 2000, 74). Deepening the study of the role of the family in welfare provision also developed the focus on the study of the delivering of care (paid and unpaid) and the gendered access to citizenship and citizenship rights. These approaches point out the increasing importance of migration and colonial and globalization processes together with the delivering of paid care (also called the commodification of care) and paid domestic work within the welfare state and the global care chains (Williams 1987; 1995; Yuval-Davis 1991; Ungerson 1997; Hochschild 2001b).

In parallel to the feminist critique, other scholars addressed Esping-Andersen's lack of systematically including Southern European countries. This critique focused on further research on Southern European case studies, arguing for differentiating these countries from the rest of the continental welfare regime countries, and also arguing for establishing a fourth welfare regime typology: the Mediterranean (Sarasa and Moreno 1995; Ferrera 1996; Lessenich 1996; Moreno 2001). According to Ferrera (1996) and Flaquer (2004), some of the aspects that distinguish Mediterranean welfare states are, first of all, a dualistic income-maintenance system fragmented according to occupational status (with a strong protection of the core sector of the labour force versus a weak subsidization of the irregular, non-institutionalized and grey labour markets). Secondly, social protection expenses are below the European average, but social protection expenditure presents contrasting levels: high and low levels of different areas of social protection reflect that these welfare states have irregularly developed social citizenship rights. For example, they have developed a near-universalistic health system (with an extended scope of private provision) but an underdeveloped social service system that relies on the family for welfare and care provisions through private strategies and arrangements.

Whether there is a Mediterranean welfare regime or whether Southern European welfare states are a subcategory within the continental welfare regime (Esping-Andersen 2000; Katrougalos and Lazaridis 2003), the literature agrees that familism or familialism is one of the main characteristics of South European welfare states (Saraceno 1994; 1995; Esping-Andersen 1995; 2000; Flaquer 2004; amongst others). Chiara Saraceno defines familism as a 'permanent trust on the family, on its intergenerational solidarity and on its gender structure as provider of work and assistance' (Saraceno 1995, 271).[1] Familism is also understood as an 'excessive' contribution of the family to social protection, compared to other institutions such as the state (Flaquer 2000, 154).

The Mediterranean welfare state delegates to the family the responsibility of welfare provision, refraining from developing family policy itself (Valiente 1996; Esping-Andersen 2000, 74). Thus, universal social rights are circumscribed to the public health system and the public education system for three-year-olds and above. The social organization of care and domestic tasks is not an area of intervention for the Mediterranean welfare state. For example, home-based care for children is regulated within the legislation on domestic work (Valiente 1997, 112), as if it were a subsidiary task of domestic work. Care for the disabled has only recently begun to be regulated in Spain; however, it focuses on family care (named non-professional) without taking into consideration paid elderly care delivered in the home and performed by domestic workers (Peterson 2007, 276). Research shows that 'the caring function in the private sphere has not been clearly defined in social policies, nor does it provide an alternative route to access social protection' (León 2002, 155). Some argue that 'The deficit of the Mediterranean welfare systems is not so much a result of its low decommodification as it is of its low defamilialisation' (Flaquer 2004, 53). Thus, the role of the state, with its underdeveloped family policy, is to ensure that the family is the first to exercise the function of the provision of welfare (Daly and Lewis 2000), leaving the role of the market and the state as residual or subsidiary.

The subsidiarity principle is also part of familialism (Sainsbury 1999; Katrougalos and Lazaridis 2003). This principle is a legacy of post-World War II social Catholicism (Esping-Andersen 2000, 112) based on limiting public intervention to situations in which primary social networks fail. Also, the principle of subsidiarity implies that the type of support provided by the welfare state when families cannot confront social risks is biased towards money transfers rather than the development of services. In this sense, the subsidiarity principle is related to the male breadwinner–female caretaker model (Sainsbury 1999, 255). Esping-Andersen argues that familist social policy might create a division between those inside and outside the labour market, which creates gender differences due to the male-breadwinner model (2000, 31). So, familism relies on a particular gendered organization within the family for delivering welfare.

The family's caring function takes the form of intergenerational solidarity, reliance on women's role within the family, and traditional gender roles and gender relations. With regards to care, intergenerational support is reflected in the important role grandmothers play when it comes to taking care of children (Tobío 2003). This is the first private strategy used in Spain for what has been called the reconciliation of private, professional and family life. All the female family members have a crucial role in welfare provision. Flaquer (2004) identifies the adult married women as primary care providers and Saraceno (1995, 279–80) argues that familist welfare states rely not so much on the male-breadwinner model as on the female-caretaker model. That is, familism prioritizes women's responsibility in providing assistance, particularly married women and mothers, over men's responsibility in providing economic wellbeing.

The familist welfare state pictured above is going through an incipient defamilialization process in Spain. The study of the Spanish welfare state has only recently related the concept of defamilialisation to the outsourcing of care and domestic work to economic migrant women, indicating that defamilialisation results in an ethno-stratification of the labour market (Flaquer 2004, 39; Catarino and Oso 2000). Women's economic independence and trends in the outsourcing of care and domestic work in Spain is analysed below.

Defamilialization: outsourcing of care and domestic work and migration flows

Despite the fact that familism is well ingrained in Mediterranean welfare states, Spanish society has had a deep and fast transformation in the past 25 years, particularly in the lives of women. Across Western Europe, Spanish women have taken a leading part in accessing the public sphere of the labour market. According to Eurostat data, Spanish women's employment rate had the biggest percentage point increase across EU-15 between 1995 and 2006 (from 31.7 to 53.2 per cent), although it is around 4 percentage points below European averages, as opposed to Spanish men's employment rate which is above such averages. Also, women's unemployment rate had the biggest decrease between 1996 and 2007 in Spain across EU-15 (from 23.8 to 10.9 per cent). Finally, according to data from the Instituto de la Mujer (the Spanish Woman's Institute; the institutional gender equality body at national level), Spanish women had the second highest increase in activity rates between 1997 and 2006 across EU-15 (from 36.7 to 47.4 per cent). Thus, women's participation in the Spanish labour market, despite being below EU averages, is rapidly increasing, reflecting one of the most important social changes in Spain.

Spanish public institutions have stated that one of the consequences of the increasing number of employed women is a change in households' and families' organization towards a dual-earner model, a process not accompanied by equal sharing of care and domestic tasks between men and women (Consejo Económico y Social 2004). According to the Woman's Institute, the time women spend on paid labour almost doubled between 1993 and 2001, whereas time men spend on paid labour has remained stable. On the other hand, time women spend on domestic tasks has been reduced by 6 per cent in that period, whereas men's time spent on domestic tasks has increased by 26 per cent. Still, women spend, on average, almost three more hours a day than men on activities related to household maintenance and family care (Instituto Nacional de Estadística 2004). This gender gap is bigger compared to other European countries: in Belgium women spend, on average, more than 1.5 hours more a day than men; in Denmark 1 hour; in France almost 2 hours, as in Estonia, in Hungary and in Slovenia (Eurostat 2003).

However, studies show that in Spain it is becoming more difficult to rely on family members and other reliable networks for caring tasks. The shift towards the market for caring services is more frequent, particularly amongst double-earner couples and single-headed households

(Consejo Económico y Social 2006). The domestic sector (the economic sector where paid non-institutionalized care and paid domestic work takes place) is known for having a high volume of labour in the grey economy – twice as big as the one developed in the formal economy. Whether in the formal or informal labour market, this outsourcing of care and domestic tasks to the domestic sector reflects incipient changes in the familist social organization, and, as we will see next, economic migrant women play an important role in these changes.

Mediterranean countries share a shift in migration flows from being countries that exported migrants to being countries that now receive migrants (King et al. 2000, 8), especially from their former colonies. Migration growth in Spain is bigger than in any other European country and it is part of the global growth of migration flows, characterized by the UN as the second age of migrations (Pajares 2007, 18). Spain has, after the USA, the second-highest positive net migration in the world (UN 2006). In Spain, the augmentation of migration flows is marked by its feminization and by its economic nature. Although the following data do not include irregular migrants, they do reflect this increase: according to the Ministerio de Trabajo e Inmigración (Spanish Ministry of Labour and Immigration), at the end of 1996 there were over 500,000 foreigners with residence permits and by the end of 2007 almost 4 million. According to the census data of 1991 and 2001, female migration to Spain increased by 417 per cent during those 10 years. It evolved from a migration of European women settled mainly in costal touristic areas, to a migration of Latin American women who represent the *new female migration*: women travelling alone responsible for the economic wellbeing of their families back home and concentrated in the metropolitan areas of Madrid and Catalonia (Consejo Económico y Social 2003). Latin American migration in Spain is the only type where women outnumber men. Between 1998 and 2007, Latin American women represented from 11 to 16 per cent of all foreigners (women and men) with residence permits and they made up to 36 per cent of all foreign women with residence permits in 2007.

Spanish legislation on (non-EU) migrants aims at ordering migration flows and at adapting them to the labour market's needs, for example by establishing yearly quotas. However, these policies do not prevent irregular migrants from accessing the Spanish labour market, so the government has implemented several regularization processes for migrants since the beginning of the 1990s. The last one, during 2005, was a legalization process for migrants working irregularly and who were not self-employed. This process's novelty was the requirement to have a written job offer and an effective Social Security affiliation (that is, demonstrating being a contributor to the Social Security system) before obtaining work and residence permits. If we compare the data available on the affiliation of foreign women to Social Security before and after this last regularization process, we see the relevance of the Special Regime of Home Workers among migrant women. The Special Regime of Home Workers sets the contributory obligations and benefit rights of people employed in the domestic sector, and includes home-based care tasks (except for the care of people with disabilities). In January 2005 there were 76,147 foreign workers in the Special Regime of Home Workers, 92 per cent of whom were women. In January 2006, at its height in affiliation numbers, the number of foreign workers was 250,018, out of which more than 88 per cent were women (data from the Ministerio de Trabajo e Inmigración and the Ministerio del Interior, the Spanish Ministry of Internal Affairs). So, after the legalization process of 2005, there were around 184,000 new affiliations to this Special Regime, which represent over one third of the total new affiliations of this process. Although the proportion of foreign workers in this Regime has always been significant, Latin American female workers played a leading role in this increase.

In January 2005 and in January 2006 more than 65 per cent of the foreign workers in this Special Regime were from Latin America (particularly from Ecuador and Colombia, and after the regularization process a very significant increase of workers from Bolivia). Outside Latin America, a very significant increase of workers from Romania, who represent over 10 per cent of the foreign workers in this Regime, was also noticeable. Economic migrant women coming to Mediterranean countries share a common characteristic in their type of labour insertion: the main employment niche is domestic service and home-based care work. This regularization process and the legislation on home-based care and domestic tasks inform the legal frame of the defamilialization process in the Spanish welfare state.

The legal frame of the defamilialization process

Domestic work legislation in Spain applies to the outsourcing of all tasks performed within or for the home, including home-based care (except for people with disabilities). The Decree of the Social Security's Special Regime of Domestic Work of 1969[2] (nowadays known as the Special Regime of Home Workers, the term used in this chapter) established the basis for the contributory obligations and benefit rights of the sector. The original text of the Francoist (pre-democratic) regime is in force nowadays with few adjustments. The Royal Decree of the Family

Household Service of 1985[3] regulates the labour-contract aspects of this occupation. As we will see, these laws have embedded second-class citizenship and worker conceptions.

The Spanish Social Security system is segmented between the General Regime (which embraces most of the labour force) and several Special Regimes not integrated in the former, amongst which is the Special Regime of Home Workers. There is the long-term political consensus for simplifying the Spanish Social Security system into two regimes: the General Regime and the Special Regime for the self-employed. It is unclear which of the two the Special Regime of Home Workers will be integrated into in the future. However, nowadays the Special Regime of Home Workers stands by itself and has particularities with regards to affiliation, contributions, benefits and protection. The Special Regime of Home Workers establishes two ways of contributing to Social Security and accessing social protection, depending upon the number of households where the work is delivered and the number of hours of work. That is, there is a clear distinction between domestic service delivered exclusively in or for one household for a minimum of 80 hours per month and domestic service delivered in or for several households during a minimum of 72 hours per month distributed across at least 12 days. In the first case, the head of household is responsible for registering the worker with Social Security and for paying 75 per cent of the contributions. In the latter case, the worker is responsible for registering and for the full amount of the contributions to the Social Security system.

For all of the domestic workers attached to the Special Regime, the basis of the contributions is the minimum level, and thus benefits strongly differ from those other occupations attached to the General Regime of Social Security with a higher rate of contribution. The level and type of benefits in the Special Regime of Home Workers are significantly reduced in comparison to those enjoyed in the General Regime. For example, the Special Regime does not provide access to unemployment benefits and sickness benefit does not apply as early as it does on the General Regime (the third sick-day), but as late as the 29th day. Also, while enjoying sickness benefit or during maternity leave, workers are solely responsible for paying the contributions in full. Finally, any protection against work-related accidents and illnesses is excluded within this Social Security Special Regime and there is no right to early retirement either.

The Royal Decree of the Family Household Service of 1985 establishes the contractual aspects of domestic work and home-based care tasks. The most significant aspect of this Decree is the determinant factor that the work is delivered within a private household, which is considered a special context. This particularity of the occupation subordinates workers' rights to employers' rights: the legislation appeals to the constitutional rights of privacy and private family life over labour rights. The place where care and domestic tasks are delivered is so important that the legislation associates the services delivered to the particular space of the house up to the point of regulating the possibility of attaching the worker to the actual space (the house) where work is performed. This means that the regulation includes the possibility that the contract remains when the ownership of the household changes if work is performed during seven days after this change of ownership. This aspect is reminiscent of the medieval subjection of workers to the land or to the master's house (López Gandía and Toscani Giménez 2006, 44).

The legislation on the working conditions of domestic work also argues that the labour relationship for family household services is of a special nature. Because it is delivered in the domestic sphere of the household, it is stated that the relationship is based on mutual trust and flexibility. Thus, basic aspects such as the contract's duration and other working conditions are left to a *common agreement* between the worker and the employer, and there is no obligation to establish a written contract: it can be an agreed upon, spoken contract. Still, the legislation does regulate some aspects of working conditions. For example, with regards to remuneration it establishes the minimum wage if the work is full time. However, up to 45 per cent of the wages can be paid in kind (housing, food, and so on) instead of in cash. When it comes to working time, full-time work is 40 hours a week; however these 40 hours are of *effective work*, which means that time of presence is excluded. Time of presence is understood as non-working time but with permanent availability for unforeseen needs. Thus, flexibility and availability are considered *natural* to the working conditions but are not reflected in wages and nor are they accounted for in working time. Finally, the legislation on the labour aspects of family household services does not include any collective rights.

The Spanish familist welfare state has loosely regulated private market arrangements for the delivery of home-based care and domestic services. The analysis of the contractual aspects and of the social rights attached to the occupation makes clear that it is under-protected (for example, there are no basic benefit rights such as unemployment) and under-regulated (for example, there are no collective agreements, no requirement for formalizing the contract, no professional categories, and the law for preventing labour-related accidents does not apply to this economic sector). Its under-protection and under-regulation place the occupation within the private arrangements of the informal economy rather than in the formal labour market and subject to workers' legislation. This unequal treatment of the occupation compared to other, more regulated, occupations has been considered a case of indirect gender discrimination (López Gandía and Toscani Giménez 2006, 58). Recently there has been a political debate on the need to reform the legislation on domestic work. The political debate started in 2005 and sometimes was linked to the regularization process of migrant workers done that same year, which is analysed below.

The last regularization process of migrant workers took place in Spain in 2005. This process targeted those irregular migrant workers who were not self-employed. This process was considered of an exceptional nature; a transitory openness of the 'second' gate of admission 'to full or partial [citizenship] membership, with its associated rights and obligations' (Lister 2003, 47), granted under particular circumstances.

The government justified this process because of the high number of foreigners in Spain and because of the will to *normalize* their presence. As stated in the Royal Decree[4] shaping the process, *normalization* was bounded to labour market participation: 'Due to the high number of foreigners that are today in the Spanish territory without authorization, the stable [official] channels of workers' admission must be temporarily excepted in order to consider a normalization measure of the situation of such workers, in any case bound to a future labour relationship.' The process established that irregular migrants who had a demonstrable job offer and who could also prove they had been living in Spain for the previous six months, could access a preliminary residence and work permit for one year. This also applied to foreigners with a deportation order. Such permits would come into effect when the first contributions to Social Security were made. The demonstrable job offer had certain requirements: it had to be written and signed by both parties and, generally, the job offer had to be at least equivalent to six months of full-time employment.

The administrative requirements[5] established two paths within the regularization process: some requests had to be made by the employers (the intention being to ensure that the job offers were real) and others by the migrant workers. The latter applied only to domestic workers in more than one household because the two paths were based on who was responsible for fulfilling the Social Security contributions. That is, requests were made by employers only when they were responsible for paying for the migrant workers' Social Security, and requests were made by migrant employees when it was their responsibility. So, the regularization process established a distinction between domestic workers working for one or more households: the same distinction made in this occupation's legislation.

Thus, domestic workers working for one household depended upon the head of household's will and agency to be *normalized* since, in this case, the head of household is responsible for registering the worker with Social Security and for paying 75 per cent of the contributions. Domestic workers working for more than one household had to gather something similar to letters of intent signed by the different heads of household guaranteeing working activity during six months. However, they depended upon their active role to initiate the regularization process since, in this case, the worker was responsible for registering with Social Security and paying the full contributions. These differentiated procedures reflect the emphasis put on Social Security contributions as proof of the required commitment to labour market participation. Payments made to Social Security were pursued until the working permit expired.

The regularization process established requirements for a written and demonstrable job offer *even* in the case of hiring domestic workers. This could be seen as a step further towards regulating working agreements in the domestic sector, because this written requirement had to include some aspects of the working conditions that otherwise could have been left to a verbal and informal agreement. For example, the written requirement had to include the starting day of the job, the working hours per month, and the number of working months when work was delivered in one household or the number of monthly working hours when work was delivered in several households. However, in both cases this information was required only to ensure that the minimum working hours were met and thus the obligation was discharged to contribute to Social Security. As we shall see, while the requirements of the regularization process focused on payments of contributions and on ensuring minimum working hours adjusted to these contributions, the regularization process placed less emphasis on controlling working conditions; it thus focused more on workers' duties than on workers' rights.

The regularization process exemplifies how gendered and origin-based is the domestic sector in Spain. As stated earlier, around one third of regularized migrant workers belonged to the domestic sector and almost all of them were women (in the informal labour market, which is twice as big as the formal, migrant women are also the most numerous). While the regularization process provides a chance to obtain social rights, regularization in the domestic sector provides limited access to these rights compared to other occupations. It provides work and residence permits, which indeed are cherished for irregular migrants, but only provides access to limited social rights because it is an occupation not truly recognized nor regulated as labour. It is interesting to note that rights obtained through work performed in the private sphere of the home are always restrictive, whether this work is unpaid or is commodified in the formal or informal labour market, and this affects mainly women (native and migrant). Historically, across Europe domestic work and home-based care have not been regulated as other jobs have been in the public sphere and have provided limited access to rights (Sarti 2006; Platzer 2006). In this sense, future research should analyse the extent to which regular domestic work has or can qualitatively improve working conditions for regularized economic migrant women, beyond the limited access to social rights that it provides, and which has been explained in this chapter.

Conclusions

This chapter has explored the legal frame of households' outsourcing of care and domestic tasks in an incipient defamilialization process of the Spanish welfare state. As we have seen, the defamilialization process of the Spanish welfare state relies on a gendered and origin-based outsourcing of care and domestic tasks. These and other processes aimed at ordering migration flows are responsible for a gendered and origin-based access to partial substantive social citizenship rights amongst economic migrant workers. Migrant women's access to partial substantive social citizenship rights is more restricted, since the majority of them migrate to work in the private sphere of other countries, where families' needs and the rights of the private sphere of the home prevail over any other rights available in the labour market and gained through the commodification of labour. Thus, defamilialization via the market is not de-gendered: women are still the main (paid) care providers and the main (paid) domestic workers.

Although the state in familist welfare regimes does not develop family policies directly and delegates to the family the responsibility of welfare provision, it does have an important role in facilitating defamilialization via the market and contributing to fostering economic migrant women's role in the outsourcing and commodification of care and domestic work. The new care mix developing in the Spanish welfare state (as well as in other Southern European countries) has led some scholars to refer to a transition from a 'family' to a 'migrant-in-the-family' model of care

(Bettio et al. 2006, 272). I argue that in this transition the state resists taking responsibility for welfare provision, for which commodified care and domestic work (loosely regulated and under-protected so that it is inexpensive for both households and the state) and economic migrant women are both instrumental. In this sense, familist welfare states are in a transition towards facilitating that the family turns to the market for the purchase of welfare provision (thus maintaining a private responsibility for the delivering of care and domestic work) as opposed to shifting towards a public (state) responsibility for welfare provision. Thus, familist welfare states seem to follow the path of liberal welfare states rather than the path of social-democratic welfare states. In this transition, globalization as migration, as exemplified by the Spanish case, plays a major role in redesigning the welfare state.

Notes

1. The original text is in Spanish. All the quotes from original texts in Spanish are translated by me.
2. The original name is: 'Decreto 2346/1969, de 25 de noviembre, por el que se regula el Régimen Especial de la Seguridad Social del Servicio Doméstico'.
3. The original name is: 'Real Decreto 1424/1985, de 1 de agosto, por el que se regula la relación laboral de carácter especial del Servicio del Hogar Familiar'.
4. 'Real Decreto 2393/2004, de 30 de diciembre, por el que se aprueba el Reglamento de la Ley Orgánica 4/2000, de 11 de enero, sobre derechos y libertades de los extranjeros en España y su integración social.'
5. As stated in the ministerial order 'Orden PRE/140/2005, de 2 de febrero, por la que se desarrolla el procedimiento aplicable al proceso de normalización previsto en la disposición transitoria tercera del Real Decreto 393/2004, de 30 de diciembre, por el que se aprueba el Reglamento de la Ley Orgánica 4/2000, de 11 de enero, sobre derechos y libertades de los extranjeros en España y su integración social'.

10
Privatizing Neo-Colonialism: Migrant Domestic Care Workers, Partial Citizenship and Responsibility

Joan Tronto

Care work now

In autumn 2006, the Austrian conservative People's Party (ÖVP) and the opposition Social Democrats (SPÖ) agreed to issue temporary permits for thousands of illegal foreign care workers. 'Thousands of older people and those in need of care privately engage the services of illegal foreign workers for geriatric nursing and care purposes in the home; this is generally because they cannot afford to use licensed professional services' (Adam 2007). The Austrian change of heart occurred not as a result of a large-scale public discussion of this question but because the mother of the ÖVP's leader employed such a worker in her home. And so, the state did and did not acknowledge a problem: its reimbursement for care work was too low for Austrian citizens to pay for Austrian care workers. Rather than provide a greater welfare benefit, though, the state solved its crisis by looking the other way at the employment of cheaper border-crossing workers.

In 2008 in Italy, days after he approved a 'fast track' for immigrant home helps and carers, Welfare Minister Maurizio Sacconi stated that the Italian government was 'determined' to reduce the number of immigrants arriving in Italy (*Corriere della Sera* 2008; ANSA 2008).

* * * * *

As European Union members have succeeded over the past 20 years to include more women in the labour force, this success has opened a gap in caring labour that is difficult to fill. As Helma Lutz writes,

> Moreover, the re-evaluation of the asymmetrical relation between care work and gainful unemployment has never been on the agenda

of the EU or national state policies. All in all, care work has remained a female domain, reflecting the fact that many states now discuss the **compatibility** of gainful employment and family work as women's problem. (Lutz 2007, 188)

In many European states, either through conscious policy or a default lack of policy, migrant women workers, from other European states and beyond, have come to fill these gaps (Lutz 1997; 2002; 2008c; Hrženjak 2007). While European states vary greatly in their welfare regimes that provide public services for care that might substitute for home care and in their recognition and in their willingness to recognize migrant workers who are doing caring work, the reality is that with increasingly neo-liberal policies throughout Europe, the result is similar. In most European states, either through conscious policy or default of policy, migrant women workers have come to fill these caring gaps, working in circumstances that are different from those that protect workers in other spheres (Lutz 1997; 2002; 2008c).

The solution so far seems to be to hold to one set of principles and to act in a way inconsistent with those principles. Whenever government policies seem so contradictory, it suggests that there is a problem that does not fit easily within the existing political frameworks. In most of the social welfare states in Europe, long-term policy has been to provide relatively high wages to workers. Yet, when faced with the great expense of care work (especially caring that used to be provided by women outside of the formal labour market), governments have been reluctant to pay more and have looked the other way at illegal and temporary care workers. Why is this seeming contradiction tolerable?

The key moral and political question in this framing of the question is to notice the way in which responsibility for this problem has been assigned. It would be possible to frame this question as one of justice, or rights, or law. Yet, as will be shown below, those formulations have largely failed to make complete sense of this issue. An ethic of care would suggest that we focus on the care itself. In this context, that focus would require that we are attentive to the scope and context of migrant care work from its most intimate setting of the actual work itself to the broadest context of its place within the global systems of economic and political power. The meeting point of such narrow and broad concerns can be found in the question of responsibility: who is responsible for caring work? Once we think through this problem from this view, a clear pattern emerges. European states are privatizing responsibility by leaving the conundrum of 'work/life balance' to individual citizens, primarily women, to resolve.

To put responsibility at the centre of our inquiry requires that we change the moral framework that we use to approach a question. In her account of two types of *Moral Understandings*, Margaret Urban Walker contrasts a theoretical-juridical model of morality with an expressive-collaborative model. The theoretical-juridical model, in which principles are first fixed and then applied, 'shields from view the historical, cultural, and social location of the moral philosopher, and that of moral philosophy itself as a practice of intellectual and social authority' (Walker 1998, 35). In contrast, the expressive-collaborative model presumes that there is no single and unchallenged authority in moral thought. Instead, this model 'looks at moral life as a continuing negotiation *among* people' (Walker 1998, 60). This approach 'displaces formulaic deduction from theoretical principles with negotiated understandings; and displaces legislation from first principles or categorical imperatives with cooperative engagement in producing habitable communities, environments, and ways of life' (Code 2002, 160).

From the standpoint of Walker's 'ethic of responsibility', the Austrian and Italian cases cannot be studied only as a change in administration or legislation, but must be studied in terms of the complexity of the relationships they entail. But what is interesting is that all of those engaged in these cases were not parties to the ongoing discussion. The transnational migrants, who did the actual work of caring, were not parties in the discussion. What does their exclusion signify? Might an ethic of care, an ethic of responsibility, help us to see this exclusion differently?

The important theme for this chapter is that there is a link between two different levels of responsibility, and understanding the nature of care in the modern world will help us to make this link. There is a connection between the narrative of 'global inequality' and the narrative of 'taking care of my family'. These two conceptions of responsibility might clarify why international care workers pose a central challenge to the interrelated conceptions of what constitutes citizenship, what is just, and what is adequately caring.

The nature of contemporary migration

Currently, 2.9 per cent of the world's population are international migrants. In many more developed countries, the percentage of the population that is immigrant is much higher; in Europe as a whole, 6.4 per cent of the population are international migrants (International Organization for Migration 2005).

Immigration can be and often is, in itself, desirable. But as the UN High-level Dialogue on International Migration and Development stated early in their work, there is a difference between migration undertaken by choice and by necessity:

> Participants felt that it was essential to address the root causes of international migration to ensure that people migrated out of choice rather than out of necessity. They observed that people often had to migrate because of poverty, conflict, human rights violations, poor governance or lack of employment. (General Assembly of the United Nations 2006, 2)

Yet the distinction between choice and necessity is not an easy one to draw. The realities about care-worker migrants are complex.

Not all migrants are low-skilled care workers. Indeed, there are two different trends with care-worker immigrants, those who are highly skilled and those who are relatively low-skilled. Both advanced medical personnel and relatively low-skilled workers, such as orderlies and home-help workers, cross national borders. The reasons for the crossings might also be complex. In some cases, such as our Austria case above, or the case of a Czech nurse who does additional work across the border in Germany, the incentive may be the 'choice' to make more money. In some cases, skilled workers who cross international borders find themselves underemployed in their new location (Lutz 2008c). Historically, decisions to travel to do care work may have coincided with religious or other commitments (Yeates 2004). In other cases, though, the 'choice' may be less of an individual choice. It may result from a national policy to collect foreign remittances by sending workers abroad (Parreñas 2001). Sometimes, the 'choice' may result from a systemic problem: doctors and nurses trained in a developing nation may find that their ability to perform their duties are so severely compromised by the incapacities of their native health-care systems that they leave to be able to practise their profession competently (Garrett 2007). As a result, in Africa, 3 per cent of the world's trained health workers combat 24 per cent of the global disease burden (Physicians for Human Rights 2006). This 'brain drain' creates a problem in the nations from which those workers exit, not for the developed countries that benefit from trained medical personnel whom they have not borne the expense of training; in the end, Laurie Garrett (2007, 26–29) warns that as such workers leave for the west, the developing world will grow even more desperate in its needs for health-care professionals.

But there is another side to this question, which scholars call the 'care drain'. Increasingly, the work demanded by the more developed countries is more informal care work, that is, maintenance of the health and lifestyles of those who live in more advanced economies in order that those workers can be freed up to work more. This situation also has a pronounced effect on the lives of people around the globe. In Europe, domestic migrant workers move from East to West, from South to North, both within and beyond European borders.

Rhacel Parreñas (2001) called this situation a new kind of colonialism in which the extracted raw material is care labour. Now, people in the developed world benefit from a new product imported from the formerly colonial world – the labour of the individuals who come to do care work. The 'care drain' continues not only because of the desirability of these moves for individuals, but also because of national policies in sending countries that encourage them (Parreñas 2001). Indeed, remittances are the second largest source of income in developing countries (only surpassed by direct capital investment), well outstripping foreign aid of all kinds and from all sources, amounting to an estimated $232 billion in 2005 (United Nations Department of Economic and Social Affairs 2006). In some countries in the third world, remittances from abroad constitute a huge proportion of the national income; for example, in Jamaica, over 20 per cent of the GDP arrives from abroad (source: World Bank).

In this chapter, I cannot do justice do the various conditions of care workers in a global setting. I shall concentrate on some of the moral issues raised when European and non-European women serve as domestic migrant workers in European households.

Privatized neo-colonialism?

Despite the *economic* centrality of the new migrants in the global economy, their economic importance does not translate into a political status nor into any appropriate form of *moral* reflection upon their place in society. If we think of immigration as primarily an economic issue, or even as one in which necessity and choice are the key categories, we are apt to miss the critical point that immigration is also about human relationships and continues to reflect the acceptance and denial of responsibility by (among others) individuals, economic entities, groups, nation-states, the European Union, and the world community. By turning the question of immigration into primarily an economic decision of choice by particular individuals, we are apt no longer to see the connections among people at work. If we look for such connections, what might we see? In this chapter, I want to make the claim that we need to look beyond political economy (cf. Yeates 2004) and consider a relational analysis that starts from responsibility as a key angle for viewing this issue. Here, I consider the moral implications of looking at migrant care workers who work in households, primarily cleaning and tending to children and the elderly.

The first point that we need to be aware of is that patterns of migration are not accidental. They are often influenced by questions of proximity, by similarities of language, culture, religion, and other cultural factors. Often these connections exist because of a legacy of colonialism. Within Francophone Africa, France seems a natural destination. To former members of the British Empire, the UK seems an appropriate place to which to emigrate, and earlier British policies emphasized the importation of colonial workers to keep women from having to enter the workforce (Williams and Gavanas 2008).

I want to push this point a bit further, and to place it in the context of *colonialism and neo-colonialism*. If we return to the question of whether such immigration is a result of necessity or choice, it is clear that a large part of the 'necessity' is caused by economic inequality in global terms. Such global inequality and global underdevelopment is a lasting legacy of colonialism. So now, when well-trained medical personnel from the third world leave home and come to work as doctors or other medical personnel in Canada (Attaran and Walker 2008), the USA or Europe, the poor nations that trained them suffer because their health systems are underdeveloped, but this underdevelopment, at least in part, is a legacy of colonialism and lack of resources. Nevertheless, this is not any longer a deliberate colonialist policy. The decisions of previously colonial powers to divest themselves of responsibility for the health and wellbeing of the people who live in their former colonies is a political, not a moral, decision. And yet, when those same people must move to the metropole in order to earn enough money to live, the connection between these two conditions is not seen as a public or political process. Former colonial powers have thus divested themselves of responsibility for a situation that they helped to create.

Indeed, as was argued nearly 20 years ago, the very language that we use to describe immigration is meant to communicate its somewhat uncontrollable 'natural' qualities. Teun van Dijk pointed out that our metaphors to describe immigration are often hydraulic, for example, 'flood', 'tide', 'stream'; such metaphors communicate that immigration is something inhuman, dangerous and barely controllable (van Dijk 1989). Such language signals to its users that they need not think about such 'processes' as engaging their own complex moral and political relationships. They function, in the phrase of W. O. Brown, as an 'inoculation against insight' (Brown 1933).

Not all European states were colonial powers or colonial powers in the same way. Nevertheless, beyond the colonial legacy per se, other processes of political change will also affect the care balance. The moral and political implications of these changes are often parallel to the neo-colonial ones, but they also remain somewhat unobserved. One oft-mentioned effect of greater European integration has been the growth of the view that northern and western welfare states will not be able to afford their current generous welfare benefits if these must be provided to every citizen of Europe who happens to come to reside in their states. Even as the European welfare states become less generous about welfare provision, people living in these states still need care. This political change does not mean that the need to care for people, and increasingly an elderly population, will disappear in the European states with more constrained welfare budgets. It does mean, however, that the demand for cheap care workers, and perhaps increasingly privatized care workers, will increase. The end result will be a system of privatized neo-colonialist care. When we consider the historical association of women with the private sphere, the conditions for privatizing neo-colonial care have implications for gender relations as well as for citizenship, in complex ways.

So, imagine that European nations follow the lead of Sweden in providing tax incentives for middle-class wives (the responsibility falls to women within the household) to hire someone to do the cleaning while they pursue more lucrative paid work (Bowman and Cole 2009). One thing that such a policy does is to transfer responsibility from the state to the private sector. In a way, the Austrian government's concession to the actual practices of families in hiring illegal workers from other European countries is a formal acknowledgment of this trend. But it is also a transfer to individual women, who now must negotiate a series of complex interactions of class, culture and so forth within their own homes (McDowell 2007). The question I wish to consider now is this: what is lost or gained in transforming this responsibility away from the society as a whole and to individuals (mainly women still in charge of managing their households)?

Although within the European Union, citizens of each state are also citizens of the EU, the question of determining whether new extra-European citizens will be admitted still rests with each sovereign government. In this way, policies about citizenship vary across the EU, though the EU also has moved some states toward more 'normal' practices. Some European states have closed citizenship options in the past generation (for example, the UK's exclusion of automatic citizenship for Commonwealth members) and others have opened citizenship options (for example, Germany in 2001). For migrant care workers who work in domestic settings, Spain, Italy and Greece have made provisions for routes to citizenship; in some states they are openly admitted (the UK and Ireland) while in other European countries, including Germany, the Nordic states and the Netherlands, their presence is not officially acknowledged (Lutz 2008a).

In creating an informal market for care workers, in order to cover up the consequences of the official policies of workforce attachment, European states have transferred the responsibilities for fixing the care deficit to individual women and men in private households. What is disturbing about this solution, though, is that it will recreate a form of unequal regard for migrants whose presence is marked by their privatized place in the society. Many dimensions of this arrangement work together to make it reproduce patterns of inclusion and exclusion that work to the detriment of newcomers.

Of course, migration itself puts newcomers in a defensive position. Despite arguments by such thinkers as Joseph Carens, who has argued for around 20 years that immigrants have rights to immigrate (Carens 1987), the prevailing attitude towards migrants more closely follows Michael Walzer's view from *Spheres of Justice* that membership in a community is ultimately a local matter and 'being there first' confers on people a right to make the decision about who should belong (Walzer 1983). Even John Rawls's *The Law of Peoples* (Rawls 1999) goes no further than to endorse this position that a people have a right to limit immigration. And Walzer's description is politically accurate; decisions about admitting immigrants to citizenship are ultimately made by those who are already citizens of a sovereign state. 'Being there first', though, carries no moral weight, especially when we consider how difficult it is to disentangle historical movements of peoples. Some there 'first', for example, aboriginal peoples in North America and Australia, have never counted as 'first' in this sense. In other places, the argument about who was there 'first' continues to this day. But even if being there first was always easy to determine, it still raises a different set of issues. The use of this criterion turns all immigrants permanently into 'the other', since 'they' were not there first. Thus, it prejudges the argument about multiculturalism. It contains an implicit endorsement of assimilation (or 'integration') as against creating a more open and diverse society.

Contemporary accounts of citizenship also reinforce exclusions of domestic migrant workers. In post-war thinking about citizenship, the most important measure of citizenship has been that offered by T. H. Marshall, in which citizenship grows out of one's work status. Many feminists have criticized this view, because of its implicit endorsement of a family structure in which the male breadwinner is paired with a female care-giver whose task is to maintain the household (see, for example, Knijn and Kremer 1997; Lewis 2006; Pascall and Lewis 2004; Bussemaker and van Kersbergen 1994). This view of the contribution of labour rarely carries over to conferring citizenship to domestic workers who are immigrants. They are workers for whom work is not enough to make them into citizens, and who only enjoy the benefits of what Rhacel Parreñas (2001) calls 'partial citizenship'.

Nor can this problem be solved simply by expanding the notion of work to include domestic migrant workers' tasks. Citizenship is partial because the 'work' that domestic migrant workers do cannot be transformed into the kind of productive work that Marshall had in mind (Luxemburg 2004; Tronto 2002; Lutz 2008b). This is so for several reasons. First, care work itself is undervalued in Western society. This may be more true in North America than in the welfare states of Western Europe, but the devaluation of care work per se has long been noted by feminist scholars (Bubeck 1995).

Second, domestic care work is clearly distinguishable from other kinds of work. The institutional setting of the household is a different setting than the market. Because domestic service takes place in a private home, it is often not regarded as employment at all (Hondagneu-Sotelo 2001; Romero 1992). Michael Walzer writes: 'The principles that rule in the household are those of kinship and love. They establish the underlying pattern of mutuality and obligation, or authority and obedience. The servants have no proper place in that pattern, but they have to be assimilated to it' (Walzer 1983, 52). Feminist scholars have been more dubious than Walzer about the rule of kinship and love; nonetheless, the personalistic rule in the household makes this a work relationship that is distinctive. Insofar as domestic servants are conceived as a substitute for the wife in a traditional household, they are expected to conform to a notion of their work that is only partly real 'work'. As Hondagneu-Sotelo observes, employers were often shocked to realize that their child care workers were 'only in it for the money'.

Not only is the household a different institution from a market, but the relationships within a household are considerably more immediate and more intimate than in a market. The status of quasi-family member means that the domestic servant is enmeshed in the complete details of the lives of the people served. Domestic workers not only do work, then; they are also expected to reflect the values (for example, in raising children or performing household duties), tastes (for example, in purchasing food, cleaning products and other commodities for the household) and other aspects of the lives of their employers. The space in which they do their work is not a public work space, but someone else's most private space. Thus, the level of control that employers expect to be able to exert over domestic workers is very great, and noncompliance is often emotionally and psychologically charged (Rollins 1985; Romero 1992; Hondagneu-Sotelo 2001). One of the reasons that domestic work defies professionalization is because it is so dependent upon the whims of the employer (Lutz 2008b, 50).

There is a third factor that distinguishes domestic service from other market relations. Insofar as the work of domestic service is care, one of the 'products' of care is that it creates ongoing relationships among the care-givers and care-receivers. The quality of these relationships is thus one of the measures of the quality of the work that is done (Stone 2000). Thus, part of the work of domestic service itself is to nurture and maintain care relationships. While some such concerns exist in market relations of care (for example, among nursing home aides and their charges), they are presumed to be paradigmatic of domestic relations, and thus form a central part of domestic service.

Finally, domestic work reveals, as will be discussed more fully below, a kind of vulnerability. The masters must therefore control the domestic workers so that their needs, and vulnerability, are masked. Thus, domestic work requires an elaborate pantomime in which the worker's need for the tutelage of the master disguises the fact that the master needs this work to be performed. The resulting relationship is thus premised on an inequality that resembles the colonial relationship of knowing master and ignorant colonial.

This unflattering description may seem an exaggeration. However, when we connect citizenship to nationalism, a failure to address this problem of domestic workers becomes more acute, since it is in the home that the nation is reproduced. All immigrants are expected to learn the language, and they are suspect if they are differentiated by religion, race, ethnicity or other differences. The 'Metropolis' conference report contains this anecdote:

'What does it mean to you to be British?' A young Muslim woman responded *'It just means I live here, and it's on my passport. It doesn't describe me, how can it, I'm not white'.* (Jorgensen 2003, 12)

What is telling about this comment is that the speaker has understood that her status as 'British' is only conditional and partial, and insofar as she will never be white, she will never be fully British. But the situation is more acute for domestic workers. Insofar as care workers are under the control of their employers, perhaps the perception is that the 'foreign influence' they can exert is controlled. That household workers end up in something of a struggle with their employers has a long history, but it is also newly observed (McDowell 2004). In Canada, generally a welcoming country, there are special restrictions for those who arrive to do domestic work (Bakan and Stasiulis 1997; Giles and Arat-Koç 1994; Cohen 2000). Even in the UK, which has committed itself to become more welcoming, domestic work is exempted from the Race Relations Act (Williams and Gavanas 2008).

Although some European states have adopted policies affecting migrant domestic workers, other countries have no policy (Lutz 2008b), and there is no European-wide policy. The default positions reinforce existing patterns of inequality.

Who is responsible?

When states follow a policy of encouraging women's labour market participation without providing for care work as well, this irresponsibility is a serious matter. The exploitation of care workers rarely rises to the level of 'international relations'. Some scholars have proposed solutions to these problems, but they have not been completely convincing.

One solution to this problem is to provide such workers with a special status as 'guest workers'. Wendy Sarvasy and Patrizia Longo argue that guest workers should be understood as world citizens and thus accorded the right of hospitality described by Immanuel Kant. Kant had argued that because 'all nations are *originally* members of a community of the land' we all remain members not of 'a legal community of possession' but of 'a community of reciprocal action (*commercium*)' in which members have 'constant relations with all the others' (Sarvasy and Longo 2004, 396–97).

There is a problem with the image of guests and hospitality, of course (and while the critique is mine, the metaphor is Kant's, drawing a parallel between the household and the state). The problem is that it depends upon the 'friendly agreement' by which strangers will be made into a member of the household. Sarvasy and Longo take this argument to suggest that the visitors thus have a *political* role to play in making themselves welcome. The problem with this approach is that it still leaves the burden to the guest workers to demonstrate that they *deserve* membership. Kant also does suggest (according to Sarvasy and Longo) that we have a duty to be sociable, but the burden still remains on the outsiders to explain why they should be admitted. And then, who shall be the judge? The right to hospitality never de-centers the position of the original citizen and never challenges the basically unequal standing between original citizens and guest workers. What will make them (original citizens) challenge their own ethical views? I suggest that it asks too much that the newcomers alone 'make the case' for their inclusion.

A second solution is offered by Nancy Fraser. In 'After the Family Wage: A Postindustrial Thought Experiment' (in Fraser 1997) she presciently posits the need for welfare states to go beyond the 'universal breadwinner' and 'caregiver parity' models. Fraser's argument here is that the welfare state's gendered solutions to the problem of integrating women into the paid labour force, following either the 'universal breadwinner' model or the 'caregiver parity' model, do not achieve gender justice. Instead, she proposes a notion of a 'Universal Care Giver' in which men must engage in care work as well as women. But at least two problems emerge. First, given the gendered nature of caring, how can Fraser ignore the resistance of men to being labelled, in any way, as care givers? Second, as Cynthia Willett also observes, Fraser 'does not include the issue of immigrant labour or disposable workers among her focal criteria for the evaluation of models of citizenship' (Willett 2001, 88).

Fraser (1997, 61) writes, 'The key to achieving gender equity in a post-industrial welfare state, then, is to make women's current life-patterns the norm for everyone.' But her norm does not apply to everyone; she means able-bodied adults. And she ignores the fact that 'women's current life-patterns' involve a great deal of off-the-books, indirect, intra-gender exploitation and domination.

Alison Weir tries to rehabilitate Fraser's model and 'to encompass a larger feminist imagination' by including global care workers in Fraser's 'universal care giver' model. Weir makes clear that the issues of justice and shirking do not end if we allow the employment of globally cheaper care workers to address the problem. While Weir is correct to notice that the rhetoric of 'choice' is no solution, her solution, 'that carework should not be a matter of free choice' (Weir 2005, 321), does not explain how a wholesale rethinking of the nature of care work might proceed. Weir argues that citizenship rights should be extended to care workers, and that they should be permitted to bring family members with them. As she proceeds further, Weir suggests that de-privatizing care and transforming work will require greater attention to the redrawing of public and private spheres. As she ends, she also recommends transforming the nuclear family and admits, 'These are, of course, all dreams' (327).

The limit to Weir's adjustment of Fraser's 'universal care giver' model is a problem that also inheres in Fraser's initial account. Care is not only about giving care, it is also about receiving care. In her account of colonialism as a care discourse, Uma Narayan observed that often systems of exploitation are justified by those who do the exploiting through a claim that their exploitation serves some higher purpose (Narayan 1995). We can well imagine then, a claim that the 'universal care giver' needs the assistance of others in order to meet the demands for him/her to give care. From the perspective of this chapter, such a model of 'care giver' can quickly turn into another kind of 'inoculation against insight'.

Citizenship and care immigrants

What can be done? As many have argued, granting the right to real and full citizenship is the first step towards addressing this problem (Cyrus 2008). In so doing, proposals to extend citizenship rights to workers who do care work is an expansion of the work basis for citizenship. But the danger of this approach is that, rather than disappearing, the exploitation gets shifted to some other site.

In a recent criticism of the approach that would extend citizenship through care, Nira Yuval-Davis observed that while citizenship might be an important beginning, it does not yet change the difficulty of making migrant care workers actually a part of their new society, of 'belonging'. Further, she observes, since these workers are likely to be women, they are likely to be written in to a gender script that continues the existing separations of public and private life, and thus 'facilitate and oil, rather than obstruct and resist, the smooth working of globalized neo-liberalism' (Yuval-Davis 2007, 96).

Elsewhere, I have tried to extend the moral reach of the view of citizen-as-carer by arguing that citizenship should be extended to anyone involved in a relationship of care with a citizen (Tronto 2005). The radical nature of this proposal is that it does not only extend citizenship to care workers, but also to care receivers who happen also to receive care from these new care-worker citizens. Consider the case of a care worker who crosses the border to care for an elderly person at home in Austria but who travels back and forth and also is in an ongoing relationship of care with her home family in Poland (Morokvasic 2004). Through the proposal I am suggesting, not only the care worker but her family in Poland become eligible for Austrian citizenship. My suggestion flies in the face of accepted views that it is the work of care giving that should create the condition for citizenship. But it is precisely this Marshall-ian account of work, and of what kind of work matters, that I want to challenge fundamentally. This suggested policy exposes states' casual willingness to take in care labour without acknowledging any responsibility for the effects in the real lives of the women and men who are doing the caring work. It would force a re-thinking of the nature of citizenship, and one which makes Yuval-Davis's concerns about the complex meanings of 'belonging' a more central issue in defining citizenship.

Among the virtues of Yuval-Davis's focus on 'belonging' is that it disrupts the sense that citizenship is about national unity and opens up questions of what it means to be a citizen, and what citizens might be able to expect of one another. The Marshall-ian conception of citizen as worker is not sufficiently strong, we have seen, to alleviate concerns about domestic workers. In this absence of stronger content, Yuval-Davis is correct to worry how gender constructions enter into our views of citizenship. While caring might be a 'feminine' way to confer citizenship, Yuval-Davis notes, it ignores the 'heart of modern masculinities' that is also at 'the heart of collective membership' (Yuval-Davis 2007, 96). But Yuval-Davis's concern is more properly directed at the earlier generation of care theorists who associated care more closely with women's work and values (Hankivsky 2004). More recent care theorists have also expressed concern about the masculine bias of citizenship (Leonard and Tronto 2007).

Indeed, rather than taking Yuval-Davis's point as a critique of the connection of care and citizenship, we might use it as an opening to understanding another way to think through questions of citizenship as belonging. Belonging requires a willingness to accept the existence of different subgroups, with different (religious, cultural, economic, political) values, and to see the contours of different ways of organizing one's life as nonetheless consistent with being citizens together. The approach of care commends itself as a way to understand such differences because of the nature of care itself. On the one hand, all care requires that the needs of the one being cared for be met; in this way, concerns such as watching small children and tending to the infirm are universal within the framework of care. On the other hand, though, since good care is highly variable – even down to the level of individual personalities who prefer to be cared for one way or another – an honest focus on care opens the prospects that others' ways of caring might be best for them. While the questions over one form of care or another are open questions, then, the agreement that care is necessary provides a starting point for discussions of what differences are acceptable.

In this way, speaking and acting about very concrete matters, people from different backgrounds are able to agree and disagree without coming to intractable disagreements. Through such a process of concrete care practices shared and negotiated, then, one can see the ways in which care requires and creates trust. Because they are intimate, care work relations might result in the creation of trust and understanding. This, not a focus on work and equity, is the starting point for the creation of belonging. 'At the most basic level, a culture of exchange among new-comers and established communities [that is, integration] depends on establishing a baseline level of trust' (Goździak and Martin 2005).

The current mode of thinking about domestic care relations, though, in which a workforce-engaged woman in Europe discharges her caring duties by replacing her time and labour with a migrant woman, pro-vides none of these opportunities for exchange. For this reason, Knijn and Kremer's (1997) excellent argument for a right to care and a right to time to care is not yet sufficiently far-reaching. If relations of intimate care continue to reproduce the neo-colonial understanding of which set of values, habits, ways-of-doing are worthy (the European workforce model), and the choices and values of the women doing the labour are taken as inconsequential, then the conditions are set for lack of under-standing, miscommunication, disrespect.

If we take care-as-citizenship seriously, it requires that all of the com-munities, newcomers and established community members alike, rethink what should count as a contribution to the society based on attitudes towards care. For example, immigrant girls (and boys) are sometimes the primary baby-sitters for their younger siblings at home. As a result, college admissions officers may be wary that they have no regular after-school activities. How should this factor count when they apply to college and university? If caring for an elderly parent is socially useful, then migration policies need to be attentive to transnational care for elderly parents.

But a more serious problem arises as we attempt to think about care-as-citizenship. There is one way in which this view departs radically from the image of worker-as-citizen. The caring citizen is also a care *receiver*, and not simply a care giver. Receiving care is an ongoing part of the caring relationships in which we are engaged. It is for this reason pri-marily that we need to go beyond Fraser's 'universal care giver' model, for Fraser's model fails to recognize that we are also, all and always, care receivers. When we add care receiving into what it means to be a citizen, the images we can conjure to describe citizenship change substantially.

Consider: if a working middle-class woman in Germany hires a migrant from Eastern Europe to clean her house, who is giving to whom and who is receiving care from whom? If all we think about is whether or not the work gets done, then this arrangement seems no different from the housewife doing the work herself. But if the house must be clean to meet the expectations of her husband, or mother, or neighbours, or her own perceived class status, then the relationship becomes more complex. Whose standards of cleanliness matter? These are difficult questions to answer, and as with many care decisions, there are many idiosyncratic qualities that contribute to an answer. Indeed, perhaps these questions seem trivial. But if we ask, who is harmed if the house is not cleaned? Now we see the hiring housewife as vulnerable. This is perhaps a minor vulnerability; this example is not as concerning than if we had asked, who is harmed if the children are not watched or an elderly person's medications are not administered in a timely manner. But the fact remains: to be a care receiver requires that one has a need; that is, it is a form of vulnerability. Marshall-ian worker citizens have so exaggerated the sense of selves as active, productive citizens that they are unable to admit to vulnerability. On a deep level, to dismiss such vulnerability out of hand plays into the masculinized nationalistic conceptions of citizenship and unity that Yuval Davis described (Young 2003). And it makes much more complicated the difficult but necessary processes of listening to others.

From such a political position – that we are all equally potentially vulnerable – it may become possible for us to change our attitude towards the exploitation of others and of others who are immigrants. When we look at immigrants from this perspective of care, they take on a different appearance. The peddlers and day labourers, mostly men but also women, who now live on the edge of most western cities, are also engaged in care practices. They send money back home, remain engaged in families, and interweave their own lives with those of their 'receiving' countries. As a result, they bring with them new attitudes about work, family, about raising children, about basic human needs. They deserve, as people engaged in activities that contribute to their own care, to be included in citizenship.

Immigrants, too, are vulnerable and deeply entrenched in their own sets of care relationships. My hope is that the universal need for care that characterizes all humans will also let us recognize our commonality with the immigrants who might otherwise be exploited, in an unthinking way, along paths of gender, race and nationality that follow historic patterns of colonialism and global inequality.

In the end, my argument expands substantially the meaning of citizen. I do so deliberately, with the hopes that such a re-visioning of citizenship will allow 'those who were here first' (Walzer 1983) to see more clearly the limits of their own judgments as they look upon the 'others' in their midst. The neo-colonial attitudes of one's own superiority can be challenged only when people are able to recognize their own vulnerability as they go about their lives. Only when migrant domestic care workers are treated fully as citizens might it become possible for them to appear to us as fully human. And only then can we begin to accept our responsibilities that connect our most intimate lives with the brutal forms of global inequality from which people who live in the developed western world benefit every day.

Concluding Remarks

Hanne Marlene Dahl, Marja Keränen and Anne Kovalainen

This book has focused on varieties of care in present-day diversified Europe. If at times care has been seen as something personal, intimate, familial and private, the chapters in the book display the fact that the idea of care can no longer exclusively be understood as personal and intimate, nor within a nation-state container, but needs a transnational perspective encompassing broad and complex processes of Europeanization and globalization.

Care relations have existed both informally and formally, the latter being regulated at different levels of state through municipalities, regions and nation-states, the former existing as interwoven into the lives of families and women and informal dependency relations of various kinds. Care relations have always been changing in time and space, being organized differently in various places and related to different ideological understandings. In that existence care relations have been part of the normalized structure of social life. Therefore the questions related to the changing nature of care cannot be understood detached from the contextual understandings, and understandings of the past, present and future of care work, the role of the state, the voluntary or the private sectors and the changing positions of the family. As argued in the introduction and shown in detail throughout the chapters, there cannot be one single idea of care relations and their arrangement throughout the European Union member states. There may be strong political rhetoric and a general political wish for this aim, but it is not backed up by research and analysis of the current situations throughout the member states, nor through comparative studies on a larger scale, focusing on structures, mechanisms, time-use and other features carving out the different valuations and solutions related to care.

Yet, attempts to find a common solution for a unified model and idea of the European welfare strategy have been considerable. In 2001, a working group submitted a report to the Belgian presidency of the EU, titled 'A New Welfare Architecture for Europe' (Esping-Andersen et al. 2001). The report set out to solve the Gordian knot of 'How to sustain Europe's normative commitments to social justice while aspiring to be a truly competitive force in the evolving knowledge economy'. The basic principles of the welfare architecture designed by the group were to start from three cornerstones of people's lives, childhood, work life and old age (Esping-Andersen et al. 2001, 3). The attempts of universal solutions such as this are several, but they all seem to relate to another era and time: a time of continuous growth, and a prosperous and homogenized Europe. In the second decade of the 21st century none of these conditions prevail any longer in Europe or beyond.

How well do these aims presently meet the general ambition for a globally competitive European Union are yet to be seen, as many of the member states are struggling now with high public sector deficits and expenditure-related debts and slow economic recovery from the global downturn of 2008. For many countries, the maintenance of the level of public expenditure – coverage for the cornerstones' in people's lives – and further public sector investments are seen as an economic 'cure' that has helped to ameliorate the worst outcomes of the recession. However, the overall growth of the elderly population, trends of lowering the retirement ages among the working population, and general lack of workforce in the future public sector services are major problems and might weaken the general recovery. The global economic downturn from 2008 onwards has also created severe pressures to slim down public expenditure throughout the European Union member states. Even if welfare services and care arrangements are not solely economic questions and cannot be solved with money alone, the economic aspects of care go hand in hand with the practical arrangements of the care throughout the EU.

Indeed, the questions and issues originally raised in this book have turned out to be much more complex than we imagined when starting this project. Many of the previously adept categorizations and theoretical bases for research seem inadequate and need to be readjusted and critically re-evaluated. The problems discussed in relation to care and care arrangements no longer necessarily fit into available categorizations of the research fields in question, or they only get a bleak explanation through traditional analysis. The contemporary issues of care cannot be adequately discussed in terms of migration flows in neat categories of migration regimes, welfare regimes and the push and pull factors causing those flows. Neither can these problems be discussed solely in terms of 'old' welfare regimes and welfare state models of a stable nature. Furthermore, issues raised in this book cannot be discussed by relying on European integration as an economic project that would leave member states with autonomous capacities for social redistribution and regulation of their own kinds.

While the original aim of the European integration process was to establish a single market and ascertain the free movement of goods, services and capital, the consequent free movement of labour opens up far more complicated issues. The aim of the EU internal migration policy was to secure access to a transnational labour force – with this leading to a need for regulating the rights of this labour force in all member states. The need for reconciliation of care and paid work has also put gender equality fairly high on the European political agenda. This is clearly visible in the chapters in this volume as well.

Strengthening women's employment and labour force participation had earlier been a social policy safety measure that enhanced any private family economy, brought about economic efficiency, guaranteed better living standard for families and kept social exclusion at bay. This is no longer the case. Due to many overlapping processes, the women's labour market reserve no longer 'exists' in many countries, and as part of modernization, individualistic life patterns blur the picture even more. While gender equality is seen as central to achieving high economic activity and high birth rates, it is the overly 'policy'-related aspect that ignores current lifestyles and the multitude of life patterns where balancing various requirements at the same time may not always be easy.

Even if originally driven by economic interests, the European Union has, during its development, come to deepen its understanding of integration from economic issues to politico-institutional and even some social issues, making it possible to discuss a future European citizenship. While the content of that citizenship may, in Marshall's terms, concern civil rights or political rights, the issue of social rights being included in European citizenship has at best been a vague and ambivalent project, if it ever has been 'a project' in its own right for citizenship only. Presently, with the idea of 'flexible citizenship' (Ong 1999; Kwok-bun 2005), it is more difficult for nation-states to equate nationality and citizenship as membership rights as defined on the basis of human rights and on the basis of residence, and no longer on the basis of community or birth (Eder and Giesen 2001). And while many of us would agree with social issues being better solved at the nation-state level, separating different policy fields may not be that simple: advancing economic integration and free movement of labour indeed also have social and cultural consequences. Those consequences may be different for member states sending or receiving labour, and they might be global in a sense that the questions of 'otherness', 'minority' or 'cultural coherence' all come into the open as part of the process. The indeterminate nature of globalization means that outcomes may be different for the individual citizen – the actual people – moving house and country in search of employment and income. And they may still vary depending on situational factors where sending and receiving – the basic categories of migration studies – are no longer to stable locations but to rapidly changing and fluctuating, contingent positions.

Throughout this book, through the various chapters and introductory remarks, it has been argued that gender occupies a key position in defining care, relating to the variety of care arrangements and social and political articulations of it. The outlook of the European Union has in many respects been aiming for equal opportunities, and seeking just regulation of the rights of women, the disabled and minority ethnic or faith groups. There is increasing regulation of member state activities for protection against discrimination on the basis of gender or ethnicity. There are also various action programs for opening up opportunities for marginalized citizens. The union has been active in establishing policies for gender mainstreaming (Pollack and Hafner-Burton 2000), and gender equality and gender mainstreaming have indeed been fairly high on the EU agenda. Now it seems that attempts to advance the dual-breadwinner model may have ended up undermining the rights of, for example, migrant care workers, whether in grey markets, in homes in private employment, or in public employment. Promotion of the free movement of labour within the EU may in fact have ended up in leaving thousands of children in Eastern European new member countries without parents (Gheaus 2008). As family care in one location of the EU gets promoted, families at the other end are dissolved due to this promotion. The EU aims at guaranteeing civil, political and even social rights to the new Europeans, but which jobs are available for them?

The gradually advancing process of European integration has been an effort to establish a single market with free movement of goods, capital and labour. This advancing process of deepening integration has occurred in parallel with the enlargement of the EU, while at the same time requiring new member states to adapt to 'western' criteria of economic and politico-institutional arrangements in the EU, but also bringing in more variety and 'difference' in the palette of member states, coming from many kinds of traditions and societal arrangements, histories and historical experiences. At the same time as the EU is pushing the new member states to become neo-liberal economies, a 'care chain' has developed between member states. The effects of this are many: new inequalities in the cost of labour, inequalities in the receiving countries, overall commercialization of intimate relationships, but also freedom of movement, mobility of the labour force and, possibly, even slow unification of the union. What possibly started as a project of equality may have ended up with the birth of new frictions and problems. In the turns taken between political and economic integration, Eastern European countries have come to provide the cheap labour force required in Western Europe in care services, and for industrial production the transfers of enterprises to Eastern European countries have provided a cheaper expense structure. While enlargement was intended to be a process of democratization and the countries entering the EU were required to conform to necessary levels of democratization, this process can also be seen as a case of western neo-colonial rule, whereby western norms were set to be fulfilled by the entering countries (see Melegh 2006).

Is there, then, need for a European care strategy? Would there be any possibility for a joint view on care at the European Union level? We do not know and do not necessarily wish to propose a solution to this question. However, we suggest that there is a need for an academic and political debate that takes into consideration the sometimes conflicting interests of children and the elderly, women and men in the East and the West, the ethnic or religious groups of the various member states, and carers and the cared for, whether in families or public institutions. It seems that issues of care might act as a Litmus test for outcomes of many conflicting policies.

Original attempts to develop a European social dimension have failed and are not likely to succeed in the foreseeable future. External pressures, such as economic crises and their effects on national budgets, demographic changes and, overall, the different pace of development throughout the European Union, have made it difficult, if not impossible, to synchronize the common social dimension. While originally deemed fairly successful in regulating equal opportunity matters and promoting women's overall participation in the labour force, the market-led process of integration leaves social protection and issues of democracy to the nation-states, and the nation-states no longer can be regarded as autonomous actors isolated from a global context (Fraser 2008). The parallel process of enlargement has brought in countries with a variety of societal gender orders, first the Nordic countries, sometimes deemed to have been the predecessors of equality policies (Hernes 1987) and, later, Eastern European countries with strong traditions of women's participation in the labour market, but in some cases failing economies and societal infrastructure. While one could assume that, in principle, the division of functions between nation-states and EU institutions is clear, or that the functions of the market and political regulation can be separated, none of these 'divisions of labour' seem to hold in real life. Instead, they co-act in complicated and conflicting ways.

All societies have developmental possibilities in the process of trans-formation that is presently taking place in Europe and beyond. In this process, Europe has a very special tradition to carry forward that is at the core of the idea of the 'caring state' (Daly 1998), which includes the ideas of gender specificity, formal recognition of care, and strong emphasis on citizenship, equality and welfare. By identifying the emerg-ing problematic fields at the nexus of European states, care arrange-ments and gender, we hope to have been able both to set new research agendas and capture issues that call for political solutions in the future Europe, for the benefit of its citizens.

Bibliography

Abrahamson, P., Boje, T. P. and Greve, B. (2005) *Welfare and Families in Europe* (Aldershot: Ashgate).

Adam, G. (2007) *Temporary Work Permits Issued to Illegal Foreign Care Workers*, EIRO Online 2007, available at: www.eurofound.europa.eu/eiro/2007/01/articles/at0701019i.html, accessed 10 June 2007.

AFP, Sweden, Interview with Swedish Minister (2007) available at: www.sr.se/cgi-bin/isidorpub/PrinterFriendlyArticle.asp?programID=2054&Nyheter=0&grupp=3574&artikel=976610, accessed 15 June 2007.

Ahtela, K. (2004) 'Promoting Equality in the Workplace: Legislative Intent and Reality', in E-M. Svensson, A. Pylkkänen and J. Niemi-Kiesiläinen (eds), *Nordic Equality at the Crossroads*, Feminist Legal Studies Coping with Difference (Aldershot: Ashgate).

Alber, J. (1995) 'A Framework for the Comparative Study of Social Services', *Journal of European Social Policy*, Vol. 5, No. 2, pp. 131–49.

Alhadeff, G. (1998) *The Origins and Development of Waling-Waling (Overseas Domestic Workers Organisation)*, available at: http://ourworld.compuserve.com/homepages/kalayaan/lh_euro_2.htm, accessed 3 July 2006.

Andall, J. (2000) *Gender, Migration and Domestic Service. The Politics of Black Women in Italy* (Aldershot: Ashgate).

Anderson, B. (2000) *Doing the Dirty Work? The Global Politics of Domestic Labour* (London: Zed Books).

Anderson, B. and O'Connell Davidson, J. (2003) 'Is Trafficking in Human Beings Demand Driven? A Multicountry Pilot Study', *IOM Migration Research Series*, no. 15 (Geneva: IOM [International Organization for Migration]).

ANSA (2008) 'Italy "To Curb Immigrant Influx"', ANSA.it 2008, available at: www.ansa.it/site/notizie/awnplus/english/news/2008-11-13_113, accessed 13 November 2008.

Anti-Slavery International (2006) *Trafficking in Women, Forced Labour and Domestic Work in the Context of the Middle East and Gulf Region*, Working Paper (London: Anti-Slavery International), available at: www.antislavery.org/includes/documents/cm_docs/2009/t/traffic_women_forced_labour_domestic_2006.pdf, accessed 13 March 2011.

Anttonen, A. and Sipilä J. (1996) 'European Social Care Services: Is It Possible to Identify Models?', *Journal of European Social Policy*, Vol. 6, No. 2, pp. 87–100.

Asch, A. (1999) 'Prenatal Diagnosis and Selective Abortion: A Challenge to Practice and Policy', *American Journal of Public Health*, Vol. 89, No. 11, pp. 1649–57.

Attaran, A. and Walker, R. (2008) 'Shoppers Drug Mart or Poachers Drug Mart?', *Canadian Medical Association Journal*, Vol. 178, No. 3, pp. 265–68.

Bacchi, C. L. (1999) *Women, Policy and Politics* (London: Sage).

Baier, A. C. (1992) 'Trusting People', *Philosophical Perspectives*, Vol. 6, pp. 137–53.

Baier, A. C. (1995) *Moral Prejudice* (London: Harvard University Press).

Bakan, A. B. and Stasiulis, D. (eds) (1997) *Not One of the Family: Foreign Domestic Workers in Canada* (Toronto: University of Toronto Press).

Baldwin, S. and Twigg, J. (1991) 'Women and Community Care: Reflections on a Debate', in D. Groves and M. Maclean (eds), *Women's Issues In Social Policy* (London: Routledge).

Beasley, C. and Bacchi, C. (2007) 'Envisaging a New Politics for an Ethical Future: Beyond Trust, Care and Generosity Towards an Ethic of "Social Flesh"', *Feminist Theory*, Vol. 8, No. 3, pp. 270–98.

Beck, U. (2002) 'The Cosmopolitan Society and Its Enemies', *Theory, Culture and Society*, Vol. 19, Nos 1–2, pp. 17–44.

Beck, U. (2006) *The Cosmopolitan Outlook* (Cambridge: Polity Press).

Begum, N. (1992) 'Disabled Women and the Feminist Agenda', *Feminist Review*, Vol. 40, pp. 70–84.

Bercusson, B. (1999) 'Democratic Legitimacy and European Labour Law', *The Industrial Law Journal*, Vol. 28, No. 2, pp. 153–70.

Bercusson, B. (2008) 'Transnational Labour Regulation: Process and Substance', in K. Ahlberg, B. Bercusson, N. Bruun, H. Kountouros, C. Vigneau, and L. Zappalà (eds), *Transnational Labour Regulation, A Case Study of Temporary Agency Work* (Brussels: P.I.E. Peter Lang), pp. 11–36.

Berger, P. L. and Luckman, T. (1966) *The Social Construction of Reality* (Garden City: Anchor Books).

Bergqvist, C. and Jungar, A-C. (2000) 'Adaptation or Diffusion of the Swedish Gender Model?', in L. Hantrais (ed.), *Gendered Policies in Europe. Reconciling Employment and Family Life* (Basingstoke: Palgrave Macmillan), pp. 160–79.

Bernard, N. (2000) 'Legitimising EU Law: Is the Social Dialogue the Way Forward? Some Reflections around the UEAPME Case', in J. Shaw (ed.), *Social Law and Policy in an Evolving European Union* (Oxford and Portland: Hart Publishing), pp. 279–302.

Bettio, F. and Plantenga, J. (2004) 'Comparing Care Regimes in Europe', *Feminist Economies*, Vol. 10, No. 1, pp. 85–113.

Bettio, F., Simonazzi, A. and Villa, P. (2006) 'Change in Care Regimes and Female Migration: The Care Drain in the Mediterranean', *Journal of European Social Policy*, Vol. 16, No. 3, pp. 271–85.

Beveridge, F. (2007) 'Building against the Past: The Impact of Mainstreaming on EU Gender Law and Policy', *European Law Review*, Vol. 32, No. 2, pp. 193–212.

Beveridge, F. and Nott, S. (2002) 'Mainstreaming: A Case for Optimism and Cynicism', *Feminist Legal Studies*, Vol. 10, No. 3, pp. 299–311.

Beveridge, F. and Velluti, S. (2008) (eds) *Gender and the Open Method of Coordination, Perspectives on Law, Governance and Equality in the EU* (Aldershot and Burlington: Ashgate), pp. 191–208.

Björnberg, U. (2002) 'Ideology and Choice between Work and Care: Swedish Family Policy for Working Parents', *Critical Social Policy*, Vol. 22, No. 1, pp. 33–52.

Bleijenbergh, I., de Bruijn, J. and Bussemaker, J. (2004) 'European Social Citizenship and Gender: The Part-time Work Directive', *European Journal of Industrial Relations*, Vol. 10, No. 3, pp. 309–28.

Boje, T. P. (2007) 'Work and Welfare. The Gendered Organization of Work and Care in Different European Countries', *European Review*, Vol. 15, No. 3, pp. 373–96.

Boje, T. P. and Almqvist, A-L. (2000) 'Citizenship, Family Policy and Women's Pattern of Employment', in T. P. Boje and A. Leira (eds), *Gender, Welfare State and Market* (London and New York: Routledge).

Boje, T. P. and Ejrnæs, A. (2011) 'Fertility, Mothers' Employment and Family Policy – What Kind of Relationship?', forthcoming in P. Abbott and C. Wallace (eds), *Social Quality and Work-Care Relations*.

Borchorst, A. (2008) 'Gender Interest and Scandinavian Welfare Policies', in Kathleen B. Jones and Gunnel Karlsson (eds), *Gender and the Interests of Love – Essays in Honour of Anna G. Jonasdottir* (Örebro: Centrum for feministiska samhällsstudier), pp. 26–29.

Borras, S. and Greve, B. (2004) 'Concluding Remarks: New Methods or Just Cheap Talk?, *Journal of European Public Policy*, Vol. 11, No. 2, pp. 329–36.

Bowman, J. R., and Cole, A. M. (2009) 'Do Working Mothers Oppress Other Women? The Swedish "Maid Debate" and the Welfare State Politics of Gender Equality', *Signs: Journal of Women in Culture & Society*, Vol. 35, No. 1, pp. 157–84.

Brennan, D. (2007) 'The ABC of Child Care Politics', *Australian Journal of Social Issues*, Vol. 42, No. 2, pp. 213–55.

Brewer, M. and Shaw, J. (2004) 'Childcare Use and Mothers' Employment: A Review of British Data Sources', DWP Working Paper, No. 16 (London: HMSO).

Brown, S. (2006) 'Can Remittances Spur Development? A Critical Survey', *International Studies Review*, Vol. 8, No. 1, pp. 55–75.

Brown, W. O. (1933) 'Rationalization of Race Prejudice', *International Journal of Ethics*, Vol. 43, No. 3, pp. 294–306.

Brunning, G. and Plantenga, J. (1999) 'Parental Leave and Equal Opportunity Experiences in Eight European Countries', *Journal of European Social Policy*, Vol. 9, No. 3, pp. 195–209.

Bruun, N. (2000) 'The Finnish System of Industrial Relations and Labour Law', in A. C. Neal (ed.), *European Social Policy and the Nordic Countries* (Aldershot: Ashgate), pp. 77–109.

Bubeck, D. (1995) *Care, Justice and Gender* (Oxford: Oxford University Press).

Bulmer, M. (2008) 'Theorizing Europeanization', in P. Graziano and M. P. Vink, *Europeanization – New Research Agendas* (Basingstoke: Palgrave Macmillan), pp. 46–58.

Burchell, D. (1995) 'The Attributes of Citizens: Virtue, Manners and the Activity of Citizenship', *Economy and Society*, Vol. 24, No. 4, pp. 540–58.

Bussemaker, J. and van Kersbergen, K. (1994) 'Gender and Welfare States: Some Theoretical Reflections', in D. Sainsbury (ed.), *Gendering Welfare States* (London: Sage).

Cancedda, A. (2001) *Employment in Household Services* (Dublin: European Foundation for the Improvement of Living and Working Conditions).

Carens, J. H. (1987) 'Aliens and Citizens: The Case for Open Borders', *The Review of Politics*, Vol. 49, No. 2, pp. 251–73.

Catarino, C. and Oso, L. (2000) 'La inmigración femenina en Madrid y Lisboa: hacia la etnización del servicio doméstico y de las empresas de limpieza', *Revista Papers*, Vol. 60, pp. 183–207.

Charles, N. (2000) *Feminism, the State and Social Policy* (Basingstoke: Macmillan).

Cichowski, R. A. (2007) *The European Court and Civil Society: Litigation, Mobilisation and Governance* (Cambridge: Cambridge University Press).

Code, L. (2002) 'Narratives of Responsibility and Agency: Reading Margaret Walker's Moral Understandings', *Hypatia*, Vol. 17, No. 1, pp. 156–73.

Cohen, R. (2000) '"Mom is a Stranger": The Negative Impact of Immigration Policies on the Family Life of Filipina Domestic Workers', *Canadian Ethnic Studies*, Vol. 32, No 3, pp. 76–88.

Conaghan, J. (2005) 'Work, Family and the Discipline of Labour Law', in J. Conaghan and K. Rittich (eds), *Labour Law, Work, and Family* (Oxford and New York: Oxford University Press), pp. 19–42.

Consejo Económico y Social (2003) 'La inmigración femenina en España', *Panorama sociolaboral de la mujer en España*, Vol. 31 (Primer trimestre), available at: http://cdd.emakumeak.org/ficheros/0000/0120/eco_13.pdf.

Consejo Económico y Social (2004) 'Conciliación de trabajo y vida familiar: licencias parentales', *Panorama sociolaboral de la mujer en España*, Vol. 38 (Cuarto trimestre).

Consejo Económico y Social (2006) 'Conciliación entre la vida laboral y familiar', *Panorama sociolaboral de la mujer en España*, Vol. 45.

Cooper, D. (2007) '"Well, You Go There to Get Off": Visiting Feminist Care Ethics through a Women's Bathhouse', *Feminist Theory*, Vol. 8, No. 3, pp. 243–62.

Corriere della Sera (2008) 'Green Light for 170,000 More Immigrants – Priority for Home Helps and Carers' (Notizie di cronaca del Corriere della Sera) available at: www.corriere.it/english/08_noviembre_03/immigrants/_801538ee, accessed 8 November 2008.

Cox, R. (2006) *The Servant Problem* (London and New York: I.B. Tauris).

Crenshaw, K. (1991) 'Mapping the Margins: Intersectionality, Identity Politics, and Violence against Women of Color', *Stanford Law Review*, Vol. 43, No. 6, pp. 1241–99.

Cyrus, N. (2008) 'Being Illegal in Europe: Strategies and Policies for Fairer Treatment of Migrant Domestic Workers', in H. Lutz (ed.), *Migration and Domestic Work: A European Perspective on a Global Theme* (Aldershot: Ashgate).

Dahl, H. M. (2004) 'A View from the Inside: Recognition and Redistribution in the Nordic Welfare State from a Feminist Perspective', *Acta Sociologica*, Vol. 47, No. 4, pp. 325–37.

Dahl, H. M. (2005) 'A Changing Ideal of Care in Denmark: A Different Form of Retrenchment?', in H. M. Dahl and T. R. Eriksen (eds), *Dilemmas of Care in the Nordic Welfare State – Continuity and Change* (Aldershot: Ashgate), pp. 47–61.

Dahl, H. M. (2009) 'New Public Management, Care and Struggles about Care', *Critical Social Policy*, Vol. 29, No. 4, pp. 634–54.

Daly, M. (1998) 'A More "Caring State"?', in J. Lewis (ed.), *Gender, Social Care and Welfare State Restructuring in Europe* (Aldershot: Ashgate), pp. 25–50.

Daly, M. (2002) 'Care as a Good for Social Policy', *Journal of Social Policy*, Vol. 31, No. 2, pp. 251–70.

Daly, M. and Lewis, J. (2000) 'The Concept of Social Care and the Analysis of Contemporary Welfare States', *British Journal of Sociology*, Vol. 51, No 2, pp. 281–98.

Daly, M. and Rake, K. (2003) *Gender and the Welfare State* (Oxford: Blackwell Publishing).

De Beauvoir, S. (1949 [1970]) *The Second Sex* (Oslo: Pax Publishing).

Delanty, G. and Rumford, C. (2005) *Rethinking Europe: Social Theory and the Implications of Europeanization* (London: Routledge).

de la Porte, C. and Nanz, P. (2004) 'The OMC – a Deliberative-Democratic Mode of Governance? The Cases of Employment And Pensions', *Journal of European Public Policy*, Vol. 11, No. 2, pp. 267–88.

Dean, M. (1998) 'Questions of Method', in I. Velody and R. Williams (eds), *The Politics of Constructionism* (London: Sage).

Dean, M. (1999) *Governmentality, Power and Rule in Modern Society* (London: Sage).

den Dulk, L. and van Doorne-Huiskes, A. (2007) 'Social Policy in Europe: Its Impact on Families and Work', in R. Crompton, S. Lewis and C. Lyonette (eds),

Women, Men, Work and Family in Europe (New York: Palgrave Macmillan), pp. 35–58.

Duncan, S. (2002) 'Policy Discourses on "Reconciling Work and Life" in the EU', *Social Policy & Society*, Vol. 1, No. 4, pp. 305–14.

Dwyer, P. (2004) 'Creeping Conditionality in the UK: From Welfare Rights to Conditional Entitlements?', *Canadian Journal of Sociology*, Vol. 29, No. 2, pp. 265–87.

Dybbroe, B. (2008) 'A Crisis in Learning, Professional Knowledge and Welfare in Care', in S. Wrede, L. Henriksson, H. Høst, S. Johansson and B. Dybbroe (eds), *Care Work in Crisis – Reclaiming the Nordic Ethos of Care* (Malmö: Studentslitteratur), pp. 50–73.

Eder, K. and Giesen, B. (eds) (2001) *European Citizenship: National Legacies and Transnational Projects* (Oxford: Oxford University Press).

Ehrenreich, B. and Hochschild A. R. (eds) (2002) *Global Woman: Nannies, Maids and Sex Workers in the New Economy* (London: Granta Books).

Ejrnæs, A. (2010) 'The Impact of Family Policy and Career Interruptions on Women's Perceptions of Negative Occupational Consequences of Full-Time Home Care', *European Societies*, 2010, e-published 4 November 2010, at: DOI 10.1080/14616696.2010.514354.

Ejrnæs, A. and Boje, T. P. (2010) 'Flexibility, Employment Regulation, and Working Time', unpublished paper.

Ellingsæter, A. L. (1998) 'Dual Breadwinner Societies: Provider Models in the Scandinavian Welfare States', *Acta Sociologica*, Vol. 41, pp. 59–73.

Eräranta, K. (2009) 'The Promotion of Family Friendly Workplace Policies In Finland – Europeanization of Welfare Government?', paper presented at the conference 'European Ideas and Action, Their Impacts on Social and Health Policy, and on the Nordic and other European Models', 26–27 March 2009, Stockholm.

Esping-Andersen, G. (1990) *The Three Worlds of Welfare Capitalism* (Cambridge: Polity Press and Princeton: Princeton University Press).

Esping-Andersen, G. (1995) 'Welfare Status without Work: The Impasse of Labour Shedding and Familialism in Continental European Social Policy', *Estudio/ Working Paper* 1995, Fundación Juan March.

Esping-Andersen, G. (1999) *Social Foundations of Postindustrial Economies* (Oxford: Oxford University Press).

Esping-Andersen, G. (2000) *Fundamentos sociales de las economías postindustriales* (Barcelona: Ariel).

Esping-Andersen, G. (2007) 'Conclusions', in G. Esping-Andersen (ed.) *Family Formation and Family Dilemmas in Contemporary Europe* (Bilbao: Foundacion BBVA), pp. 265–74.

Esping-Andersen, G., Duncan, C., Hemerijk, A. and Myles, J. (2001) *A New Welfare Architecture for Europe?* Report submitted to the Belgian Presidency of the European Union.

European Commission (1993) *Growth, Competitiveness, and Employment. The Challenges and Ways forward into the 21st Century*, available at: www.ena.lu/ commission_white_paper_growth_competitiveness_employment_1993-020000113. html, accessed 28 November 2010.

European Social Survey (2003), at: www.europeansocialsurvey.org

Eurostat (2003) 'How Women and Men Spend Their Time. Results from 13 European Countries', *Statistics in Focus. Population and Social Conditions*, Theme 3, 12/2003, available at: http://epp.eurostat.ec.europa.eu, accessed 6 April 2007.

Eurostat (2008)

Falkner, G. (2000) *EU Social Policy in the 1990s: Towards a Corporatist Policy Community* (London and New York: Routledge).

Falkner, G. (2008) 'Social Policy', in P. Graziano and M. P. Vink (eds), *Europeanization – New Research Agendas* (Basingstoke: Palgrave Macmillan), pp. 253–65.

Ferrera, M. (1996) 'The "Southern Model" of Welfare in Social Europe', *Journal of European Social Policy*, Vol. 6, No. 1, pp. 17–37.

Finch, J. (1989) *Family Obligations and Social Change* (Cambridge: Polity).

Finch, J. and Groves, D. (1983) *A Labour of Love: Women, Work and Caring* (London: Routledge and Kegan Paul).

Finch, J. and Mason, J. (1993) *Negotiating Family Responsibilities* (London: Routledge).

Fine, M. and Glendinning, C. (2005) 'Dependence, Independence or Interdependence? Revisiting the Concepts of "Care" and "Dependency"', *Ageing & Society*, Vol. 25, pp. 601–21.

Fish, J. N. (2006) *Domestic Democracy. At Home in South Africa* (London: Routledge).

Flaquer, L. (2000) *Las políticas familiares en una perspectiva comparada*, Fundación "La Caixa", Colección Estudios Sociales, No. 3 (Barcelona: Fundación "La Caixa").

Flaquer, L. (2004) 'La articulación entre familia y Estado de bienestar en los países de la Europa del sur', *Revista Papers*, Vol. 73, pp. 27–58.

Foucault, M. (1984) 'Nietzsche, Genealogy, History', in P. Rabinow (ed.), *The Foucault Reader. An Introduction to Foucault's Thought* (London: Penguin Books).

Foucault, M. (1991) 'Governmentality', in G. Burchell, C. Gordon and P. Miller (eds), *The Foucault Effect. Studies in Governmentality* (Chicago: University of Chicago Press), pp. 87–104.

Fraser, N. (1997) *Justice Interruptus: Critical Reflections on the "Postsocialist" Condition* (New York and London: Routledge).

Fraser, N. (2003) 'Social Justice in the Age of Identity Politics', in N. Fraser and A. Honneth (eds), *Redistribution or Recognition? A Political-Philosophical Exchange* (London: Verso), pp. 7–109.

Fraser, N. (2008) *Scales of Justice: Reimagining Political Space in a Globalizing World* (New York: Columbia University Press).

Fredman, S. (1998) 'Social Law in the European Union: The Impact of the Lawmaking Process', in P. Craig and C. Harlow (eds), *Lawmaking in the European Union* (London: Kluwer Law International).

Garrett, L. (2007) 'The Challenge of Global Health', *Foreign Affairs*, Vol. 86, No. 1, pp. 14–38.

Gavanas, A. (2006) 'De Onämnbara: Jämlikhet, "Svenskhet" och Privata Hushållstjänster i Pigdebattens Sverige', in P. de los Reyes (ed.), *Arbetslivets (O)synliga Murar in Utredningen om Makt. Integration och Strukturell Diskriminering*, SOU 2006: 59 (Stockholm: Statens Offentliga Utredningar).

General Assembly of the United Nations (2006) *Chairperson's Summary of the High-level Dialogue on International Migration and Development* (New York: United Nations).

Germanavičius, A. et al. (2005). *Žmogaus teisių stebėsena uždarose psichikos sveikatos priežiūros ir globos institucijose* (Vilnius: Zmogaus teisiu stebejimo institutas, Globali iniciatyva psichiatrijoje, Lietuvos sutrikusio intelekto zmoniu globos bendrija "Viltis", Vilniaus psichosocialines reabilitacijos centras).

Gheaus, A. (2008) 'Care Drain and Women's Citizenship: Who Should Provide for the Children Left Behind?', paper presented at the CINEFOGO conference, 2–3 April, Roskilde. Available at: http://cinefogo.cuni.cz/index.php?&id_result= 86315&l=0&w=15&id_out=399.

Giddens, A. (1992) *The Transformation of Intimacy: Sexuality, Love and Eroticism in Modern Societies* (Stanford: Stanford University Press).

Giles, W. and Arat-Koç, S. (eds) (1994) *Maid in the Market: Women's Paid Domestic Labour* (Halifax, NS: Fernwood Publishing).

Glendinning, C. (2008) 'Increasing Choice and Control for Older and Disabled People: A Critical Review of New Developments in England', *Social Policy & Administration*, Vol. 42, No. 5, pp. 451–69.

Glover, S., Gott, C., Loizillon, A., Portes, J., Price, R., Spencer, S., Srinivasan V. and Willis C. (2001) 'Migration: an Economic and Social Analysis', RDS Occasional Paper 67 (Home Office: London).

Gordon, T. (2006) 'The Nordic Approach to the Promotion of Equality', *Scottish Affairs*, Vol. 56 (summer 2006), pp. 57–68.

Gornick, J. C. and Meyers, M. K. (2003) *Families that Work* (New York: Russell Sage Foundation).

Gorz, A. (1988) *Critique of Economic Reason* (London and New York: Verso).

Goździak, E. and Martin, S. F. (2005) 'Challenges for the Future', in E. Goździak and S. F. Martin (eds), *Beyond the Gateway: Immigrants in a Changing America* (Lanham: Lexington Books).

Graham, H. (1983) 'Caring: A Labor of Love', in J. Finch and D. Groves (eds), *A Labor of Love: Women, Work and Caring* (London: Routledge and Kegan Paul).

Gray, D. E. (2001) 'Accommodation, Resistance and Transcendence: Three Narratives of Autism', *Social Science & Medicine*, Vol. 53, No. 9, pp. 1247–57.

Gregson, N. and Lowe, M. (1994) *Servicing the Middle Classes: Class, Gender and Waged Domestic Labour in Contemporary Britain* (London and New York: Routledge).

Greve, B. (1996) 'Welfare States Research Core: Overview and Synthesis', in B. Greve (ed.), *Comparative Welfare Systems: The Scandinavian Model in a Period of Change* (Basingstoke and London: Macmillan).

Guerrina, R. (2008) 'Employment Policy, Women's Labour Market Activation and Demographic Trends', in F. Beveridge and S. Velluti (eds), *Gender and the Open Method of Coordination, Perspectives on Law, Governance and Equality in the EU* (Aldershot and Burlington: Ashgate), pp. 35–54.

Haahr, J. H. (2004) 'Open Co-ordination as Advanced Liberal Government', *Journal of European Public Policy*, Vol. 11, No. 2, pp. 209–30.

Haas, B., Hartel, M., Steiber, N. and Wallace, C. (2006) 'Household Employment Patterns in an Enlarged European Union', *Work, Employment and Society*, Vol. 20, No. 4, pp. 751–72.

Haas, L. (1999) 'Families and Work', in M. Sussman, S. Steinmetz and G. Peterson (eds), *Handbook of Marriage and the Family* (New York: Plenum Press), pp. 571–612.

Haas, L. (2003) 'Parental Leave and Gender Equality: Lessons from the European Union', *The Review of Policy Research*, Vol. 20, No. 1, pp. 89–114.

Hamnett, C. (1996) 'Social Polarisation, Economic Restructuring and Welfare Regimes', *Urban Studies*, Vol. 33, No. 8, pp. 1407–30.

Hankivsky, O. (2004) *Social Policy and the Ethic of Care* (Vancouver: University of British Columbia Press).

Hantrais, L. (2000) 'From Equal Pay to Reconciliation of Employment and Family Life', in L. Hantrais (ed.), *Gendered Policies in Europe, Reconciling Employment and Family Life* (Basingstoke and New York: Palgrave Macmillan), pp. 1–26.

Heichel, S., Pape, J. and Sommerer, T. (2005) 'Is There a Convergence in Convergence Research? An Overview of Empirical Studies on Policy Convergence', *Journal of European Public Policy*, Vol. 12, No. 5, pp. 817–40.

Helén, I. and Jauho, M. (2003) 'Terveyskansalaisuus ja elämän politiikka', in I. Helén and M. Jauho (eds), *Kansalaisuus ja kansanterveys* (Helsinki: Gaudeamus).

Hernes, H. M. (1987) *Welfare State and Woman Power. Essays in State Feminism* (Oslo: Norwegian University Press).

Hiilamo, H. (2005) 'Subjektiivisen päivähoito-oikeuden toteutuminen Ruotsissa ja Suomessa 1990-luvulla', in P. Takala (ed.), *Onko meillä malttia sijoittaa lapsiin?* (Helsinki: Kela).

Hobson, B. (2002) *Making Men into Fathers. Men, Masculinities and the Social Politics of Fatherhood* (Cambridge: Cambridge University Press).

Hobson, B. and Lister, R. (2002) 'Citizenship', in B. Hobson, J. Lewis and B. Siim (eds), *Contested Concepts in Gender and Social Politics* (Cheltenham: Edward Elgar).

Hochschild, A. R. (1983) *The Managed Heart: Commercialization of Human Feeling* (Berkeley: University of California Press).

Hochschild, A. R. (1995) 'The Politics of Culture: Traditional, Cold Modern, Post Modern and Warm Modern Ideals of Care', *Social Politics: International Studies in Gender, State, and Society*, Vol. 2, No. 3, pp. 331–46.

Hochschild, A. R. (2001a) 'Global Care Chains and Emotional Surplus Value', in W. Hutton and A. Giddens (eds), *On the Edge. Living with Global Capitalism* (London: Vintage).

Hochschild, A. R. (2001b) 'Las cadenas mundiales de afecto y asistencia y la plusvalía emocional', in W. Hutton and A. Giddens (eds) *En el límite. La vida en el capitalismo global* (Barcelona: Tusquets), pp. 187–208.

Hochschild, A. R. (2002) 'Love and Gold', in B. Ehrenreich and A. R. Hochschild, *Global Woman. Nannies, Maids and Sex Workers in the New Global Economy* (New York: Metropolitan Books).

Hochschild, A. (2003) *The Commercialization of Intimate Life. Notes from Home and Work* (Berkeley: University of California Press).

Holden, C. (2002) 'The Internationalization of Long Term Care Provision: Economics and Strategy', *Global Social Policy*, Vol. 2, No. 1, pp. 47–67.

Holli, A. M. (1992) 'Why the State? Reflections on the Politics of the Finnish Equality Movement Association 9', in M. Keränen (ed.), *Gender and Politics in Finland* (Aldershot: Avebury), pp. 69–88.

Hondagneu-Sotelo, P. (2001) *Doméstica: Immigrant Workers Cleaning and Caring in the Shadows of Affluence* (Berkeley: University of California Press).

Hrženjak, M. (2007) *Invisible Work*, translated by O. Vuković (Ljubljana: Politike).

Hvinden, B., Heikkilä, M. and Kankare, I. (2001) 'Towards Activation? The Changing Relationship between Social Protection and Employment in Western Europe', in M. Kautto (ed.), *Nordic Welfare States in the European Context* (London: Routledge).

ILO International Standard Classification of Occupations (1990) available at: www.ilo.org /public/english/bureau/stat/isco/index.htm

International Organization for Migration (2005) *World Migration Report* (Geneva: IOM).

INE (Instituto Nacional de Estadística) (2004) 'Encuesta de Empleo del Tiempo 2002–2003. Resultados Definitivos', *Notas de Prensa*, 1 de julio 2004. Instituto de la Mujer, at: www.inmujer.es, accessed 22 March 2011.

Isaksen, L. W. (2002) 'Toward a Sociology of (Gendered) Disgust. Images of Bodily Decay and the Social Organization of Care Work', *Journal of Family Issues*, Vol. 23, No. 7, pp. 791–811.

Isaksen, L. W., Devi, S. U. and Hochschild, A. R. (2008) 'Global Care Crisis: A Problem of Capital, Care Chain, or Commons?' *American Behavioral Scientist*, Vol. 52, No. 3, pp. 405–25.

ISMU, 'The Third Italian Report on Migrations' (2007) *Polimetrica* (Milan: International Scientific Publishers).

Jenson, J. (2008) 'Diffusing Ideas for After-Neoliberalism: The Social Investment Perspective in Europe and Latin America', paper presented at the RC19 Conference of the International Sociology Association, September 2008, Stockholm.

Jorgensen, P. (2003) *Report on the Eighth International Metropolis Conference*, Vienna, Austria, 14–19 September, available at: http://pcerii.metropolis.net/ViennaConference/li_wkshp.pdf

Katrougalos, G. and Lazaridis, G. (2003) *Southern European Welfare States. Problems, Challenges and Prospects* (Basingstoke: Palgrave Macmillan).

Katzman, D. J. (1978) *Seven Days a Week* (New York: Oxford University Press).

Keith, L. and Morris, J. (1995) 'Easy Targets: A Disability Rights Perspective on the "Children as Carers" Debate', *Critical Social Policy*, Vol. 15, No. 44–45, pp. 36–57.

Kelly, S. E. (2005) '"A Different Light" – Examining Impairment through Parent Narratives of Childhood Disability', *Journal of Contemporary Ethnography*, Vol. 43, No. 2, pp. 180–205.

King, R., Lazaridis, G. and Tsardanidis, C. (eds) (2000) *Eldorado or Fortress? Migration in Southern Europe* (Basingstoke: Macmillan Press).

Kittay, E. F. (1999) *Love's Labour: Essays on Women, Equality and Dependency* (New York: Routledge).

Knijn, T. (2004) 'Commodifying Care: New Risks and Opportunities', paper read at 'Europe and the World: Integration, Interdependence, Exceptionalism?', Palmer House, Chicago.

Knijn, T. and Kremer, M. (1997) 'Gender and the Caring Dimension of Welfare States: Toward Inclusive Citizenship, *Social Politics: International Studies in Gender, State & Society*, Vol. 4, No. 3, pp. 328–61.

Kofman, E., Phizacklea, A., Raghuram, P. and Sales, R. (2000) *Gender & International Migration in Europe: Employment, Welfare & Politics* (London: Routledge).

Kofman, E. (2003) 'Political Geography and Globalization as We Enter the Twenty-first Century', in E. Kofman and G. Youngs (eds), *Globalization: Theory and Practice* (London: Continuum, 2003), pp. 17–31.

Kovalainen, A. (2004) 'Rethinking the Revival of Social Capital and Trust in Social Theory', in B. Marshall and A. Witz (eds), *Engendering the Social: Feminist Encounters with Sociological Theory* (London: Open University Press), pp. 151–71.

Kovalainen, A. and Sundin, E. (2008) 'The Transforming Nordic Welfare Services – Voluntary, Skilled and Marketable: What Happens for Women's Work?', paper presented at the ISTR 8th International Conference and 2nd EMES-ISTR European Conference in partnership with CINEFOGO, Barcelona, 9–12 July 2008.

Krizsan, A. (2007) Presentation at the seminar *Domestic Service and Social Economy in the Eastern European Region*, Ljubljana: Peace Institute, unpublished.

Kröger, T. (2001) *Comparative Research on Social Care: The State of the Art* (Brussels: European Commission).

Kwok-bun, C. (2005) *Chinese Identities, Ethnicity and Cosmopolitanism* (London: Routledge).

Lacoff, G. and Johnson, M. (1980) *Metaphors We Live By* (Chicago: University of Chicago Press).

Landsman, G. (2003) 'Emplotting Children's Lives: Developmental Delay vs. Disability', *Social Science & Medicine*, Vol. 56, No. 9, pp. 1947–60.

Larner, W. (2000) 'Neo-liberalism: Policy, Ideology and Governmentality', *Studies in Political Economy*, Vol. 63, No. 3, pp. 5–26.

Lehtonen, T-K. (2003) 'Historiallisesta ontologiasta', *Tiede & edistys*, Vol. 28, No. 1, pp. 1–11.

Leira, A. (2002) *Working Parents and the Welfare State* (Cambridge: Cambridge University Press).

Leiter, V. (2004) 'Dilemmas in Sharing Care: Maternal Provision of Professionally Driven Therapy for Children with Disabilities', *Social Science & Medicine*, Vol. 58, No. 4, pp. 837–49.

León, M. (2002) 'Equívocos de la solidaridad. Prácticas familiaristas en la construcción de la política social española', *Revista Internacional de Sociología*, Vol. 31, pp. 137–66.

Leonard, S. and Tronto, J. C. (2007) 'The Genders of Citizenship', *American Political Science Review*, Vol. 101, No 1, pp. 33–46.

Lessenich, S. (1996) 'España y los 'Regímenes' de Estado del Bienestar', *Revista Internacional de Sociología*, Vol. 13, pp. 147–61.

Levine, C. (2005) 'Acceptance, Avoidance, and Ambiguity: Conflicting Social Values about Childhood Disability', *Kennedy Institute of Ethics Journal*, Vol. 15, pp. 371–83.

Lewis, J. (1992) 'Gender and the Development of Welfare Regimes', *Journal of European Social Policy*, Vol. 2, No. 3, pp. 159–73.

Lewis, J. (ed.) (1993) *Women and the Social Politics in Europe: Work, Family and the State* (Aldershot: Edward Elgar).

Lewis, J. (1997) 'Gender and Welfare Regimes: Further Thoughts', *Social Politics*, Vol. 4, No. 2, pp. 160–77.

Lewis, J. (ed.) (1998) *Gender, Social Care and Welfare State Restructuring in Europe* (Aldershot: Ashgate).

Lewis, J. (2001) 'The Decline of the Male Breadwinner Model: Implications for Work and Care', *Social Politics*, Vol. 8, No. 2, pp. 152–69.

Lewis, J. (2002) 'Gender and Welfare State Change', *European Societies*, Vol. 4, No. 4, pp. 331–57.

Lewis, J. (2004a) 'The State and the Third Sector in Modern Welfare States: Independence, Instrumentality, Partnership', in A. Evers and J. L. Laville (eds), *The Third Sector in Europe* (Cheltenham: Edward Elgar), pp. 169–87.

Lewis, J. (2004b) 'Individualization and the Need for New Forms of Family Solidarity', in T. Knijn and A. Komter (eds), *Solidarity between the Sexes and the Generations* (Cheltenham: Edward Elgar), pp. 51–67.

Lewis, J. (2006) 'Perceptions of Risk in Intimate Relationships: The Implications for Social Provision', *Journal of Social Policy*, Vol. 35, No. 1, pp. 39–57.

Lewis, J. (2009) *Work–Family Balance, Gender and Policy* (Cheltenham: Edward Elgar).
Lewis, J., Campbell, M. and Huerta, C. (2008) 'Patterns of Paid and Unpaid Work in Western Europe: Gender, Commodification, Preferences and the Implications for Policy, *Journal of European Social Policy*, Vol. 18, No. 1, pp. 21–37.
Lister, R. (1990) *The Exclusive Society: Citizenship and the Poor* (London: CPAG).
Lister, R. (1997) *Citizenship: Feminist Perspectives* (Basingstoke: Macmillan).
Lister, R (2002) 'The Dilemmas of Pendulum Politics: Balancing Paid Work, Care and Citizenship', *Economy and Society*, Vol. 31, No. 4, pp. 520–32.
Lister, R. (2003) *Citizenship: Feminist Perspectives* (Basingstoke: Palgrave Macmillan).
Lister, R., Williams, F., Anttonen, A., Bussemaker, M., Gerhard, U., Johansson, S., Heinen, J., Leira, A., Siim. B., Tobio C. and Gavanas, A. (2007) *Gendered Citizenship in Western Europe: New Challenges for Citizenship Research in a Cross-National Context* (Bristol: The Policy Press).
López Gandía, J. and Toscani Giménez, D. (2006) *Los trabajadores al servicio del hogar familiar. Aspectos laborales y de Seguridad Social. Propuestas de reforma* (Albacete: Editorial Bomarzo).
Lupton, D. and Barclay, L. (1997) *Constructing Fatherhood: Discourses and Experiences* (London: Sage).
Lutz, H. (1997) 'The Limits of European-ness: Immigrant Women in Fortress Europe', *Feminist Review*, Vol. 57, No. 1, pp. 93–111.
Lutz, H. (2002) 'At Your Service Madam! The Globalization of Domestic Service', *Feminist Review*, Vol. 70, pp. 89–104.
Lutz, H. (2007) 'Editorial: Domestic Work', *The European Journal of Women's Studies*, Vol. 14, No. 3, pp. 187.
Lutz, H. (2008a) 'Introduction: Migrant Domestic Workers in Europe', in H. Lutz (ed.), *Migration and Domestic Work: A European Perspective on a Global Theme* (Aldershot: Ashgate), pp. 1–11.
Lutz, H. (2008b) 'When Home Becomes a Workplace: Domestic Work as an Ordinary Job in Germany?', in H. Lutz (ed.), *Migration and Domestic Work: A European Perspective on a Global Theme* (Aldershot: Ashgate), pp. 43–60.
Lutz, H. (ed.) (2008c) *Migration and Domestic Work: A European Perspective on a Global Theme* (Aldershot: Ashgate).
Lutz, H. and Schwalgin, S. (2003) 'Living in the Twilight Zone: Illegalised Migrant Domestic Workers in Germany', available at: www.servantproject. com/abstractEssex.htm, accessed 3 July 2006.
Luxemburg, R. (2004) *The Rosa Luxemburg Reader*, ed. P. Hudis and K. B. Anderson (New York: Monthly Review Press).
Macklin, A. (1994) 'On the Outside Looking in: Foreign Domestic Workers in Canada', in W. Giles and S. Arat-Koc (eds), *Maid in the Market* (Halifax: Fernwood Publishing), pp. 13–40.
Mahon, R. (2002) 'Child Care Policy: Toward What Kind of "Social Europe"?', *Social Politics*, Vol. 9, No. 3, pp. 343–79.
Mahon, R. (2008) 'Learning, Forgetting, Rediscovering: the OECD's "New" Family Policy Produced for Volume on the OECD', in K. Martens and A. Jakobi (eds), *Mechanisms of OECD Governance – International Incentives for National Policy Making* (Oxford: Oxford University Press).
Mantu, S. A. (2008) *The Boundaries of European Social Citizenship* (Nijmegen: WPL).
Marcussen, M. (2002) *OECD og idespillet – Game Over?* (Copenhagen: Hans Reitzels forlag).
Marshall, T. H. (1975) *Social Policy in the Twentieth Century* (London: Hutchinson).

Martinsen, D. (2009) 'Conflict and Conflict Management in the Cross-border Provision of Healthcare Services', *West European Politics*, Vol. 32, No. 4, pp. 792–809.

Matten, D. and Crane, A. (2005) 'Corporate Citizenship: Towards an Extended Theoretical Conceptualization', *Academy of Management Review*, Vol. 30, No. 1, pp. 166–79.

May, J., Wills, J., Datta, K., Evans, Y., Herbert, J. and McIlwaine, C. (2007) 'From Coping Strategies to Tactics: Global Cities, the British State, and London's New Migrant Division of Labour', *Transactions of the British Institute of Geographers*, Vol. 37, No. 2, pp. 151–67.

Mayo, M. (2005) *Global Citizens: Social Movements and the Challenge of Globalization* (London: Zed Books).

McDowell, L. (2004) 'Work, Workfare, Work/Life Balance and an Ethic of Care', *Progress in Human Geography*, Vol. 28, No. 2, pp. 145–63.

McDowell, L. (2007) 'Spaces of the Home: Absence Presence, New Connections and New Anxieties', *Home Cultures*, Vol. 4, No. 2, pp. 129–46.

McGlynn, C. (2005) 'Work, Family, and Parenthood: The European Union Agenda', in J. Conaghan and K. Rittich (eds), *Labour Law, Work and Family* (Oxford and New York: Oxford University Press), pp. 217–36.

McKie, L., Gregory, S. and Bowlby, S. (2002) 'Shadow Times: The Temporal and Spatial Frameworks and Experiences of Caring and Working', *Sociology*, Vol. 36, No. 4, pp. 897–924.

McLaughlin, E. and Glendinning, C. (1994) 'Paying for Care in Europe: Is There a Feminist Approach?', in L. Hantrais and S. Mangen (eds), *Family Policy and the Welfare of Women. Cross-National Research Papers* (Leicestershire: The Cross-National Research Group), pp. 52–69.

McLaughlin, J. (2003) 'Screening Networks: Shared Agendas in Feminist and Disability Movement Challenges to Antenatal Screening and Abortion', *Disability & Society*, Vol. 18, No. 3, pp. 297–310.

McLaughlin, J. (2006) 'Conceptualising Intensive Caring Activities: The Changing Lives of Families with Young Disabled Children', *Sociological Research Online*, 11.

McLaughlin, J., Goodley, D., Clavering, E. K. and Fisher, P. (2008) *Families Raising Disabled Children: Values of Enabling Care and Social Justice* (Basingstoke: Palgrave Macmillan).

Meagher, G. (2003) *Friend or Flunkey? Paid Domestic Workers in the New Economy* (Sydney: UNSW Press).

Melegh, A. (2006) *On the East-West Slope: Globalization, Nationalism, Racism and Discourses on Central and Eastern Europe* (Budapest: Central European University Press).

Meuser, M. and Nagel, U. (1991) 'Experteninterviews – vielfach erprobt, wenig bedacht', in D. Garz and K. Kraimer (eds), *Qualitativ-empirische Sozialforschung* (Opladen: Westdeutscher Verlag).

Ministerio del Interior (2001) *Anuario Estadístico de Extranjería*.

Ministerio de Trabajo y Asuntos Sociales: http://extranjeros.mtas.es and www.seg-social.es, date of access: 12 February 2008.

Moreno, L. (2001) 'La "vía media" española del modelo de bienestar mediterráneo'. *Revista Papers*, Vol. 63/64, pp. 67–82.

Morokvasic, M. (2004) '"Settled in Mobility": Engendering Post-Wall Migration in Europe', *Feminist Review*, Vol. 77, No. 1, pp. 7–25.

Morris, J. (1993a) 'Feminism and Disability', *Feminist Review*, Vol. 43, Spring, pp. 57–70.

Morris, J. (1993b) *Independent Lives* (Basingstoke: Macmillan).

Mouffe, C. (1992) 'Democratic Citizenship and the Political Community', in C. Mouffe (ed.), *Dimensions of Radical Democracy* (London and New York: Verso).

Narayan, U. (1995) 'Colonialism and Its Others: Considerations on Rights and Care Discourses', *Hypatia*, Vol. 10, No. 2, pp. 133–40.

Nelson, J. L. (2002) 'Just Expectations: Family Caregivers, Practical Identities and Social Justice in the Provision of Healthcare', in R. Rhodes, M. P. Battin and A. Silvers (eds), *Medicine and Justice: Essays on the Distribution of Health Care* (New York: Oxford University Press).

Nere, L. (2006) *Social Networks and the Politics of Everyday Life – Ukrainian and Polish Immigrant Women in South Italy* (work in progress), Department of Sociology, University of Helsinki, Finland.

Nussbaum, M. (2003) 'Capabilities as Fundamental Entitlements: Sen and Social Justice', *Feminist Economics*, Vol. 9, No. 2/3, pp. 33–60.

O'Brien, M. (2007) 'Mothers' Emotional Care Work in Education and Its Moral Imperative', *Gender and Education*, Vol. 19, No. 2, pp. 159–77.

O'Connor, J. (1993) 'Gender, Class and Citizenship in the Comparative Analysis of Welfare State Regimes: Theoretical and Methodological Issues', *The British Journal of Sociology*, Vol. 44, No. 3, pp. 501–18.

O'Connor, J. (1996) 'From Women in the Welfare State to Gendering Welfare State Regimes', *Current Sociology*, Vol. 44, No. 2, pp. 1–130.

OECD (2001) 'Balancing Work and Family Life: Helping Parents into Paid Employment', *OECD Employment Outlook* (Paris: OECD), pp. 129–66.

OECD (2003) *Babies and Bosses – Reconciling Work and Family Life (Vol. 2) Austria, Ireland and Japan* (Paris: OECD).

OECD (2005) *Babies and Bosses – Reconciling Work and Family Life (Vol. 4) Canada, Finland, Sweden and the United Kingdom* (Paris: OECD).

Ong, A. (1999) *Flexible Citizenship: The Cultural Logics of Transnationality* (Durham: Duke University Press).

Ong, A. (2006) 'Mutations of Citizenship', *Theory, Culture & Society*, Vol. 23, No. 2–3, pp. 499–505.

ONS (2007) *Unpaid Care: Cohabiting Couples Provide Less Unpaid Care* (London: Office for National Statistics).

Orloff, A. S. (1993) 'Gender and the Social Rights of Citizenship: The Comparative Analysis of Gender Relations and Welfare States', *American Sociological Review*, Vol. 58, No. 3, pp. 303–28.

Orme, J. (2001) *Gender and Community Care* (Basingstoke: Palgrave Macmillan).

Ozyegin, G. (2001) *Untidy Gender: Domestic Service in Turkey* (Philadelphia: Temple University Press).

Pajares, M. (2007) *Inmigración y mercado de trabajo. Informe 2007*, Documentos del Observatorio Permanente de la Inmigración, Ministerio de Trabajo y Asuntos Sociales.

Parreñas, R. (2001) *Servants of Globalisation: Women, Migration and Domestic Work* (Stanford: Stanford University Press).

Pascall, G. and Lewis, J. (2004) 'Emerging Gender Regimes and Policies for Gender Equality in a Wider Europe', *Journal of Social Policy*, Vol. 33, No. 3, pp. 373–94.

Pearson, R. (2000) 'Rethinking Gender Matters in Development', in T. Allen and A. Thomas (eds), *Poverty and Development into the 21st Century* (Oxford: Open University in association with Oxford University Press).

Peeno, L. (1996) 'Managed Care Ethics: The Close View', submission prepared for the US House of Representatives Committee on Commerce Subcommittee on Health and Environment, Michael Bilirakis, Chair.

Pelkonen, V. (ed.) (1993) *Hyvinvointioikeus* (Helsinki: Suomen kaupunkiliitto, Suomen kunnallisliitto).

Peterson, E. (2007) 'The Invisible Carers. Framing Domestic Work(ers) in Gender Equality Policies in Spain', *European Journal of Women's Studies*, Vol. 14, No. 3, pp. 265–80.

Pfau-Effinger. B. (2004) 'Welfare State Policies and the Development of Care Arrangements', *European Societies*, Vol. 7, No. 2, pp. 321–47.

Physicians for Human Rights (2006) *Bold Solutions to Africa's Health Care Worker Shortage* (Boston: Physicians for Human Rights).

Place, B. (2000) 'Constructing the Bodies of Critically Ill Children: An Ethnography of Intensive Care', in A. Prout (ed.), *The Body, Childhood and Society* (Basingstoke: Palgrave Macmillan).

Plantenga, J. and Hansen, J. (1999) 'Assessing Equal Opportunities in the European Union', *International Labour Review*, Vol. 138, No. 4, pp. 351–79.

Plantenga, J., Remery, C., Siegel, M. and Sementini, L. (2007) 'Reconciling Work and Private Life. The Barcelona Targets and Provision of Childcare Services in 25 European Member States, paper presented at the LSE Conference at CINEFOGO.

Platzer, E. (2006) 'From Private Solutions to Public Responsibility and Back Again: the New Domestic Services in Sweden', *Gender & History*, Vol. 18, No. 2, pp. 211–21.

Poiares Maduro, M. (2000) 'Europe's Social Self: "The Sickness Unto Death"', in J. Shaw (ed.), *Social Law and Policy in an Evolving European Union* (Oxford and Portland: Hart Publishing), pp. 325–49.

Pollack, M. A. and Hafner-Burton, E. (2000) 'Mainstreaming Gender in the European Journal', *Journal of European Public Policy*, Vol. 7, No. 3, pp. 432–56.

Pylkkänen, A. (2004) 'Constructions of Legal Persons in a "Communitarian" Context: The Modernisation of Law in Finland', in V. Puuronen, A. Häkkinen, A. Pylkkänen, T. Sandlund and R. Toivanen (eds), *New Challenges for the Welfare Society* (University of Joensuu: Publications of the Karelian Institute), pp. 63–89.

Pylkkänen, A. (2007) 'Pohjoismainen työn ja yksityiselämän yhdistämisen malli: millaista tasa-arvoa?', *Janus*, Vol. 16, No. 3, pp. 200–14.

Radaelli, C. (2000) 'Whither Europeanization? Concept Stretching and Substantive Change', *European Integration Online Papers*, Vol. 4, No. 8, available at: http://eiop.or.at/eiop/tex-te/2000-008a.htm.

Radaelli, C. and Pasquier, R. (2008) 'Conceptual Issues', in P. Graziano and M. P. Vink (eds), *Europeanization – New Research Agendas* (Basingstoke: Palgrave Macmillan), pp. 35–45.

Rapp, R. and Ginsburg, F. (2001) 'Enabling Disability: Rewriting Kinship, Reimagining Citizenship', *Public Culture*, Vol. 13, No. 3, pp. 533–56.

Rawls, J. (1985) 'Justice as Fairness: Political Not Metaphysical', *Philosophy and Public Affairs*, Vol. 14, No. 3, pp. 223–51.

Rawls, J. (1999) *The Law of Peoples* (Cambridge MA: Harvard University Press).

Regulating domestic help (A5-0301/2000) Brussels: European Parliament.

Rehm, R. S. and Bradley, J. F. (2005) 'Normalization in Families Raising a Child Who Is Medically Fragile/Technology Dependent and Developmentally Delayed', *Qualitative Health Research*, Vol. 15, No. 6, pp. 807–20.

Report on Equality Between Women and Men (2006) (Brussels: EU Commission), available at: http://europa.eu.int/comm/employment_social/emplweb/news/news_en.cfm?id=129, accessed 7 January 2009.

Report on Equality Between Women and Men (2008) (Brussels: EU Commission), available at: http://ec.europa.eu/employment_social/publications/2008/keaj08001_en.pdf, accessed 7 January 2009.

Robinson, F. (1999) *Globalizing Care* (Boulder: Westview Press).

Robinson, F. (2006a) 'Beyond Labour Rights: the Ethics of Care and Women's Work in the Global Economy', *International Feminist Journal of Politics*, Vol. 8, No. 3, pp. 321–42.

Robinson, F. (2006b) 'Care, Gender and Global Social Justice', *Journal of Global Ethics*, Vol. 2, No. 1, pp. 5–25.

Rollins, J. (1985) *Between Women. Domestics and their Employers* (Philadelphia: Temple University Press).

Romero, M. (1992) *Maid in the USA* (New York: Routledge).

Rose, N. (1999) *Powers of Freedom, Reframing Political Thought* (Cambridge: Cambridge University Press).

Rosenmayr, L. and Køckeis, E. (1963) 'Propositions for a Sociological Theory of Ageing and the Family', *International Social Science Journal*, Vol. 15, No. 3, pp. 410–26.

Ruhs, M. and Anderson, B. (2006) 'Semi-compliance in the Migrant Labour Market', *COMPAS Working Paper WP0630*, University of Oxford, available at: www.compas.ox.ac.uk/publications/working-papers/, accessed 1 August 2010.

Rumford, C. (2003) 'European Civil Society or Transnational Social Space? Conceptions of Society in Discourses of EU Citizenship, Governance and the Democratic Deficit: An Emerging Agenda', *European Journal of Social Theory*, Vol. 6, No. 1, pp. 25–43.

Rummery, K. (2002) *Disability, Citizenship and Community Care: A Case for Welfare Rights?* (Aldershot: Ashgate).

Ruškus, J. (2002) *Negalės fenomenas* (Šiauliai: Šiaulių universiteto leidykla).

Rutherford, F. (1989) 'The Proposal for a European Directive on Parental Leave: Some Reasons for Why It Failed', *Policy and Politics*, Vol. 27, No. 4, pp. 301–10.

Sahlin-Anderson, K. (2002) 'National, International and Transnational Constructions of New Public Management', in T. Christensen and P. Lægreid (eds), *The Transformation of Ideas and Practice* (Aldershot: Ashgate), pp. 43–72.

Sainsbury, D. (ed.) (1994) *Gendering Welfare States* (London: Sage).

Sainsbury, D. (1996) *Gender, Equality, and Welfare States* (Cambridge: Cambridge University Press).

Sainsbury, D. (ed.) (1999) *Gender and Welfare State Regimes* (Oxford: Oxford University Press).

Saraceno, C. (1994) 'The Ambivalent Familism of the Italian Welfare State', *Social Politics*, Vol. 1, pp. 60–82.

Saraceno, C. (1995) 'Familismo ambivalente y clientelismo categórico en el Estado de bienestar italiano', in S. Sarasa and L. Moreno (compilers), *El Estado del bienestar en la Europa del sur* (Madrid: CSIC), pp. 261–88.

Saraceno, C. (1997) 'Family Change Policies and the Restructuring of Welfare', in *Family, Market and Community. Equity and Efficiency in Social Policy*, OECD Social Policy Studies, No. 21 (Paris: OECD).

Sarasa, S. and Mestres, J. (2007) 'Women's Employment and the Adult Caring Burden', in G. Esping-Andersen (ed.), *Family Formation and Family Dilemmas in Contemporary Europe* (Bilbao: Foundacion BBVA), pp. 185–222.

Sarasa, S. and Moreno, L. (compilers) (1995) *El Estado del bienestar en la Europa del Sur* (Madrid: CSIC).

Sarti, R. (2005) *Domestic Service and European Identity, Final Report,* available at www. uniurb.it/scipol/drs_servant_project_conclusion, accessed 20 March 2007.

Sarti, R. (2006) 'Domestic Service: Past and Present in Southern and Northern Europe', *Gender & History,* Vol. 18, No. 2, pp. 222–45.

Sarvasy, W. and Longo, P. (2004) 'The Globalization of Care – Kant's World Citizenship and Filipina Migrant Domestic Workers', *International Feminist Journal of Politics,* Vol. 6, No. 3, 392–415.

Sassen, S. (1996) 'New Employment Regimes in Cities: The Impact on Immigrant Workers', *New Community,* Vol. 22, No. 4, pp. 579–94.

Sassen, S. (2007) *A Sociology of Globalization* (New York: W.W. Norton).

Schecter, T. (1998) *Race, Class, Women and the State: The Case of Domestic Labour* (Montreal, New York and London: Black Rose Books).

Senden, L. (2004) *Soft Law in European Community Law* (Oxford: Hart Publishing).

Sevenhuijsen, S. (1998) *Citizenship and the Ethics of Care* (London: Routledge).

Silvers, A. and Francis, L. P. (2005) 'Justice through Trust. Disability and the "Outlier Problem" in Social Contract Theory', *Ethics,* Vol. 116, No. 1, pp. 40–76.

Silvers, A., Wasserman, D., and Mahowald, M. (1998) *Disability, Difference, Discrimination: Perspectives on Justice in Bioethics and Public Policy* (Lanham: Rowman and Littlefield).

Simmel, G. (1908) 'The Stranger', in K. Wolff (1950) (ed.) *The Sociology of Georg Simmel* (New York: The Free Press).

Simonen, L. and Kovalainen, A. (1998) 'Paradoxes of Social Care Restructuring: The Finnish Case', in J. Lewis (ed.), *Gender, Social Care and Welfare State Restructuring in Europe* (Aldershot: Ashgate), pp. 229–35.

Skeggs, B. (1997) *Formations of Class and Gender: Becoming Respectable* (London and New York: Sage Publications).

Skřivánková, K. (2006) *Trafficking for Forced Labour, UK Country Report* (London: Anti-Slavery International).

Smart, C. (1989) *Feminism and the Power of Law* (London: Routledge).

Smismans, S. (2008) 'The European Social Dialogue in the Shadow of Hierarchy', *Journal of Public Policy,* Vol. 28, No. 1, pp. 161–80.

Spain (1969), 'Decreto 2346/1969, de 25 de noviembre, por el que se regula el Régimen Especial de la Seguridad Social del Servicio Doméstico', *Boletín Oficial del Estado,* 15 de octubre 1969, No. 247, p. 16109.

Spain (1985), 'Real Decreto 1424/1985, de 1 de agosto, por el que se regula la relación laboral de carácter especial del Servicio del Hogar Familiar', *Boletín Oficial del Estado,* 13 de agosto de 1985, No. 193, p. 25617.

Spain (2000), 'Ley Orgánica 4/2000, de 11 de enero, sobre derechos y libertades de los extranjeros en España y su integración social', *Boletín Oficial del Estado,* 12 de enero de 2000, No. 10, p. 1139.

Spain (2004), 'Real Decreto 2393/2004, de 30 de diciembre, por el que se aprueba el Reglamento de la Ley Orgánica 4/2000, de 11 de enero, sobre derechos y libertades de los extranjeros en España y su integración social', *Boletín Oficial del Estado,* 7 de enero de 2005, No. 6, p. 485.

Spain (2005), 'Orden PRE/140/2005, de 2 de febrero, por la que se desarrolla el procedimiento aplicable al proceso de normalización previsto en la disposición transitoria tercera del Real Decreto 2393/2004, de 30 de diciembre, por el que se aprueba el Reglamento de la Ley Orgánica 4/2000, de 11 de enero, sobre derechos y libertades de los extranjeros en España y su integración social', *Boletín Oficial del Estado*, 3 de febrero de 2005, No. 29, p. 3709.

Squires, J. (2005) 'Is Mainstreaming Transformative? Theorizing Mainstreaming in the Context of Diversity and Deliberation', *Social Politics: International Studies in Gender, State & Society*, Vol. 12, No. 3, pp. 366–88.

Staland-Nyman, C., Alexsanderson, K. and Hensing, G. (2008) 'Associations between Strain in Domestic Work and Self-related Health: A Study of Employed Women in Sweden', *Scandinavian Journal of Public Health*, Vol. 36, No. 1, pp. 211–27.

Stone, D. (2000) 'Why We Need a Care Movement', *The Nation*, March 13, pp. 13–15.

Stratigaki, M. (2000) 'The European Union and the Equal Opportunities Process', in L. Hantrais (ed.), *Gendered Politicies in Europe: Reconciling Employment and Family Life* (Basingstoke and New York: Palgrave Macmillan), pp. 27–48.

Stratigaki, M. (2004) 'The Co-optation of Gender Concepts in EU Policies: The Case of "Reconciliation of Work and Family"', *Social Politics*, Vol. 11, No. 1, pp. 30–56.

Strauss, R. (2000) 'The Local Dimension for the European Employment Strategy', available at: www.jil.go.jp/english/events_and_information/documents/20050209/chapter4.pdf, accessed on 28 November 2010.

Sullivan, O. (2000) 'The Division of Domestic Labour: Twenty Years of Change?', *Sociology*, Vol. 34, No. 3, pp. 437–56.

Szebehely, M. (2003) *Hemhjälp i Norden* (Lund: Studentlitteratur).

Sørensen, N. N. (2002) 'Transnationaliseringen af husmoderlige pligter', *Kvinder, Køn & Forskning*, Vol. 11, No. 2, pp. 9–19.

Taylor, S. J. (2000) '"You're not a Retard, You're Just Wise": Disability, Social Identity, and Family Networks', *Journal of Contemporary Ethnography*, Vol. 29, No. 1, pp. 58–92.

Thornton Dill, B. (1994) *Across the Boundaries of Race and Class: an Exploration of Work and Family among Black Female Domestic Servants* (New York and London: Garland Publishing).

Threlfall, M. (2000) 'Taking Stock and Looking Ahead', in L. Hantrais (ed.), *Gendered Policies in Europe, Reconciling Employment and Family Life* (Basingstoke and New York: Palgrave Macmillan), pp. 180–200.

Tijdens, K., Van der Lippe, T. and De Ruijter (2003) 'Working Women's Choices for Domestic Help. The Effects of Financial and Time Resources', *AIAS Working Paper*, Utrecht University.

Tobío, C. (2003) 'Conciliación o contradicción: cómo hacen las madres trabajadoras', in *Conciliar la vida. Tiempo y servicios para la igualdad*, Consejo de la Mujer de Madrid, pp. 15–43.

Tobis, D. (2000) *Moving from Residential Institutions to Community-based Social Services in Central and Eastern Europe and the Former Soviet Union* (Washington, DC: World Bank).

Traustadóttir, R. (1991) 'Mothers who Care: Gender, Disability and Family Life', *Journal of Family Issues*, Vol. 12, No. 2, pp. 221–28.

Traustadóttir, R. (1995) 'A Mother's Work Is Never Done, Constructing a "Normal" Family Life', in S. J. Taylor, R. Bogdan and Z. M. Lutfiyya (eds), *The*

Variety of Community Experience: Qualitative Studies of Family and Community Life (Baltimore: Paul H. Brookes Publishing Co.).

Tronto, J. C. (1993) *Moral Boundaries – A Political Ethic of Care* (New York: Routledge).

Tronto, J. C. (2002) 'The "Nanny Question" in Feminism', *Hypatia,* Vol. 17, No. 2, pp. 34–51.

Tronto, J. C. (2005) 'Care As the Work of Citizens: A Modest Proposal', in M. Friedman (ed.), *Women and Citizenship* (New York: Oxford University Press).

Unalan, D. (2009) 'An Analytical Framework for Policy Transfer in the EU Context', *Policy & Politics,* Vol. 37, No. 3, pp. 439–52.

Ungerson, C. (1987) *Policy Is Personal: Sex, Gender, and Informal Care* (London: Tavistock).

Ungerson, C. (1990) *Gender and Caring: Work and Welfare in Britain and Scandinavia* (Hemel Hempstead: Harvester Wheatsheaf).

Ungerson, C. (1997) 'Social Politics and the Commodification of Care', *Social Politics: International Studies in Gender, State and Society,* Fall 1997, pp. 362–81.

Ungerson, C. (2000) 'Thinking about the Production and Consumption of Longterm Care in Britain – Does Gender Still Matter?', *Journal of Social Policy,* Vol. 29, No. 4, pp. 623–43.

Ungerson, C. and Yeandle, S. (2007) 'Conceptualizing Cash for Care: The Origins of Contemporary Debates', in C. Ungerson and S. Yeandle (eds), *Cash for Care in Developed Welfare States* (Basingstoke: Palgrave Macmillan).

United Nations (n.d.) at:www.un.org

United Nations Department of Economic and Social Affairs, Population Division (2006) *Fact Sheet: International Migration Facts & Figures* (New York: United Nations).

Valiente, C. (1996) 'The Rejection of Authoritarian Policy Legacies: Family Policy in Spain (1975–1995)', *South European Society & Politics,* Vol. 1, No. 1, pp. 95–114.

Valiente, C. (1997) 'Las políticas de cuidado de los niños a nivel nacional en España (1975–1996)', *Revista Papers,* Vol. 53, pp. 101–36.

van der Vleuten, A. (2007) *The Price of Gender Equality: Member States and Governance in the European Union* (Aldershot: Ashgate).

van Dijk, T. A. (1989) *Communicating Racism: Ethnic Prejudice in Thought and Talk* (Beverly Hills: Sage).

Verdier, Y. (1981) *Tvatterskan, kokerskan och syerskan* (The Cleaner, the Cook and the Seamstress) (Stockholm: Bokforlaget Prisma).

Walby, S. (1997) *Gender Transformations* (London: Routledge).

Walker, M. U. (1998) *Moral Understandings: A Feminist Study in Ethics* (New York: Routledge).

Wall, K. (2007) 'Leave Policy Models and the Articulation of Work and Family in Europe: A Comparative Perspective', in P. Moss and K. Wall (eds), *International Review of Leave Policies and Related Research,* Employment Relations Research Series No. 80 (London: Department for Business, Enterprise and Regulatory Reform), pp. 25–43.

Walters, W. and Haahr, J. H. (2005) *Governing Europe. Discourse, Governmentality and European Integration* (London and New York: Routledge).

Walzer, M. (1983) *Spheres of Justice: A Defense of Pluralism and Equality* (New York: Basic Books).

Wærness, K. (1987) 'On the Rationality of Caring', in A. Showstack Sassoon (ed.), *Women and the State* (London: Hutchinson).

Webster, J. (2005) *Changing European Gender Relations: The Findings of Recent Social Research and Their Implications for Gender Equality Policy, Policy Synthesis Report to the European Commission* (Brussels: DG-Research).

Weir, A. (2005) 'The Global Universal Caregiver: Imagining Women's Liberation in the New Millennium', *Constellations: An International Journal of Critical & Democratic Theory*, Vol. 12, No. 3, pp. 308–30.

Wennberg, L. (2008) *Social Security for Solo Mothers in Swedish and EU Law, On the Constructions of Normality and the Boundaries of Social Citizenship* (Uppsala: Iustus förlag).

WHO (2003) 'Mental Health in the WHO European Region', available at WHO Fact Sheet 03/03, WHO, available at: www.euro.who.int/document/mediacentre/fs0303e.pdf.

Willett, C. (2001) *The Soul of Justice: Social Bonds and Racial Hubris* (Ithaca: Cornell University Press).

Williams, F. (1987) 'Racism and the Discipline of Social Policy: a Critique of Welfare Theory', *Critical Social Policy*, Vol. 7, No. 4, pp. 4–29.

Williams, F. (1995) 'Race/Ethnicity, Gender, and Class in the Welfare State: A Framework for Comparative Analysis', *Social Politics: International Studies in Gender, State, and Society*, Vol. 2, No. 2, pp. 127–59.

Williams, F. (2007) 'How Do We Theorise the Employment of Migrant Women in Home-Based Care Work in European Welfare States?', paper presented at the RC19 Conference, Florence, September.

Williams, F. (2009) *Claiming and Framing in the Making of Care Policies: The Recognition and Redistribution of Care* (Geneva: UNRISD).

Williams, F. (2010) 'Themes and Concepts in Migration, Gender and Care', *Social Policy and Society*, Vol. 9, No. 3, pp. 385–96.

Williams, F. (2011) 'The Transnational Political Economy of Care', in R. Mahon and F. Robinson (eds), *The Global Political Economy of Care: Integrating Ethical and Social Politics* (Vancouver: UBC Press).

Williams, F. and Gavanas, A. (2008) 'The Intersection of Child Care Regimes and Migration Regimes: A Three-country Study' in H. Lutz (ed.), *Migration and Domestic Work: a European Perspective on a Global Theme* (London: Routledge).

Williams, J. (2000) *Unbending Gender. Why Family and Work Conflict and What to Do About It* (Oxford: Oxford University Press).

Windebank, J. (2007) 'Outsourcing Women's Domestic Labour: the Chèque Emploi-Service Universal in France', *Journal of European Social Policy*, Vol. 17, pp. 257–70.

Wolkowitz, C. (2006) *Bodies at Work* (London: SAGE Publications).

Yeates, N. (2004) 'A Dialogue with "Global Care Chain" Analysis: Nurse Migration in the Irish Context', *Feminist Review*, Vol. 77, pp. 79–95.

Yeates, N. (2009) *Globalising Care Economies and Migrating Workers: Explorations in Global Care Chains* (London: Palgrave Macmillan).

Young, I. M. (2003) 'The Logic of Masculinist Protection: Reflections on the Current Security State', *Signs: Journal of Women in Culture & Society*, Vol. 29, No. 1, pp. 1–24.

Yuval-Davis, N. (1991) 'The Citizenship Debate. Women, Ethnic Processes and the State', *Feminist Review*, Vol. 39, pp. 58–68.

Yuval-Davis, N. (2007) 'Nationalism, Belonging, Globalization and the "Ethics of Care"', *Kvinder, Køn & Forskning*, Vol. 16, No. 2–3, pp. 91–100.

Index

Not all author citations are listed in the index; readers requiring a complete list of authors and works cited should consult the reference list.